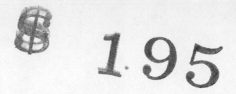

Religious Humanism
and the
Victorian Novel:

George Eliot,
Walter Pater, and
Samuel Butler

Religious Humanism and the Victorian Novel:

George Eliot,
Walter Pater,
and Samuel Butler

By U. C. Knoepflmacher

Princeton, New Jersey
Princeton University Press

To E. D. H. Johnson

Preface

MANY PEOPLE have had an active share in the making of this book. Robert Bloom, Frederick C. Crews, Thomas Flanagan, Robert B. Martin, and Edward McVey gave me invaluable advice at very different stages of its growth. The incisive suggestions made by Miss Elizabeth Walser, who supervised the preparation of the final manuscript with enthusiasm and care, were a wonderful boon. On a more passive level, I must certainly give credit to those members of the English Conference at Berkeley and the Discussion Group X of the Modern Language Association who patiently listened as I tested out some of my ideas. I am obliged also to the editors of *Victorian Studies, Modern Fiction Studies,* and *English Fiction in Transition* for their earlier critical comments and their present permission to reprint, in a considerably altered form, the fragments of Chapters II, V, and VIII which appeared in their journals.

My greatest indebtedness, however, belongs to five persons who have been responsible, not only for the evolution of the book, but also for that of its writer. This indebtedness belongs to my parents, who, at the cost of a great personal sacrifice, consented to be separated from their only son by allowing him to migrate to the United States; it belongs to John H. Raleigh, who was instrumental in the transformation of an undergraduate in architecture into a graduate student in English literature; it belongs to Cecilia Mandzuch, who endowed that student's life with new meaning, fulfillment, and stability; it belongs, finally, to E. D. H. Johnson, whose passion for and understanding of the nineteenth century helped to convert a neophyte in Victorian studies into the author of the present book. It is to him, therefore, that I most gratefully dedicate this work.

U. C. K.

Berkeley, California
July 1964

Contents

CONTENTS

Religious Humanism
and the
Victorian Novel:

George Eliot,
Walter Pater, and
Samuel Butler

I

Religion, Evolution, and the Novel

Si Dieu n'existait pas, il faudrait l'inventer.—VOLTAIRE

My dear friend, the problem of the world at this moment is—how to find a religion? —*some great conception which shall be once more capable, as the old were capable, of welding societies, and keeping man's brutish elements in check.* —MRS. HUMPHRY WARD

1. 1888 AND A LOOK BACKWARDS

WRITING IN the *Guardian*, Walter Pater demanded: "Who will deny that to trace the influence of religion upon human character is one of the legitimate functions of the novel?" "In truth," he added, "the modern 'novel of character' needs some such interest, to lift it sufficiently above the humdrum of life."[1] The date was March 28, 1888; the occasion, the publication of *Robert Elsmere* by Mrs. Humphry Ward, Matthew Arnold's niece, who until recently had been Pater's neighbor at Oxford. Pater's exhortation hardly seemed necessary: Mrs. Ward had been preceded by a host of nineteenth-century writers who, usually with greater earnestness than artistry, had portrayed "the influence of religion upon human character" in order to disseminate their own sectarian preferences for any one of the many cults warring within and without the Church of England.[2] The genre defended by Pater was neither new nor

[1] *Essays from 'The Guardian'* (London, 1910), pp. 56-57. Pater's review is discussed at greater length in connection with his own work in Chapter v, section 2, below.

[2] For a survey of the period's multiple varieties of religious fiction, consult Margaret M. Maison, *The Victorian Vision* (New York,

was its propagandistic use in need of vindication. Still, Mrs. Ward's own defiant plea for a new secular church, to be called "the brotherhood of Jesus," stirred the minds of the Victorian reading public, which was receptive yet distrustful of her extreme liberalism in matters of faith.

Spokesmen for the State, the Church, and that new power, Science, soon became embroiled in a public controversy over Mrs. Ward's melodramatic depiction of the religious doubts of Elsmere, the novel's clergyman hero. W. E. Gladstone, supported somewhat belatedly by the Bishop of Peterborough and the Reverend Dr. Henry Wace, Principal of King's College, attacked the book for its unbelief; T. H. Huxley, eager for a polemical showdown with the forces of religious orthodoxy, rushed to its rescue. In the year following the publication of the novel, a heated but decorously fought battle was waged in the pages of the *Nineteenth Century*. Mrs. Ward herself participated briefly by outlining the various trends in biblical criticism which had made orthodox belief so impossible for her novel's empirical-minded hero. But it was Huxley, the man who had once crowned Darwin and who now wore his mantle, who carried the day under the new watchword of "agnosticism." Years later, Mrs. Ward gratefully remembered "the dear and famous Professor" (he was her sister's father-in-law) "who, like my uncle, fought half the world and scarcely made an enemy."[3]

The controversy over *Robert Elsmere* was symptomatic: the book's historic significance exceeded by far its intrinsic merits. For Mrs. Ward's novel was but the culmination of two distinct though overlapping phases of Victorian specula-

---

1961); also see Joseph Ellis Baker, *The Novel and the Oxford Movement* (Princeton, 1932).

[3] *A Writer's Recollections* (London, 1918), II, 170-171.

tive thought: the one expressed in the writings of evolutionists or thinkers of a "scientific" cast of mind, the other contained in inventive attempts at reconciling the new beliefs
with the old. The 1850's and the early 1860's had seen the
final consolidation of an empirical spirit which challenged,
quite tentatively at first and then more directly, the old
Mosaic cosmogony, as well as the miraculous element, in
the Scripture. The assumptions of natural scientists and historians were quickly—though often quite superficially—
assimilated by a small elite of intellectuals. In the 1860's,
but above all in the 1870's and 1880's, there was a prolifera-
tion of imaginative efforts to reconcile the new findings
with the moral verities of the old religion. Writers such as
Mrs. Ward's famous uncle accepted the empiricist premise
that "miracles did not exist," but they enlisted their creative talents in the fashioning of "essences" of Christianity
based on a "scientific appreciation of the facts of religion."[4]
"The thing," in Arnold's words, was "to recast religion."[5]

Through the process of a dialectical balancing of the
factual and the potential, the relative and the absolute, the
"sweet" and the "reasonable," the prosaic and the poetical,
the "Hebraic" and the "Hellenic," Victorian critics of culture and religion hoped to amass truths untainted by error
and to weld them into a "natural," if necessarily eclectic,
faith. Their humanist creeds were intended as a compromise
between the orthodoxies of religion and science; actually,
they resulted in a reduction of both. Their relativism was
branded as atheistic by the Church; the conversion of this
relativism into personal cults was denounced by the genuine

[4] Matthew Arnold, *St. Paul and Protestantism with an Essay on
Puritanism and the Church of England* (New York, 1875), p. 118.
[5] Matthew Arnold, *Literature and Dogma: An Essay Towards a
Better Apprehension of the Bible* (London, 1873), p. xi.

scientist as being tantamount to the transformation of old myths into new allegories.[6]

Its negative aspects notwithstanding, the "spirit of the relative" was initially hailed by a number of writers, who saw in its applications a break with the tyranny of the absolute. In 1853 Marian Evans told herself in a rare outburst of confidence: "Heaven help us! said the old religions—the new one, from its very lack of that faith, will teach us all the more to help one another."[7] Yet the future George Eliot was to rectify this initial optimism by painfully reappraising and refining her humanist convictions throughout the entire corpus of her novels. She was not the only one to find relativism a self-divisive tool. As if anticipating the desperate mockery of an Oscar Wilde, many an "earnest" seeker exercised his irony in fruitless public debates or yielded to the allurements of paradox in a prolonged dialogue with himself: "Let us tell the truth about ourselves, even if the truth be only that there is no truth to tell."[8]

Humanism inevitably placed a burden on the individual by doing away with the security provided by established doctrines and usages. "As faith loses in extent it must gain in intensity," professed Benjamin Jowett.[9] Yet each Victorian reconciler had a different conception of this "intensity." To Matthew Arnold it was equivalent to the absorption of a

[6] T. H. Huxley disdainfully dismissed the emerging "religions of humanity" as the work of mere scientolators propounding a "new Anthropolatry" ("Agnosticism," *The Nineteenth Century*, xxv, February 1889, 354-355).

[7] *The George Eliot Letters*, ed. Gordon S. Haight (New Haven, 1954-1955), II, 82.

[8] R. H. Hutton, "Professor Tyndall on Physical and Moral Necessity," *Criticisms on Contemporary Thought and Thinkers* (London, 1894), p. 245.

[9] *The Life and Letters of Benjamin Jowett*, ed. Evelyn Abbott and Lewis Campbell (London, 1897), I, 115.

literary "sweetness and light" based on the best that had been thought and said; to John Ruskin it was to be obtained through the moral influence of the forms of Nature or of a society modeled on Nature; to Walter Pater it became analogous to the "quickened sense of life" brought on by the sensual appreciation of art.[10] To many others "intensity" was to be found in an active creed of social sympathy and humanitarianism. Yet the starting point for all the new creeds was the human "heart." "To gain religious starting points," argued none other than John Henry Newman, aware that humanist doubt could well lead to orthodox assent, "we must . . . interrogate our hearts, and (since it is a personal individual matter) our *own* hearts."[11]

What had begun as a disparagement of the old religion two decades before, ended in the 1870's and 1880's as a conservative clinging to its remains. Shortly after attacking the unscientific side of Protestant theology, Matthew Arnold found it necessary to profess in a "palinode" that Hebraic conduct, and not cultural Hellenism, was after all "three-fourths of human life."[12] George Eliot, who, in her early essays on the poet Young and the preacher Dr. Cumming, had acidly denounced the "other-worldliness" of a scriptural bibliolatry, depicted in her last novel an Old Testament righteousness based on the workings of an unknown and providential power.[13] Walter Pater revoked the Hellenism

[10] *The Renaissance: Studies in Art and Poetry* (London, 1910), p. 238.

[11] Wilfrid Ward, *The Life of John Henry Cardinal Newman* (London, 1912), II, 331.

[12] *Literature and Dogma*, p. 381. In *St. Paul and Protestantism* Arnold had praised the Apostle for his Hellenic culture and argued that it was "the scientific value of his teaching" that gave him "his permanent worth and vitality" (p. 9). Three years later, this "value" has shrunk to only "one fourth of life."

[13] Cf. "Evangelical Teaching: Dr. Cumming," *Westminster Re-*

of *The Renaissance* in order to worship in the religious "atmospheres" of Amiens and Vézelay. Samuel Butler, increasingly dissatisfied with the mechanistic world of the Darwinians, endowed it with a teleology of his own. Other writers unconsciously echoed Voltaire's famous epigram about the necessity of inventing God. "Perhaps a hypothetical religion is better than none at all," wrote Frederic Harrison, looking backward defensively at Positivism and its detractors.[14] And Stopford Brooke, likewise taking a retrospective look, mused in self-amazement about the times "when we threw everything into the seething pot and wondered what would emerge."[15]

Robert Elsmere thus arrived on the scene late enough for Mrs. Ward to capitalize on the practice of previous and more distinguished "reconcilers," but still early enough for her to believe in the efficacy of its prescriptions. Like her uncle, she intends nothing less than to "recast religion"; the search for a new binding faith still remains to her, as to Elsmere, "the problem of the world at this moment."[16] Mrs. Ward also accepts the "scientific" spirit of her predecessors. Elsmere,

---

view, LXIV (October 1855), 436-462, and "Worldliness and Other-Worldliness: the Poet Young," *Westminster Review*, LXVII (January 1857), 1-42. George Eliot's reversion in *Daniel Deronda* to a belief in the "bare possibility" of a supernatural power is discussed in Chapter IV, below.

[14] *Autobiographical Memoirs* (London, 1911), II, 92.

[15] *The Life and Letters of Stopford Brooke*, ed. Lawrence Pearsall Jacks (London, 1917), II, 628.

[16] *Robert Elsmere*, 2 vols. (London, 1888), chap. 32, p. 155. Mrs. Ward went on to explore the religious "problem" in *The History of David Grieve* (1892), *The Marriage of William Ashe* (1905), and *The Case of Richard Meynell* (1911). In her later novels she rejected her earlier plea for a new sect and adhered instead to Arnold's belief that theological reform should come within the established Church.

we are informed along the way, read Darwin's *Earthworms* and *The Origin of Species* shortly after his ordination and marriage; Mrs. Ward takes it for granted that her readers understand the significance of such an act. For soon the young clergyman lets "himself drift" into a dangerous "intellectual intimacy with one of the most distinguished of anti-Christian thinkers," the Squire Wendover.[17] Elsmere's perusal of the Squire's major work, *The Idols of the Market Place*, leads him to the writings of the German biblical critics and stimulates him to an awareness of the analogous predicament of "M. Renan."[18] The young man's religion collapses like a house of cards. His wife's broken pleas are futile, though fully exploited for their pathetic effect: " 'Do you think *nothing* is true because something may be false? Did not—did not—Jesus still live, and die, and rise again?—*can* you doubt—*do* you doubt—that He rose—that He is God —that He is in heaven—that we shall see Him?' "[19] Elsmere does not flinch from his wife's orthodox "intensity." For, unknown to her, Catherine has raised precisely those points challenged by the "Higher Criticism" in Germany and in England. Elsmere answers calmly: "I can believe no longer in an Incarnation and Resurrection . . . Miracle is a natural product of human feeling and imagination."[20]

In the words of W. H. Mallock, the popularity of *Robert Elsmere* illustrated "first, the amount of unformulated scepticism prevalent amongst the Christian public; secondly, the eagerness of this public to understand its own scepticism

[17] *Robert Elsmere*, chap. 22, p. 458.

[18] Elsmere reads the same commentary on the Book of Daniel that —as Mrs. Ward is quick to point out—drove "M. Renan out of the Church of Rome" (*ibid.*, chap. 24, p. 22). She had reviewed the Frenchman's autobiography only five years before.

[19] *Ibid.*, chap. 28, p. 87.

[20] *Ibid.*

more clearly; and lastly, its eagerness to discover that, whatever its scepticism might take from it, something would still be left it, which was really the essence of Christianity. In other words, the popularity of *Robert Elsmere* is mainly the expression of the devout idea that the essence of Christianity will somehow survive its doctrines."[21] Though Mallock directed his criticism at the drab Christian socialism preached by Mrs. Ward's renegade minister, his criticism applied also to Elsmere's more eminent prototypes. For if Mrs. Ward's attempt to "recast religion" had become a time-honored practice by 1888, her use of fiction as a vehicle for this attempt had likewise acquired a venerable ancestry. As Pater well knew in framing his question, "the influence of religion upon human character" had, in effect, become a "legitimate function" of the English novel through the efforts of a small group of writers who had preceded her in the search for a Christian "essence."

By 1888 Mrs. Ward had a variety of immediate models to choose from even without looking to America or to the Continent. Among the more important there was *John Inglesant* (1880), the religio-historical novel by J. H. Shorthouse.[22] There were also the two parts of "Mark Rutherford's" *Autobiography* (1881, 1885), written in the genre adopted by seekers as diverse as Thomas Carlyle, J. A. Froude, John Henry Newman, and William Delafield Arnold, Mrs. Ward's younger uncle, who had died in

[21] "Amateur Christianity," *The Fortnightly Review*, LVII (May 1892), 678.

[22] Charles Kingsley in his belligerently subtitled *Hypatia: Or, New Foes with an Old Face* (1853), Cardinal Wiseman in *Fabiola: Or, the Church of the Catacombs* (1855), and John Henry Newman in *Callista: A Tale of the Third Century* (1856), had all resorted to historical fiction for the purpose of religious propaganda.

1859.[23] And there was the combination of the historical novel with the spiritual "autobiography" in Walter Pater's own *Marius the Epicurean* (1885), a work reviewed by Mrs. Ward, who noted at that time that books such as "*Sartor Resartus,* or *The Nemesis of Faith, Alton Locke* or *Marius*" would one day reveal to the student of the nineteenth century "what was deepest, most intimate, and most real in its personal experience."[24] Though unaware that a satirical version of the spiritual "autobiography" had been completed two years before and lay stowed away in Samuel Butler's desk, Mrs. Ward shunned the autobiographical form in general, possibly because she distrusted it for its "intimate" and revelatory qualities (*The Way of All Flesh* would be read by future generations as its author's self-catharsis).[25] At any rate, Mrs. Ward could avail herself of an even more commanding model.

This model was none other than George Eliot, already revered as a literary classic eight years after her death. Unlike Mrs. Ward's somewhat easy acceptance of the

[23] The quasi-religious and autobiographical nature of *Sartor Resartus* (1833-1834) undoubtedly gave an impetus to works such as Froude's *Shadows of the Clouds* (1847) and *The Nemesis of Faith* (1849), Newman's *Loss and Gain* (1849), and Arnold's *Oakfield* (1853), a work published under the pseudonym of "Punjabee." Carlyle's impact on George Eliot, Pater, and Butler—writers who truly converted this form into fiction—is also undeniable; yet his relevance is ideological rather than artistic.

[24] "Marius the Epicurean," *Macmillan's Magazine,* LII (June 1885), 134.

[25] Nonetheless, Mrs. Ward did manage to generate some "biographical" interest in *Robert Elsmere*: "Grey of Oxford" was identified with T. H. Green, to whose memory the book was dedicated; Edward Langham, a languid sensationalist, was rumored by many to have been inspired by Walter Pater. Mrs. Ward did nothing to quell that rumor, although she dispelled the notion that the infidel Squire Wendover was based on Mark Pattison.

skepticism of an earlier generation, George Eliot's religious and intellectual scrutinies had been prompted by her own intimate experience. The multiple position of novelist, reviewer, poet, oracle, and observer had been arduously attained. Her scarring but fortifying encounter with the new "development hypothesis" in the "Higher Criticism" of Hennell, Strauss, and Feuerbach, as well as an almost masculine mastery of the physical sciences, made her eminently fitted for the role of Victorian authoress-sage. At first addressing herself to the audiences of Dickens and Mrs. Gaskell, George Eliot later included the public sought out by Matthew Arnold and other prophets of culture and religion, an intelligentsia composed of those increasingly disenchanted unbelievers "who now throw the Bible aside, not those who receive it on the ground supplied either by popular theology or by metaphysical theology."[26] It was this later George Eliot (as well as her uncle) whom Mrs. Ward was consciously emulating in *Robert Elsmere*.[27]

Unlike her earlier Wordsworthian reinterpretations of a rural English past, George Eliot's later novels reflect the more discursive climate of the seventies. In 1859 *Adam Bede* illustrated a covertly recast Adamic myth in light of the still unpopular theories of Feuerbach; the same novel also portrayed an "evolutionary ethic" several months before the

[26] *Literature and Dogma*, p. 127.

[27] Mrs. Ward's indebtedness to George Eliot in *Robert Elsmere* caused Pater to recommend the book to the latter's admirers. The characterization of Catherine Leyburn, the novel's puritanical heroine, is modeled on that of Dorothea Brooke in *Middlemarch*, while that of Rose, her egoist sister, bears distinct resemblances to George Eliot's portraits of Rosamond Vincy and Gwendolen Harleth. For a comparison of the ethical systems espoused by the two woman novelists see the present writer's "The Rival Ladies: Mrs. Ward's *Lady Connie* and Lawrence's *Lady Chatterley's Lover*," *Victorian Studies*, IV (December 1960), 141-158.

publication of *The Origin of Species* launched other Victorian writers on a similar search.[28] In the seventies, however, George Eliot's novels reflect the firm entrenchment of a scientific materialism and the widespread acceptance of a variety of humanist creeds. As a consequence, there is a change both in tone and in emphasis. *Middlemarch* (1871-1872) and *Daniel Deronda* (1876) are above all novels, but they are also compendia of contemporary allusions and prophetic pronouncements by a writer desirous of expanding the standard form of fiction. They are "criticism" in the fullest Victorian sense of the word and belong to a period marked by Arnold's theological essays, Morley's *On Compromise*, Huxley's lectures on the self-sufficiency of science, and Mill's posthumous *Essays in Religion*. They form part of a decade of reassessment and controversy—of debates conducted in lecture halls, journals, pamphlets, or on the premises of the "Metaphysical Society."

Unlike Mrs. Ward, George Eliot never yielded to the temptation of writing fictionalized "criticism," or, what is the same, of resorting to the *roman à thèse*. Though coming perilously close to a propagandistic use of the novel in *Daniel Deronda*, she was one of the few Victorian reconcilers who managed to preserve an artistic integrity. Two years after the publication of *Daniel Deronda* and ten years before the appearance of Mrs. Ward's novel, she protested, perhaps a trifle too much, that her role was not that of the didacticist or social reformer: "My function is that of the *aesthetic*, not the doctrinal teacher—the rousing of nobler emotions, which

[28] See Chapter II below. "Evolutionary ethics" is a term used to comprehend all theories which hold that "man's moral standards and ethical ideas" have evolved from the observable behavior of other animals (David Lack, *Evolutionary Theory and Christian Belief: The Unresolved Conflict*, London, 1957, p. 91).

make mankind desire the social right, not the prescribing of special measures."[29] It was this quality that Henry James undoubtedly had in mind when he commented, not without some reservations, on George Eliot's contribution to the development of English fiction: "Fielding was didactic—the author of *Middlemarch* is really philosophic."[30]

2. GEORGE ELIOT, WALTER PATER, AND SAMUEL BUTLER: THREE TYPES OF SEARCH

To understand how three major writers tried to present through the medium of fiction "the legitimate function" demanded by Pater without abandoning the "aesthetic function" postulated by George Eliot is the main aim of this study. Like the work of many a Victorian "reconciler," its format is the result of a compromise. Modern literary scholars tend to fall into two distinct camps. The one regards a work as a repository of ideologies and intellectual issues; the other denies the validity of an historical approach. The dangers of either extreme are evident. A study which would treat a novel like *Robert Elsmere* as the culmination of the history of an "idea" conveniently ignores the book's artistic demerits. On the other hand, the failure to apply an "ideological" type of criticism to works which, like *Middlemarch*, *Daniel Deronda*, *Marius the Epicurean*, and *The Way of All Flesh*, were intended to be "really philosophic" robs them of much of their richness. Throughout this study, therefore, an equal emphasis is given to ideas and to their artistic transmutation into a peculiar type of novel—a novel advocating a religious humanism based on the fusion of science,

---

[29] *The George Eliot Letters*, VII, 44.

[30] James's 1873 review, "George Eliot's *Middlemarch*," is reprinted in *Nineteenth Century Fiction*, VIII (December 1953), 161-170.

morality, and historicism, but essentially one prompted by "religious yearning without a religious object."[31]

George Eliot, Walter Pater, and Samuel Butler were selected as subjects because of the similarity of purpose and background which they brought to the writing of their novels, as well as for the rich contrasts provided by their ideas, their search for faith, and their art. The representativeness of these ideas, the modernity of their religious inquiries, and the artistic relevance of their novels to the later development of English fiction were equally decisive. Although all three writers turned to the novel in order to "recast religion," their respective efforts to endow an alien evolutionary cosmos with new ethical principles were remarkably dissimilar. George Eliot made use of her early contact with the new "development theory" to achieve her masterful balancing of science and religion in *Middlemarch*, a balance which gives way to her "Hebraist" synthesis in *Daniel Deronda*. Walter Pater's historicist and aesthetic theories led him, on the other hand, to concentrate on the "imaginary portrait" of a young doubter who hovers between the "atmospheres" provided by the noblest pagan philosophies and by the neo-Hellenic religion of the early Christian church. Samuel Butler, perhaps the boldest of the group, transmuted autobiography into fiction, satire into earnestness, and an Erewhonian extravaganza into an actual faith, through a utopian redefinition of the Darwinian universe.

The ideas of George Eliot, Butler, and Pater may be linked to three important currents within nineteenth-century English thought: a humanism inspired by Continental philosophers, critics, and historians; a scientism based on the

1 Eliot
2 Butler

[31] Mark Schorer, "Fiction and the 'Matrix of Analogy,'" *Kenyon Review*, IX (Autumn 1949), 539-560.

3 Pater

discoveries of native geologists and biologists; and an aesthetic movement related to its counterpart across the Channel, as well as to the Catholic revival and the Pre-Raphaelite "renaissance" in England. These three currents are not strictly separable; in fact, the ramifications of any one of them merge easily with those of the others. Yet, for the sake of simplification, it is possible to identify each novelist with the predominant concerns of one alone of these three movements.

When Henry James correctly remarked that George Eliot wished above all "to recommend herself to a scientific audience,"[32] he did not therefore assume, as did so many of her contemporaries, that her work was a mere emanation of "the New Spirit that Darwin was to breathe into the inner life of man."[33] For George Eliot enlisted the very tools that she had received from evolutionism for what amounted to a reaction against its materialist tenets. Although her "recommendations" were addressed to the scientific-minded, they were largely inspired by a second wave of the Continental humanism which, in a previous generation, had already prompted Coleridge and Carlyle to challenge science and its assumptions. Like Matthew Arnold, whose cultural traditionalism had similar origins, she attempted to conserve a Christian "essence" that would be ethical as well as empirical, "natural," or "scientific." The chapter on George Eliot's intellectual preparation shows how her conversance with science and the German "Higher Criticism" was carried into the construction of her novels.

[32] "George Eliot's *Middlemarch*," p. 169. James regarded this choice of audience rather coldly; but John Ruskin, ignoring George Eliot's admiration for his own work or for that of his master Carlyle, passionately denounced her appeal to a public steeped in and obsessed by science (See "Letter 29," in *Fors Clavigera*).

[33] Joseph Jacobs, *Literary Studies* (New York, 1896), p. xx.

It is supplemented by a comparison of George Eliot's concept of "culture" with that of Matthew Arnold.

Unlike George Eliot, Samuel Butler belongs squarely in a native English tradition. Initially a Darwinian, Butler moved from science to pseudo science in his gradual consolidation of a vitalist faith which was to be refined by Shaw and D. H. Lawrence. The chapter on Butler's intellectual background retraces the steps by which he constructed the creed of Ernest Pontifex, a creed, which for all its Lamarckian trappings, was primarily the product of his own ingenuity. Butler went beyond George Eliot in his attempt to impose design on the evolutionary universe of Darwin, Wallace, and Huxley; yet the rational world he built as a substitute was, as he admitted himself, the product of a highly irrational "dream." Butler remained a half-hearted rationalist transplanted into a neo-Romantic age. He mocked Darwin because he basically believed in him: his satire was exploratory and his utopianism the product of wishful thinking. Butler's unconventional attempts to impress harmony on a fortuitous world of natural selection resembled the far more conventional and less imaginative efforts of those late eighteenth-century writers who sought to reconcile the natural sciences with a divine purpose. It was no coincidence that, in later years, Butler should seek out the writings of Erasmus Darwin in order to confute the discoveries of his grandson.

The curious aestheticism of Walter Pater has been placed in the middle section of this study. He falls, appropriately enough, between the humanism of George Eliot or Matthew Arnold and the scientism of Samuel Butler. Like Butler, Pater was a Hellenist who rebelled against the assumptions of Arnold's and George Eliot's stoical creeds. Like Butler, he believed in the sole validity of the sensational impression. But Pater also believed with Arnold and George Eliot in the urgency of conserving a morality based on a Judaeo-Christian "essence." What is more, he was incapable of transmuting this "essence" into a new allegory such as Butler's vitalist "dream." He therefore turned to ritual and religious art in order to find in their artificial "atmospheres" a source for moral impressions. The chapter on Pater's theories examines his "religion of sanity," a creed he arrived at by the fusion of such disparate elements as Hegel's cosmic view of history, Gautier's *"L'art pour l'art,"* and the ritualism of the Oxford Apostles.

Despite this variety, these three novelists shared a large measure of experience, response, and hope. All were anti-rationalistic and anti-doctrinal. All preached an ethic based on the relativism of truth. All three began their careers by squarely rejecting the other-worldliness of the religion of their forefathers; all ended by affirming that faith alone could be a substitute for faith. Above all, however, George Eliot, Butler, and Pater were equally influenced by the idea of evolution, for the "spirit of the relative" was itself the product of the new developmental views which descended on the Victorians with such an unexpected suddenness and undermined the foundations of traditional belief. Robert Elsmere was only one of many who were converted to skepticism by the appearance of the "historical Jesus" of the "Higher Critics." George Eliot was the translator of Strauss and Feuerbach; Butler, the anonymous author of *The Fair Haven*, a work which satirically exploited the inconsistencies of the Gospels. Pater, at Oxford during the publication of *Essays and Reviews* in 1860, was only too well acquainted with German and English scriptural criticism.

The idea that the Bible was not God's unique revelation to man, but rather a partisan and often distorted account of historical facts, was in itself subordinated to the still vaster evolutionary theses of history and science. Earlier centuries had regarded history as an orderly cyclical process; the new historicism saw its movements "travel not in circles but in spirals."[34] Man was placed in a world of perpetual flux, a world in which afterlife was nonexistent, and in which existence itself was subject to implacable laws of change. To darken the picture, Darwinism regarded human progress as a mere by-product of organic evolution; it subsumed personal identity under that of the species. Heredity and "environment" determined individual life. Rooted in (and often annihilated by) physical time, man had become akin to the animals whose paragon he was once supposed to have been. The study of comparative religion, sociology, and anthropology was the result of the new "development hypothesis" which, as Walter Pater complained, threatened to invade every conception formulated by man: "Nay, the idea of development (that, too, a thing of growth, developed in the progress of reflexion) is at last invading one by one, as the secret of their explanation, all the products of mind, the very mind, itself, the abstract reason; our certainty, for instance, that two and two make four. Gradually we have come to think, or to feel, that primary certitude. Political constitutions, again, as we now see so clearly, are 'not made,' cannot be made, but 'grow.' Races, laws, arts, have their origins and end, are themselves ripples only on the great river of organic life; and language is changing on our very lips."[35]

The Victorian novelist had always been a moralist. It was logical that first George Eliot and then Pater and Butler should turn to the medium of fiction in their attempts to fashion a creed in accord with the new evolutionary world

[34] R. G. Collingwood, *The Idea of History* (Oxford, 1946), p. 114.

[35] *Plato and Platonism: A Series of Lectures* (London, 1910), pp. 20-21.

that they were faced with. This creed would be eminently "scientific," but it would also infuse poetry into an otherwise drab and prosaic age by lifting it "above the humdrum of life." To them, as to D. H. Lawrence later on, the novel was to preserve the truths of the Bible, to reshape them into a new "essence," and rehabilitate them for a future "environment." Such prophetic reconciliations demanded integrity as well as ingenuity. Despair was coupled to hope: If man was an evolutionary creature, could he not, if so induced, develop into a higher stage? If the unscientific religions of old were now obsolete, could not some of their features be retained to accommodate and guide such an evolution? The thing was not how to be, but rather how to become. If the *Zeitgeist* ruthlessly determined man's progress, an imaginative interpretation of its mechanics could provide both a guide and an inspiration. The thing was to look forward, to devise a new faith, but also to glance backward at those principles which were immutable, or at least capable of self-adjustment. Only the past could yield the prescriptions for the future. To George Eliot, Pater, and Butler these questions acquired a burning intensity: though pessimistic about their own era, they refused to portray the relentless naturalism of a Zola or a Norris or to depict a world as oppressive as that of Thomas Hardy. They would liberate a future age instead: their own "essences" were to be the heritage of saner generations.

Later generations, unemancipated by these prophets, regarded their attempts with suspicion and distrust. Pater and George Eliot fell into disrepute; Butler was hailed for his pose only. The contemporary reader is likely to be more sympathetic, aware as he is that the moral relativism of the Victorians has become a part of his own ethos, aware also that half of the world had come to believe in still another, far less compromising, nineteenth-century "faith." And yet, for all his sympathy, he cannot but regard the Victorian fusions of science and religion as highly facile. Their confident amalgam of all idealism and materialism has turned in our own times into a very brittle compound. Their optimistic belief in progress and in perfectibility has been belied by two world wars; their man-centered creeds are dampened by the crimes subsequently committed to justify the superman and the superrace; their ambitious, syncretic *summas* are distasteful to an age of specialization. Seen from an eighty-year vantage point, even their basic assumptions and proposals seem strikingly limited: Pater rejects all systems of abstract thinking, only to reduce religion to the ritualistic sensations of sympathy and joy; in order to avoid abstractions, George Eliot ultimately abstracts an Old Testament "righteousness" to such a degree as to become one-sided and unnatural; Samuel Butler, who mocks this righteousness, goes to the opposite extreme by basing morality on a "natural," vitalist creed carved out from the phantasy world of Erewhon.

But when all has been said, the modern reader finds an undeniable kinship with these three novelists—their enthusiasms, their arguments, their idioms are still very much alive. The worlds of Fielding, Jane Austen, and Scott, even Trollope or Thackeray, have assumed a remoteness, even a quaintness, which by comparison almost lends George Eliot, Pater, and Butler the shape of contemporary writers. Their precarious balancing of an inherited faith with the conclusions forced upon them by natural science, even the inconsistencies of their creeds, the evasions and compromises of their reconciliations, are our own. They foreshadow our own Freudian ethics and existentialist doctrines. Though possibly not in the sense that they would have liked to believe, they are, after all, the creators of our present.

For the student of the novel, the work of these three writers has an even greater bearing: their experimentations in the realm of fiction opened the way for later novelists who likewise chose to replace the revelations of the Bible with the prophecies of their art. The search of Marius the Epicurean, the young and "constitutionally impressible" Roman whose severe religious temperament is so much at odds with his intense desire for beauty, leads logically to that of Stephen Daedalus, the ascetic Dubliner who transforms art into a self-created faith. Similarly, the passage from faith to stoicism which chastens the ardor of a Dorothea Brooke also marks the conversion of E. M. Forster's Mrs. Moore: stripped of their provincialism, both women find that the "divine words" of their "poor little talkative Christianity" have become supplanted by the mocking rhythm of a wider, but impersonal and alien, natural order.[36] The "crossing" undertaken by an Ernest Pontifex reschooled in the ways of nature, on the other hand, anticipates the "deliverance" of many a Lawrencian hero.

The distinctly modern preoccupation with time also informs these novels. *Middlemarch* depicts the relentless "march" of human progress; *Marius*, the onslaught of the flux; *The Way of All Flesh*, the workings of an unconscious ancestral "memory." Regardless of their effectiveness as creeds, George Eliot's and Pater's reductions of religion into humanist traditions and Butler's own diminution of heritage into heredity, led them, as novelists, to new spatial and temporal forms. Dorothea Brooke and Daniel Deronda, Marius the Epicurean and Ernest Pontifex are forced by their creators to look back into the past as well as forward into the future. They must establish their identity in a shifting world oppressed by time, a world no longer offering

[36] *A Passage to India* (New York, 1924), p. 150.

the transcendence once assured by Scriptures which have themselves become only "a great confused novel" about "man alive."[37]

Victorian humanism thus brought a new dimension to the English novel which was perhaps after all the "religious function" Pater had asked for. The intensity with which Joyce, Lawrence, and Forster depicted "the influence of religion upon human character" would have been impossible without the efforts of those nineteenth-century writers who were the first to utilize the novel in their search for a principle of perpetuity. *Ulysses*, that twentieth-century compendium of the best that has been thought and said, can, like its Victorian counterpart, *Middlemarch*, be understood in terms of the Arnoldian opposites of the Hellenic and the Hebraic. For *Middlemarch*—like *Daniel Deronda*, *Marius the Epicurean*, and *The Way of All Flesh*—did not only set "a limit . . . to the development of the old-fashioned novel,"[38] but also mapped out the direction in which modern fiction would grow.

[37] D. H. Lawrence, "Why the Novel Matters," *Selected Literary Criticism*, ed. Anthony Beal (London, 1955), p. 105.
[38] "George Eliot's *Middlemarch*," p. 170.

*Eliot's transmutation of ideas into art
is her greatest contribution to literature
and most ignored by critics*

II

George Eliot:
The Search for a Religious Tradition

> *Nothing is more natural than that those who cannot
> rest content with intellectual analysis, while awaiting
> the advent of the Saint Paul of the humanitarian faith
> of the future, should gather up provisionally such
> fragmentary illustrations of this new faith as are to be
> found in the records of old.* —John Morley

> *Will you not agree with me that there is one compre-
> hensive Church whose fellowship consists in the desire
> to purify and ennoble life, and where the best members
> of all narrower churches may call themselves brother
> and sister in spite of differences?* —George Eliot

THE RECENT revival of interest in George Eliot, largely
inspired by the publication in 1954 of the first volumes of
Professor Gordon S. Haight's *The George Eliot Letters*, has
resulted in a sizable amount of literary criticism and scholarship. Yet, for the most part, individual critical attempts to
deal with George Eliot's writings have been singularly one-
sided. Critics have either concentrated on a close scrutiny
of the formal aspects of her art, or, increasingly aware of
her importance as a thinker whose work was really meant to
be "philosophic," have examined George Eliot's early essays
and reviews in order to reconstruct the ideology later exemplified in her novels in the light of Darwin, Huxley, Comte,
Mill, Lewes, Spencer, Hennell, Strauss, or Feuerbach. Both
approaches have yielded valuable and illuminating results.
And yet they have somehow perpetuated the illusion that
George Eliot's art and ideology are best examined in separa-

tion, that two divorced "principles" govern her novels, and that these principles, the one artistic and the other intellectual, must remain irrevocably apart.[1] Thus, a fine critic of George Eliot's "form" seems compelled to argue defensively that the neglect of the "strictly formal features" of her fiction merits an exclusive attention to her art,[2] while an equally able expositor of the philosophical implications of George Eliot's determinism is betrayed into self-consciousness when in his otherwise excellent discussion, he admits that he treats "George Eliot as a philosopher rather than an artist."[3]

George Eliot successfully transmuted ideas into the form and structure of her novels; it is seldom sufficiently emphasized that this transmutation is in itself a key to her "art." A grasp of the intellectual crosscurrents to which she was exposed and to which she responded in the 1840's and 1850's is indispensable not only for an understanding of her last two novels, *Middlemarch* (1871-1872) and *Daniel Deronda* (1876), but also of earlier works such as *Adam Bede* (1859) or *The Mill on the Floss* (1860), which, because of their less apparent problematic nature, have invited the attention of critics uninterested in relating them to their ideological background. That student of contemporary fiction

[1] This distinction, implicitly assumed by most of George Eliot's critics, is formulated by Neil D. Isaacs, "*Middlemarch*: Crescendo of Obligatory Drama," *Nineteenth Century Fiction*, XVIII (June 1963), 21-34. Mr. Isaacs, however, fails to relate the "philosophical principle" of the book to its "structural" counterpart or to discuss those "biographical and historical matters" that he regards as essential ingredients of the former.

[2] Barbara Hardy, *The Novels of George Eliot: A Study in Form* (London, 1959), p. 1.

[3] George Levine, "Determinism and Responsibility in the Works of George Eliot," *Publications of the Modern Language Association*, LXXVII (June 1962), 268-279.

who is concerned above all with the elucidation of "technique" examines a novel like *Adam Bede* and is elated to discover a wealth of animal imagery running through the book or to perceive the paralleling of a Christian ritual in Adam's ceremonial tasting of bread and wine. Passing on to *The Mill on the Floss*, he may find that the movement of the onrushing flood which unites Tom and Maggie in death fits into an over-all "pattern" provided by the alternation of motion and rest throughout the novel. Encouraged, he may now turn to the rest of her fiction and feel competent to discuss the totality of her "vision" (although the open intrusion of "ideas" into works such as *Romola*, *Felix Holt*, or *Deronda* may give him pause). Such a discussion must perforce be a limited one. Ready to examine a novel's use of image, ritual, or myth, quick to detect "Christ figures," eager to discourse about stasis and motion, our hypothetical critic is bound to fail unless he is able to link "techniques" to their deliberative function or to grasp their intellectual origins. The animal imagery in *Adam Bede*, for instance, is an integral part of George Eliot's Miltonic effort to endow a new and even further fallen Adam with a "natural" ethic; this ethic, in turn, is designed to remind Adam, through the example of his flawed Eve, Hetty, that man is but a fallible, though potentially noble, animal, whose only possibility of transcending a finite world lies in the survival of his species and in his contribution to its advancement.[4] Again, Adam's ritualistic supper gains an added meaning in light of the symbology and creed which George Eliot derived from Ludwig Feuerbach, whose *Essence of Christianity* she had translated only five years before the completion of her novel.[5] In *The Mill on the Floss* her symbolic identification of the river with the deterministic flow of history is readily apparent

[4] See pp. 34-37, below.   [5] See pp. 55-59, below.

to the reader acquainted with a similar representation of the *Zeitgeist* in the essays of J. S. Mill and the poetry of Matthew Arnold, or of the flux in the "imaginary portraits" of Walter Pater.

To understand how "form" and "ideology" blend in *Middlemarch* and *Daniel Deronda*, the works to be examined in Chapters III and IV of this study, as well as to understand the full significance of George Eliot's departures in the latter novel, this chapter will rehearse three important aspects of her thought which went into the making of her novels: her scientific positivism, her "humanization" of Christianity, and her Arnold-like belief in the force of tradition. Thus, George Eliot's relation to the scientific movements of her time, her indebtedness to the "Higher Criticism" of the Bible, and the similarities between her traditionalism and that of Matthew Arnold are explored in the three sections that follow, in order to evaluate the particular implications which each of these aspects holds for the substance and mode of her novels.[6]

1. George Eliot and Science

In a famous letter to Charles Kingsley, T. H. Huxley bluntly demands a conversion to the "spirit of science" by

[6] George Eliot's relation to science is examined before the consideration given to her dependence on the Higher Critics, although her acquaintance with the works of Hennell, Strauss, and Spinoza antedated—and her familiarity with Feuerbach was contemporaneous with—her full exposure to the scientific temper reigning at the *Westminster Review* in the early 1850's. Still, an evaluation of the problems raised by her adoption of the "spirit of science" must necessarily precede the discussion of the humanist remedies she derived from the Higher Critics. For a different arrangement and interpretation of some of the material discussed in sections 1 and 2 of this chapter, see Bernard J. Paris, "George Eliot's Religion of Humanity," *English Literary History*, XXIX (December 1962), 418-443.

those who, like Kingsley or F. D. Maurice, were trying to preserve the religion of "that great and powerful instrument for good or evil, the Church of England."[7] To Huxley, the budding neo-Darwinism of Kingsley is a desirable token of things to come, for, if religion "is to be saved from being shivered into fragments by the advancing tide of science . . . it must be by the efforts of men who, like yourself, see your way to the combination of the Church with the spirit of science."[8] It is highly doubtful whether at the time of his letter, 1860, Huxley would have pointed to the recent work of a new novelist, his former colleague on the *Westminster Review*, as an example of this combination. It is certain that Kingsley would hardly have cherished the work of "Miss Evans, the infidel esprit fort," for his model.[9] Yet in the years to come, a majority of Victorians were to regard George Eliot as one who combined at least the "essence" of the Church with the predominant "spirit of science." George Eliot's qualifications were unquestionable. At the end of the novelist's career, an anonymous reviewer surveyed her work and ascribed to it the empirical attitude of positivism, an attitude compressed in the simple statement that "we have no knowledge of anything but phenomena and our knowledge of phenomena is relative, not absolute."[10] Decades later, Frederic Harrison tacitly concurred with this estimate when he remembered George Eliot as "one who, possessed of an

[7] Leonard Huxley, *Life and Letters of Thomas Henry Huxley* (New York, 1901), I, 238.

[8] *Ibid.*

[9] Quoted by Margaret Thorp, *Charles Kingsley* (Princeton, 1933), p. 93. Kingsley's scorn of "Miss Evans" was partly prompted by her adverse reviews of Maurice's *Sermons* and of his own *Westward Ho!*

[10] *London Quarterly Review*, XLVII (January 1877), 447.

immense and *scientific* culture, had long meditated on burning social and moral questions."[11]

George Eliot's "scientific culture" was solidified in the early fifties when, as a contributor to the *Westminster Review*, she was surrounded by men such as Huxley, Owen, and Spencer, at a time when Spencer himself was publishing his historic essay on "The Development Hypothesis" and when George Henry Lewes began his popularization of Comte's philosophy of the sciences.[12] After her union with Lewes, a man esteemed by Darwin and Lyell for "the thoroughness of his knowledge in their departments,"[13] George Eliot remained abreast of all the major scientific and pseudoscientific developments of the time. Evolutionism confirmed her in the empiricist position she was to maintain for the remainder of her life, but it also sharpened her urgent need of imposing a new moral order on the amoral, perennially changing, and hence totally relative cosmos it had established. Her desire for clarity led her to accept the phenomenalism of the new "spirit"; yet its reduction of a purposive universe to a sequence of fortuitous evolutionary processes was distasteful to the residual religiosity of the former Evangelical enthusiast, who had already been forced to part with the mysticism of her "other-worldly" religion.

George Eliot's remarks about *The Origin of Species*, a work she read, assimilated, and correctly evaluated within

[11] *Autobiographic Memoirs* (London, 1911), II, 108 (italics added).

[12] Herbert Spencer's work appeared in the *Leader* in 1852; it anticipated some of Darwin's conclusions and earned him the support of Huxley. At the time, Marian Evans' close friendship with Spencer was expected to lead to their marriage.

[13] Quoted in a letter from Charles Eliot Norton to George William Curtis, January 29, 1869, *The George Eliot Letters*, ed. Gordon S. Haight (New Haven, 1954-1955), V, 8. Hereafter this edition shall be referred to as *GEL*.

days after its publication, reveal this same duality: her sure grasp of the book's relevance for the "spirit of science" clashes with her suddenly aroused religious sensibility—a collision quite similar to that which she was to exploit artistically, more than a decade later, through the opposed points of view of Tertius Lydgate and Dorothea Brooke. Writing to her lifelong friend, Barbara Bodichon, she prophesies that Darwin's study will make "an epoch." She welcomes the "long-celebrated naturalist" (who was to become her and Lewes's friend) as an important latecomer to the ranks of the evolutionists and applauds *The Origin of Species* as "the expression of his thorough adhesion, after long years of study, to the Doctrine of Development." By its fearless contribution to the expansion of human knowledge, the book exemplifies the very truth of the evolutionary "doctrine" tested in its pages: "So the world gets on step by step towards brave clearness and honesty!" But deep spiritual misgivings follow this shrill exclamation. The "clearness" and "honesty" of a devotion to unvarnished truth, even this truth itself, are apparently insufficient to assuage these reservations: "But to me the Development theory and all other explanations of processes by which things came to be, produce a feeble impression compared with the mystery that lies under the processes."[14]

Such pronouncements, significant as they are, must not be overestimated. Since her early childhood Marian Evans had displayed an unusual interest in the natural sciences; it was her desire for precision, however much at odds with her hankering for "mystery," which had, after all, produced her initial break with Christianity in 1842. Thus, despite her ever latent reservations about the "Development theory," she never doubted that its basic explanations of the

[14] All quotations in this paragraph are from *GEL*, III, 227.

"processes by which things came to be" had to be accepted unflinchingly. To a large extent, these explanations even acted as a partial substitute for the moral order she had lost. The Calvinism of her schooldays had instilled in her a belief in rigid laws exacted by a strict and implacable deity; it had stressed the irrevocable "consequences" of human behavior: every single act, gesture, or thought could lead to the salvation or damnation of the believer. Although science forever removed this Calvinist deity, it allowed George Eliot—and fellow Puritan renegades such as T. H. Huxley—to convert it into an equally implacable but this-wordly power as capable of punishing "the great evils of disobedience to natural laws" as of rewarding a submission to "the great and fundamental truths of Nature and [to] the laws of her operation."[15] Science reduced the salvation of the soul to the survival of the species, but its grim emphasis on "consequences" was almost identical to that of the old religion. Huxley's assumption that all conduct was to be guided by a strict observation of "the natural consequences of actions,"[16] was a belief that George Eliot (who had already absorbed Bray's crude "philosophy of necessity" and the historical determinism of Mill and Hegel) not only echoed but also translated into the complex causal sequences of her novels.

There were further links. The close introspection of her early Puritanism, with its meticulous dissection of the hidden motives which prompted men to selfish actions, its deep sense of human depravity and concomitant belief in self-denial, found outlets in the new emphasis on a man-centered order. Metaphysics had been dissolved into psychology and Vic-

[15] "A Liberal Education; and Where to Find It," *Science and Education: Essays* (New York, 1894), p. 86.
[16] *Ibid.*, p. 84.

torian psychologists such as Lewes believed that their main task consisted in a careful differentiation of man's faculties from those of the animals with which he shared a basic instinct of self-preservation and self-gratification. Man's animality, however, his innate egoism, could be tempered by a stoic acceptance of the natural order and his willingness to annul the self in the general advancement of his fellow men. The affective emotions of the "heart"— altruism and self-denial—and the thinking capacity of the "head," could allow him, as a member of the social organism, to rely on the accumulation of human experience and to rise above his instinctual nature: "Human Knowledge is pre-eminently distinguished from Animal Knowledge by this collective experience."[17]

The composition of George Eliot's first four works of fiction—*Scenes of Clerical Life* (1858), *Adam Bede* (1859), *The Mill on the Floss* (1860), and *Silas Marner* (1861)—roughly coincides with Lewes's researches for *The Physiology of Common Life* (1862), which in their meticulous examination of the limitations and potentialities of the human organism anticipate Darwin's far more famous works, *The Descent of Man* (1871) and *The Expression of the Emotions in Animals* (1872).[18] Often misread as an escape to a remote rural past, George Eliot's early novels are, despite their quiescent Wordsworthian atmosphere, a testing ground for some of the scientific assumptions of her contemporaries. Their pastoralism is deceptive, for the actions of all characters are judged, not in terms of the static eighteenth-century order to which they belong historically,

[17] George Henry Lewes, *The Study of Psychology* (London, 1879), p. 166.

[18] For a link between *Middlemarch* and Lewes's later work, *Problems of Life and Mind*, see Chapter III, section 4, below.

but in terms of the dynamic world-picture provided by the "Development theory." The old order, personified as "Old Leisure," a portly gentleman of "quiet perceptions, undiseased by hypothesis: happy in his inability to know the causes of things, preferring the things themselves," unfortunately no longer can mirror the "natural" laws of an evolutionary universe and its creatures.[19] *Adam Bede*, George Eliot's first full-length novel, illustrates her artistic transmutation of these laws and provides a typical pattern for her later work.

In one of his speeches to the London workingmen, T. H. Huxley asked his listeners to suppose "that an adult man, in the full vigour of his faculties, could be suddenly placed in the world, as Adam is said to have been, and then left to do as he best might."[20] Soon enough, Huxley asserted, Nature would become the new Adam's tutor; not only would it teach him practical truths but also act as a moral guide: "And if to this solitary man entered a second Adam, or, better still, an Eve, a new and greater world, that of social and moral phenomena, would be revealed. Joys and woes, compared with which all others might seem but faint shadows, would spring from the new relations. Happiness and sorrow would take the place of the coarser monitors, pleasure and pain; but conduct would still be shaped by the observation of the natural consequences of actions; or, in other words, by the laws of the nature of man."[21]

Adam Bede is a detailed and artistic examination of a similar "natural education." Adam, the proud perfectionist, must submit to the prosaic world into which he has been

[19] *Adam Bede*, Cabinet Edition (Edinburgh, n.d.), chap. 52, p. 341; subsequent references are given in the text.
[20] "A Liberal Education," p. 83.
[21] *Ibid.*, p. 84.

placed; like his successor in *Middlemarch*, Tertius Lydgate, he must be brought to accept his own fallibility: the egotism of his intended Eve, Hetty Sorrell, like that of Rosamond Vincy in the later novel, acts as a humiliating reminder of his own imperfections as a human animal. Unlike Lydgate the aristocratic physician, Adam is not entirely defeated by his illusive Eden. He is provided with an alternate spouse, the nunlike Dinah Morris, who, like Dorothea in *Middlemarch*, must shed her "other-worldly" religiosity.[22] By accepting a world of pain, suffering, and toil, the chastened Adam and his substitute Eve can find solace only by improving the lot of others. George Eliot's stark retelling of *Paradise Lost* contains no angelic visitations or promises of divine redemption. Thrown upon his own resources, stung by the suffering he has witnessed, Adam the craftsman must rely on the Victorian gospel of work: "I'll do the best I can. It's all I've got to think of now—to do my work well, and make the world a bit better place for them as can enjoy it" (ch. 48, p. 277). Allowing for the deliberate "rusticity" of his phrasing, Adam's resolution is almost identical to T. H. Huxley's stoic belief that "the plain duty of each and all of us is to try to make the little corner he can influence somewhat less miserable and somewhat less ignorant than it was before he entered it."[23]

The symbolism of *Adam Bede* reinforces its main theme. One of the most striking touches in the book is the recurring presentation of human beings in terms of animalistic meta-

[22] Dinah's abrupt "conversion" is far more sketchy than that of Dorothea Brooke or Romola. Her marriage to Adam was an afterthought inspired by Lewes; as we shall see, the impossibility of a similar union between Lydgate and Dorothea at the outset of *Middlemarch* informs the entire meaning of the novel.

[23] "On the Physical Basis of Life," *Method and Results: Essays* (New York, 1894), p. 163.

phors or similes. Loamshire, Adam's worldly Eden, teems
with domestic animals. Dogs herald the entries and exits of
almost all characters. There is Gyp, Adam's tailless dog;
Vixen, likened to a woman by her master, Bartle Massey;
Trot, the inseparable companion of Arthur Donnithorne's
mare Meg. With an amazing frequency animals are presented as humans and humans as animals. Marty and
Tommy Poyser are compared to "a couple of spaniels or
terriers"; Totty is referred to as a white suckling pig, while
her name is disparaged as being more fit "for a dog than a
Christian child." In a pointed allusion linking Meg and
Hetty Sorrell (whose very name carries animalistic connota-
tions), George Eliot describes the tremulous pleasure of the
mare, who, on being caressed by the young Squire, reacts
"as many others of her sex." The analogy between the inarticulate Adam and his "phlegmatic" dog is repeatedly
made. Lisbeth Bede comes to the same conclusion when she
observes that Adam's eyes follow Dinah, "welly as Gyp's
follow thee" (ch. 51, p. 324).

The analogies between beast and man are enlisted in
Adam Bede in order to point up the ironic imperfections of
the latter. Adam's unwillingness to accept the failings of
others is countered by the novelist's reminder that "These
fellow-mortals, every one, must be accepted as they are"
(ch. 17, p. 267). But Adam's idealization of Hetty is undermined even further by the barrage of animal images
which liken the young girl to a "star-brown calf," a "bright-
eyed spaniel," a "vain canary bird," a "soft-coated pet animal," while simultaneously stressing her unconcern for the
animals to which she is compared: "Hetty cared little for animals, as you know" (ch. 36, p. 128). During her flight, Hetty
meets a cart with a lonely dog on it, "a small white-and-liver
coloured spaniel," and for the first time feels "as if the help-

less timid creature had some fellowship with her" (ch. 36, pp. 127, 128). In the next chapter Hetty herself clings to life "only as the hunted wounded brute clings to it." After her unsuccessful attempt at suicide, she stumbles into the straw of a sheepfold. Her delight in life causes her to break out in "hysterical joy" over the fact "that she was still on the familiar earth, with the sheep near her" (ch. 37, p. 149). But this communion with earth, obviously paralleling the Nativity scene, does not prompt Hetty to turn toward the child she is about to give birth to; instead, "The very consciousness of her own limbs was a delight to her: she turned up her sleeves, and kissed her arms with the passionate love of life" (ch. 37, p. 149). The sheep, the humble surroundings, and, above all, her approaching motherhood are meaningless to Hetty. They merely accentuate her narcissism. The next time we hear of her, it is through the mouth of Rector Irwine, informing Adam that she is accused of having murdered her child.[24]

Hetty's story is used to impress upon Adam the necessity of the stoic creed he ultimately adopts. Her egotism, Arthur's sensuality, and Adam's aloof belief in his own infallibility, are dissimilar manifestations of the same selfish disregard of "consequences." Confessing herself to Dinah, Hetty reveals that the baby she killed felt "like a heavy weight hanging round my neck" (ch. 45, p. 249). At least one critic has noticed the relationship between this "weight" and the earlier puzzlement of Arthur Donnithorne, Hetty's seducer, over a poem

[24] An overt, if somewhat tasteless contrast between Hetty and Vixen, Bartle's bitch, who proudly nurses a litter of "babbies," is stressed by the schoolmaster himself. But his cruel remarks about Hetty (he calls her a "vermin") are soon exposed as a mere veneer when the lame misogynist, forgetting his earlier promise to drown Vixen's pups, turns lovingly to the dog he addresses as a "good-for-nothing woman."

in a "different style" called "The Ancient Mariner."[25]
Hetty is employed as an agent to convert both Arthur and
Adam into "sadder and wiser" men. Coleridge's supernatural poem is neatly incorporated into George Eliot's
"natural" novel: Adam and Dinah, like Coleridge's wedding
guests, admit to a "tinge of sadness" as the shadow of
Adam's intended bride clouds their nuptials. Hetty's inability
to love "both man and bird and beast" has singled her out
for this emblematic role to convey the book's one simple
moral: "There are so many of us, and our lots are so different: what wonder that Nature's mood is often in harsh contrast with the great crisis of our lives? We are children of
a large family, and must learn, as such children do, not to
expect that our hurts will be made much of—to be content
with little nurture and caressing, and help each other the
more" (ch. 27, pp. 4-5).

The severity of *Adam Bede* is the direct result of the
potentially tragic world given to George Eliot by the new
"spirit of science." Adam's fall is buttressed by his stoic creed
and by the comic vitality of the rustics who surround him.
But in depicting the fall of the "House of Tulliver" (the
intended title of her next novel), George Eliot explored the
tragic implications of the "Development theory," by em-
phasizing, as Professor Haight puts it, "that the survival of
the fittest is not always the survival of the best."[26] In *The
Mill on the Floss*, Tom and Maggie Tulliver are also
forced to "go out of the garden,"[27] but, unlike Adam, they
find no worthwhile substitute: their exile from the "golden
gates of their childhood" into the "thorny wilderness" of

[25] Reva Stump, *Movement and Vision in George Eliot's Novels*
(Seattle, 1959), p. 56.
[26] Introduction, *The Mill on the Floss* (New York, 1961), p. xix.
[27] *The Mill on the Floss*, Cabinet Edition (Edinburgh, n.d.),
chap. 10, p. 152; subsequent references are given in the text.

maturity is fraught with tragic consequences. For, in George Eliot's tragedy of heredity, the mixture of Dodson and Tulliver "blood" which determines the death of Tom and Maggie is as irrevocable as the *ate* of the Greeks. "Maggie's destiny," George Eliot informs us, will "reveal itself like the course of an unmapped river" (ch. 45, p. 211); at the conclusion of the novel, the river Floss becomes the executioner of the "natural" *deos* which Maggie and Tom have offended.

George Eliot's intense idealism, so similar to that which drives Dinah Morris to her "Methody" crusades or that which impels Maggie to seek refuge in the writings of Thomas à Kempis, remained unsatisfied by the rigorous logic of the system to which her demands for "clearness" and "honesty" had led her. Desperately in need of an aesthetic-moral order that would bridge the gap between her empiricism and her residual religiosity, she became temporarily attracted to pseudoscientific attempts to reconcile the two, such as the phrenological creed of her friend Charles Bray and that more popular mid-century cult, Comte's Positivist Religion of Humanity. In either case, however, her precisionist search for truth ultimately forbade the artistic use of "unscientific" ideas.

Charles Bray's phrenological studies appealed to George Eliot's own concern with the correlation between psychology and ethics. In his treatise on *How To Educate the Feelings*, Bray held that ethical "faculties" located in specific areas of the brain determined an individual's personality; thus, a recognition of these faculties (and presumably a "natural selection" based on this recognition) could ultimately bring about an "aristocracy of feeling" which would be a "real Christianity."[28] Although man embodied "all of the faculties

[28] *How to Educate the Feelings or Affections, and Bring the Dispositions, Aspirations, and Passions into Harmony with Sound Intelli-*

found in the lower animals," he could thus strip himself of his animality.[29] The characters in *Adam Bede* occasionally seem to personify categories listed in Bray's treatise, which, in a later edition, smugly referred the reader to the authority of "the distinguished author of *Adam Bede*."[30] But George Eliot could not accept his simplified presentation of human nature. Lewes's denunciation of phrenology contributed to her eventual rejection of Bray's system.[31]

George Eliot's relationship to the Comtean religion of humanity was more complex. Dubbed "Catholicism *minus* Christianity" by Huxley, defended as "Catholicism *plus* Science" by Dr. Richard Congreve, the leader of its English branch, Positivism had initially been hailed as a new *summa*, a unification of all verifiable truths, acceptable, as it was thought, both to the religious- and to the scientific-minded. But, in Basil Willey's words, Comteism "proved an Icarus-flight."[32] On the Continent it was outstripped by Marxism, the sister-ideology with which it was at deadly strife.[33] In

---

gence and Morality (New York, 1883), p. 224. (Lengthy as it is, the full title of Bray's book more than adequately summarizes the key question faced by the characters of George Eliot's novels!)

[29] *Ibid.*

[30] *Ibid.*, p. 82. The symptoms of "Love of Approbation" or "Approbativeness" are reproduced in the characterization of Arthur Donnithorne, while those listed under "Philoprogenitiveness" (Parental Love) are mentioned by George Eliot as being absent in Hetty.

[31] See Anna Theresa Kitchel, *George Lewes and George Eliot: A Review of Records* (New York, 1933), pp. 92-93.

[32] "Auguste Comte," *Nineteenth Century Studies: Coleridge to Matthew Arnold* (London, 1960), p. 187.

[33] Lewes was one of the first to contrast the aims and methods of Positivism and Communism. In the series of articles first published in the *Leader* in 1852 and later reprinted under the title of *Comte's Philosophy of the Science* (London, 1853), he deprecated Communism as a purely political solution of problems embracing moral and religious questions. George Eliot's similar reaction to Communism

England, where Comte's ideas had been propagated by
Lewes and Harriet Martineau, their rigid codification (as
well as the dictatorial rule of Dr. Congreve) soon alienated
earlier sympathizers, such as Mill, Morley, Arnold, Huxley,
and Lewes himself. Under the influence of the latter and of
the weightiness of Mill's and Huxley's critiques, George
Eliot never became a full convert to Dr. Congreve's secular
church, although she befriended him and identified herself
with the general aims of his "religion." She even toyed with
some of its more extravagant rituals by drawing up, at least
on one occasion, a highly elaborate liturgical calendar of
"Saints of Humanity."[34]

George Eliot was attracted to the muted idealism of the
Comteans. She shared their central belief that the individual
was subordinated to the influences of a contemporary social
organism and of the dead but "alive" figures of the past.
Her essays and novels show her acquaintance with Comte's
new science of sociology,[35] while the portrayal of her Romola
bears some parallels to the emblematic banner of the Posi-
tivists.[36] Yet, in Dr. Congreve's measured words, "Mrs.

is expressed in "The Natural History of German Life," *Westminster
Review*, LXVI (July 1856), 51-79.

[34] This calendar is in the notebook George Eliot kept for *Daniel
Deronda*, now in the Berg Collection of the New York Public
Library.

[35] For an excellent analysis of the possible effects of Comte's
"Social Statics" and "Social Dynamics" (the study of order and
progress, respectively) on George Eliot's thought, see Michael Wolff,
"Marian Evans to George Eliot: The Moral and Intellectual Foundations of her Career" (unpubl. diss., Princeton University, 1958),
pp. 282-326.

[36] The Comtean banner bore the emblem of a woman of thirty
holding a child in her arms and the inscription "We live for
others: love is our principle, order our method, progress our aim."
George Eliot's *Romola* ends with a vision of the widowed heroine

Lewes never accepted the details of the system, never went beyond the central idea."[37] And this central idea, as we shall presently see, was not too far removed from the ideas of thinkers such as Feuerbach and Arnold.

On the whole, then, George Eliot accepted the "spirit of science" which had reduced "mystery" to a series of verifiable processes. Though far more reluctantly than T. H. Huxley or John Tyndall, the optimist Mr. Stockton of Mallock's *New Republic*, she believed that the future advancement of society would have to be founded on the "natural knowledge" provided by empiricism. In his epoch-making Belfast *Address*, Tyndall proclaimed that this knowledge was sufficient to cope with man's major problems, all of which, he admitted, may well be "the manifestation of a Power absolutely inscrutable to the intellect of man."[38] This strict adherence to empirical truth has a twofold value: it concentrates on tangible realities and it also eliminates that inscrutable "Power" from its domain. This separation, Tyndall argued, is absolutely necessary. Though science is "able to comprehend the machinery" of all organic matter, including that of man, the prime mover "which sets it in motion" eludes its scrutiny (pp. 23-24). "Man the *object* is separated by an impassable gulf from man the *subject*. There is no motor energy in intellect to carry it without logical rupture from the one to the other" (p. 59).

---

carrying a foundling on her arms and spreading a similar gospel of love.

[37] *GEL*, I, lxii. Dorothea Brooke's remarriage to Will Ladislaw and George Eliot's own remarriage, in real life, to J. W. Cross after Lewes's death, were in direct contravention of the Comtean ideal of widowhood.

[38] *Address Delivered before the British Association Assembled at Belfast* (London, 1874), pp. 57-58. Subsequent page references to this work are given in the text.

With the exception of *Daniel Deronda,* where an inscrutable "Power" seems to operate, George Eliot's novels respect Tyndall's gulf of separation. The chain of events that governs *Adam Bede* or *The Mill on the Floss,* whether labeled as Bray's moral "law of consequences" or as Tyndall's intelligible "machinery," is reducible to component links of cause and effect, although its prime mover remains unexamined. In *Middlemarch* this causality assumes even larger proportions, but, although it extends to the extramundane reach of Casaubon's "Dead Hand," it is again worked out within the limits of verifiable evidence. By a characteristic Victorian manipulation, free will coexists with determinism and an immortality of sorts with spiritual extinction.[39] For George Eliot, like Tyndall, is eager to leave the "immovable basis of the religious sentiment" untouched (p. 60). To her, even more than to the jubilant scientist proclaiming the future absorption of religion by science, a "reasonable satisfaction" of this sentiment is "the problem of problems at the present hour" (p. 60).

To Tyndall this problem is easily resolved. The scientist, he feels, may, after all, cross the "boundary of the experimental evidence" and worship in "that Matter" which the religions of the past "have hitherto covered with opprobrium," "the promise and potency of all terrestrial Life" (p. 55). And here science can simply appropriate the sensibility of those dying "religious theories, schemes and systems" whose cosmogonies it has already replaced: "And grotesque in relation to scientific culture as many of the religions of the world have been and are—dangerous, nay destructive, to the dearest privileges of freemen as some of them undoubtedly have been, and would, if they could, be again—it

[39] See "The Metaphysics of *Middlemarch,*" Chapter III, section 4, below.

will be wise to recognize them as the forms of a force, mischievous, if permitted to intrude on the region of *knowledge*, over which it holds no command, but capable of being guided to noble issues in the region of *emotion*, which is its proper and elevated sphere" (pp. 60-61).

How this "region of emotion" is to be reached, Tyndall does not say. But his statements provide a gloss to George Eliot's novels. Her ideal religious characters are those ministers—the Tryans, Irwines, Kenns, or Lyons, who are willing to exclude their dogmatic convictions from the realm of emotional fellowship, or those who, like the astronomer Sephardo in *The Spanish Gipsy* or the Reverend Mr. Farebrother in *Middlemarch*, balance their scientific understanding of "man the object" with a compassionate feeling for "man the subject." On the other hand, the characters whose zealotry intrudes upon the "regions of knowledge," such as Savonarola in *Romola* or Bulstrode in *Middlemarch*, are inevitably punished by the consequences engendered by their actions. Even those idealists, like the ethereal Dinah Morris or Dorothea Brooke, who deny the realities of physical knowledge in their religious enthusiasm, must become re-educated in the ways of Nature.

And yet, in the over-all weighting of *Middlemarch*, though still respecting Tyndall's basic separation, George Eliot very deliberately tips the scales towards the "religious sentiment." In *Daniel Deronda*, which was published two years after the Belfast *Address*, she crosses the "boundary of experimental evidence," enters "the region of emotion," and tries to satisfy the "problem of problems at the present hour" by rejecting many of the standards she had shared with Huxley or Tyndall. For science alone was unable to conduct her into this region: Darwin persisted in a wholly "unscientific" personal religion; Huxley adopted an aloof and dispassionate stoicism.

Even Comte's utilitarian disregard for the Bible was distasteful to a writer brought up on its poetry. It was George Eliot's need to recover this poetry that gave her the power to go beyond Tyndall and made her traditionalism so similar to that of Matthew Arnold. It was her schooling in the biblical criticism of her time and the work of Ludwig Feuerbach in particular which allowed her to retain an "essence" of Christianity and provided her with a new symbology for her novels.

2. GEORGE ELIOT AND THE "HIGHER CRITICISM"

George Eliot's reluctant acceptance of the "relative" man of biological science had been preceded and, to some extent, prepared for by her earlier assent to the "relative" Christ of the "Higher Criticism." In 1841 Marian Evans read Charles Hennell's *Inquiry Concerning the Origin of Christianity,* shortly after she had suddenly abandoned a religious project of her own, an elaborate chart of church history. The negative implications of her subsequent break with her father's faith, her despair over "leathery Strauss," her typical refuge in the pantheism of Spinoza and Wordsworth, and, finally, her confrontation with the anti-theological theology of Feuerbach have all been analyzed so scrupulously and so well,[40] that it is often forgotten that, much as the "Higher Critics" helped to undermine George Eliot's belief, they also provided her with substitute values and ideals she incorporated into her novels.

[40] See Gordon S. Haight, *GEL,* I, xliii-xlv, lv-lxi; Humphry House, "Qualities of George Eliot's Unbelief," *Ideas and Beliefs of the Victorians* (London, 1948), pp. 157-163; Paris, "George Eliot's Religion of Humanity"; Willey, "George Eliot: Hennell, Strauss, and Feuerbach," *Nineteenth Century Studies,* pp. 204-236; Michael Wolff, "Marian Evans to George Eliot," pp. 54-146.

Hennell, Strauss, and Feuerbach saw themselves as the preservers of an altered but vital Christian "essence." Despite the vast differences between them, all three men proclaimed the "positivity" of their religious views. Hennell, whose *Inquiry* had sprung from a small Unitarian minority still leaning toward the Deism of the eighteenth century, assured his readers, rather unprophetically, that science and philosophy would only confirm his own vague belief in "an ever-present Logos."[41] Strauss and Feuerbach were the disciples of Hegel and, through him, the indirect heirs of the romantic impulse of an earlier generation of German philosophers and poets. Strauss gloomily conceded that his researches seemed to signify "God divested of his grace, man of his dignity, and the tie between heaven and earth broken," but he indignantly dissociated himself from the "naturalistic theologian" and the "free-thinker" by professing his veneration for "the sublimest of all religions, the Christian"—a religion "identical with the deepest philosophical truth."[42] Although Feuerbach went far beyond Strauss and Hennell in his unconventional interpretation of this "truth," his naturalistic religion of humanity was still condemned by scientific Hegelians, such as Marx and Engels, as being too idealistic.

For all their professed "positivity," the "Higher Critics" were proud of their systematic refutation of a belief based on scriptural revelation. They replaced faith in a revealed religion with their own developmental view of history, which regarded all religions as evolving "processes" originating in

[41] Charles Hennell, *An Inquiry Concerning the Origin of Christianity*, 2nd ed. (London, 1841), p. 489.

[42] D. F. Strauss, *The Life of Jesus Critically Examined*, trans. George Eliot (London, 1846), pp. 757-758. Subsequent page references to this work are given in the text.

time and subordinated to the laws of change. The evolutionary bias of Hennell, Strauss, and Feuerbach thus corresponded to that which George Eliot was to encounter, a decade after the publication of their works,[43] in the "spirit of science" of the 1850's. Indeed, Hennell, Strauss, and Feuerbach, and their German contemporaries, anticipated later English critics such as the "Seven Against Christ," Bishop Colenso, J. S. Mill, and Matthew Arnold, whose reassessment of the Bible came after the consolidation of the "Development theory." When John Morley in his *Recollections* praised Mark Pattison's 1860 essay as a pioneering application of the idea of "self-development" to religion "in this country," he was overlooking Hennell's truly original work written twenty-two years before, as well as George Eliot's translations of Strauss and Feuerbach, and the bearing that these were to have on her essays and novels.[44]

The new critics of the Bible held that religion, though the product of man's "higher" aspirations, depended on the very same "chain of causes and effects" that connected "natural phenomena with each other" (p. 39). The Gospels thus had to be re-examined dispassionately in terms of their causal "origins": the circumstances surrounding the life of Jesus, the environment of his time, the influences of earlier prophets, or the messianic expectations of the Apostles. A Christology based on revelation and miracle seemed impossible. If the narratives of the Evangelists had suddenly become "relative," the dogmas they had inspired through the centuries appeared to have lost all their validity. Working on her chart of ecclesiastical history, Marian Evans only saw,

[43] Hennell's *Inquiry* appeared in 1838; Strauss's *Leben Jesu* went through four editions from 1835 to 1840; Feuerbach's *Das Wesen des Christenthums* was published in 1841.

[44] *Recollections* (New York, 1917), I, 72.

as John Henry Newman was to see in his own attempt to trace the convolution of Christian dogmatics, a succession of conflicting doctrines, schisms, claims and counterclaims. Soon, Hennell's theories, and then those of Strauss, only confirmed her worst doubts. Her idealism, like that of Newman, felt challenged. Newman gave his assent to the least fallible of Christian churches; in the name of clarity, George Eliot rejected a Christianity which had become fallible. Yet her reaction, like his, was prompted by a need for affirmation. First Hennell and Spinoza, then Strauss, and finally Feuerbach, promised new creeds. Hennell and Strauss did not fulfill her expectations. But Feuerbach's theology, based on "processes" analogous to those of the evolutionists and yet retaining some of the poetry of the old belief, proved to be more rewarding than a bare belief in the "spirit of science."

Writing to Hennell's sister Sara in 1870, George Eliot acknowledged her own "obligations" to the *Inquiry*. She praised the book for its "grave sincerity" but cautiously hinted that its value was "independent of the opinions that might be held as to the different degrees of success in the construction of probabilities, or in particular interpretations."[45] Cryptic as it is, the passage suggests George Eliot's reservations about Hennell's particular "construction of probabilities"—reservations which must have crept in soon after she read his work. For George Eliot soon went beyond Hennell's moderate ideas. His ontologism, his belief in a "Creator both omniscient and omnipotent," as well as his assurances of "an existence beyond the grave,"[46] must have seemed at variance to her, even in the 1840's, with the psychologism of a critical method which questioned the credibility of divine revelation and of the Resurrection.

[45] *GEL*, v, 96.
[46] Hennell, *Inquiry*, p. 486.

The translation of D. F. Strauss's *Das Leben Jesu* engaged George Eliot from 1844 to 1846. Strauss shared neither Hennell's pronounced theism nor the optimism of his conclusions. In fact, his book was devoid of the positive conclusion he had anticipated. Writing in the tradition of Hegel's essays on the "Life of Jesus" and the "Positivity of Christianity," the Tübingen critic had conceived an elaborate dialectical framework in which a thesis and an antithesis based on the scriptural interpretations of the Rationalists of speculative philosophy and the supernaturalists of the Church would give way to his own "critical" synthesis. But, unfortunately, only "the first part of this programme, the antithesis, was meticulously executed."[47] In it, Strauss went far beyond Hennell in refuting the claims of the supernaturalists, for he contended that the factual record of Christ's life had been converted into wishful myths by disciples eager to identify their Master with the Jewish Messiah.

Instead of his intended synthesis, however, Strauss merely appended a few final observations attesting to his despair of reconciling faith with historical evolution. Faith, he argued in these concluding remarks, arises from the senses "and therefore contemplates a temporal history." Yet man's religiosity soon converts this contemplation of "external fact" into some "spiritual and divine idea, which has its confirmation no longer in history but in philosophy." A new theology thus is needed to lead the age "to the idea in the fact, to the race in the individual: a theology which, in its doctrines on the Christ, stops short at him as an individual [and] is not properly a theology, but a homily" (pp. 780-781).

But, unlike Feuerbach, Strauss feels incapable of advancing a "homiletic" theology of his own. This is the burden of

[47] Karl Barth, *Protestant Thought: From Rousseau to Ritschl* (New York, 1959), p. 365.

the Church and not of a secular laity. Thus, Strauss ends his book on a pathetic note by formulating the dilemma of the clergyman-theologian who, like many a minister in George Eliot's novels, is "at once critical and speculative"—"critical," in that he knows that the evangelical myths are not based on absolute fact; "speculative," in that he holds these myths to be the expression of perennial ideals attaining their "existence in the totality of individuals" (p. 782). This clergyman must somehow remain faithful to the relativism of history and to the value of ideals falsely based on history. But Strauss foresees little success for a self-divided preacher who, like Robert Elsmere, could easily "betray" himself into leaving "the ministerial profession" (p. 784).

Marian Evans's own morbidity—frowned upon by the far more confident Hennell[48]—was aggravated by Strauss's inconclusive ending. *The Life of Jesus*, far from answering her religious doubts, only added to her questioning. Yet it is easy to oversentimentalize the "tragic" impact of the man and the book, as Albert Schweitzer does when he pleads that "to understand Strauss one must love him."[49] Karl Barth has said that "one must love the question Strauss raised, in order to understand it. It has been loved only by a few; most people have feared it."[50] George Eliot was one of these few. She did not love Strauss but she appreciated the relevance of his questions. Though presumably despairing over his Teutonic "leatheriness," she also found him "so klar und ideenvoll."[51] Her grasp of his ideas had immediate repercussions. As Strauss's translator, Marian Evans gained stature in the eyes of John Chapman and the small circle which

[48] See *GEL*, I, 307.
[49] *The Quest of the Historical Jesus* (London, 1911), p. 68.
[50] Barth, *Protestant Thought*, p. 389.
[51] *GEL*, I, 218.

gathered at his home on 142 Strand. At the *Westminster Review*, she was called upon to review the only two English efforts at "Higher Criticism" of the period, R. W. Mackay's *The Progress of the Intellect* (1850) and W. R. Greg's *Creed of Christendom* (1851). Her training earned her the right to review Carlyle's *Life of Sterling* and Maurice's *Sermons*; it also provided the basis for her later essays on the Reverend Dr. John Cumming and on the poet Edward Young.

George Eliot's *Westminster* essays time and again call her public's attention to the new scriptural criticism. Her otherwise unsympathetic review of F. D. Maurice's *Sermons* states: "The leading idea, however, of the work, as of all Mr. Maurice's writings, is a good one. . . . The Jewish nation and the 'man Christ Jesus' are regarded, not as exceptional cases in the world's history, but as types of the normal relations to God."[52] Again, her denunciation of Dr. Cumming's bibliolatry is founded on a harsh attack on his outmoded "principles—or, we should rather say, confused notions—of Biblical interpretation."[53] In her review of Mackay's book, she predicts with false confidence: "England has been slow to use or to emulate the immense labours of Germany in the departments of Mythology and Biblical Criticism; but when once she does so, the greater solidity and directness of the English mind ensure a superiority of treatment."[54] George Eliot's desire is clear: she wants English critics to go beyond the unresolved questions posed by Strauss—questions now sharpened by the emerging theories of a native "spirit of science." But the *Essays and Reviews* were almost a decade away; John Stuart Mill, who possessed

[52] *Westminster Review*, LIX (April 1853), 587.
[53] *Ibid.*, LXIV (October 1855), 451.
[54] *Ibid.*, LIV (January 1851), 354-355.

the "solidity" she demanded, was not yet ready to risk the "directness" of an undisguised search for a new theology; Matthew Arnold, still a poet, had hardly divined the polemical potentialities of biblical criticism. George Eliot was forced to take matters into her own hands. She decided to rely on her solid "English mind," but, simultaneously, turned to the work of still another German critic. In June 1853 two works by the "Translator of Strauss's Life of Jesus" [sic] were announced as being in preparation. One was to be an original work entitled, significantly enough, *The Idea of a Future Life*; it never materialized. The other was a translation of Feuerbach's *Das Wesen des Christenthums*; it appeared in July of 1854.

George Eliot's choice in 1853 of a book published twelve years earlier was almost as remarkable as the book's history. Hailed and reviled with equal passion in the Germany of 1841, the work quickly underwent a second edition in 1843. Then its fame ebbed. After the social upheaval of 1848, Feuerbach's ideas were ignored until their rediscovery by later thinkers such as Nietzsche and Freud. George Eliot's own "discovery" shocked the handful of Victorian reviewers who took note of her translation. Even the liberal James Martineau—a Unitarian like Hennell and Greg, and hence sympathetic to the aims of biblical criticism—could hardly conceal his sarcasm: "It is a sign of 'progress,' we presume, that the lady-translator who maintained the anonymous in introducing Strauss, puts her name in the title-page of Feuerbach. She has executed her task even better than before: we are only surprised that, if she wished to exhibit the new Hegelian Atheism to English readers, she should select a work of the year 1840, and of quite secondary philosophical repute in its own country."[55]

[55] Quoted in *GEL*, II, 187, n.8.

Martineau's evaluation of Feuerbach was of course mistaken; but the reasons for his mistake, as well as his indignation, are telling. Unlike Strauss or the other Tübingen critics, Ludwig Feuerbach was an exegete and allegorist. Unconcerned with disputations as to how or when the Christian dogmas had arisen, uninterested in an antiquarian investigation of the exact causes for the spread of the Gospels or in the exact proportioning of their Hellenism or Hebraism, Feuerbach attempted to refashion Christianity in terms of the neo-Romantic subjectivism of his era. To him, "God is the manifested inward nature, the expressed self of a man,— religion the solemn unveiling of a man's hidden treasures."[56] Thus for Feuerbach, as for Renan later on, "the *truth*, the *essence* of religion" can be isolated by a recognition of Christianity's symbolic expression of concrete psychological needs (p. xxxvii). Religion is the anthropomorphic formulation of man's highest aspirations. Man has objectified his consciousness, thereby setting "God before him as the antithesis of himself" (p. 33). He has consequently alienated himself from the God of his own creation. But he can recover Christianity, the religion of suffering, by recognizing in it his own subjective veneration of human solidarity, the "Love" which Feuerbach detects in all its doctrines, sacraments, and practices.

Despite his clear Hegelian bias, Feuerbach solemnly proclaimed that his subjective worship of a God-Man was opposed to all metaphysical systems of thought. His philosophy was, in effect, "*the negation of philosophy*"; it was "realistic" because it was based on verifiable psychological truths:

[56] Ludwig Feuerbach, *The Essence of Christianity*, trans. George Eliot; Introductory Essay by Karl Barth; Foreword by H. Richard Niebuhr (New York, 1957), pp. 12-13. Subsequent page references to this edition are given in the text.

"This philosophy has for its principle, not the Substance of Spinoza, not the *ego* of Kant and Fichte, not the Absolute Identity of Schelling, not the Absolute Mind of Hegel, in short, no abstract, merely conceptional being, but a *real* being, the true *Ens realissimum*—man; its principle, therefore, is in the highest degree positive and real" (p. xxxv). It is easy to see how Feuerbach's brand of "positivism," unlike the systematized *philosophie positive* of Comte, would appeal to that hereditary British distrust of abstract metaphysical reasoning evident in the literary lineage which descends from Bacon, Swift, and Dr. Johnson down to Matthew Arnold and George Eliot. With no little metaphysical deception on his own part, Feuerbach insisted that he was to be merely regarded as an anthropologist or psychologist: "I am nothing but a *natural philosopher in the domain of mind*" (p. xxxiv). His sole purpose, he argued, was the revitalizing of symbols that Christianity had objectified. In actuality, like Freud after him, Feuerbach reduced the Judaeo-Christian ethos into a secularized and anti-transcendental phenomenalism. He compressed the "I" and "Thou" relation of man to God into a synthetic One; he fused the first and second Persons of the Trinity into the "completed self-consciousness of the *alter-ego*" (p. 67).

In 1854, shortly before her elopement with Lewes, George Eliot, according an indebtedness she seldom granted to any author, wrote: "With the ideas of Feuerbach I everywhere agree."[57] This agreement is everywhere exemplified in her novels. Feuerbach and the "Higher Criticism" had taught her that Christianity was a fable, a beautiful fiction which contained only a "Religion of Humanity," teaching the perennial truth of human love and selflessness. In her own fiction, begun two and a half years later, she sought to

[57] *GEL*, II, 153.

recreate this "truth" with something of the fierce intensity which marked her evangelical upbringing. George Eliot's novelistic creed of realism, best expressed in the oft-quoted passage in the seventeenth chapter of *Adam Bede*, as well as her recurrent biblical overtones, stems from a Feuerbachian insistence on recovering "the true or anthropological essence of religion."[58] Feuerbach's contention that the "Love" which was the primary "essence" of his Christianity could not exist outside a material clothing of "flesh and blood" is precisely the basis for George Eliot's defense of her characterization of Rector Irwine and of the quality of the clergyman's own "essential" religion: "These fellow-mortals, every one, must be accepted as they are: you can neither straighten their noses nor brighten their wit, nor rectify their dispositions; and it is these people—amongst whom your life is passed—that it is needful you should tolerate, pity and love" (*Adam Bede*, ch. 17, p. 267).

Feuerbach's insistence that man alone was the "*Ens realissimum*," around which his theology was built, was highly acceptable to George Eliot, who had come to regard scientific positivism as an indispensable requisite for any new creed. On the other hand, Feuerbach's contention that his man-centered faith would only further the primacy of "Love" in the world of change, suffering, and total extinction, softened considerably the evolutionary ideas that she had so stoically accepted. In *Adam Bede*—in a pattern later improved on in *Middlemarch*—the selflessness and sympathy of Dinah Morris clearly prevail over the animalism of Hetty Sorrel. Still, the young preacher's perception of Feuerbach's "Love" is faulty. Sharing the German's disapproval of "celibacy" and "monachism," George Eliot corrects Dinah's nunlike love of Christ and transforms it into the "essential" love of the

[58] The first part of Feuerbach's book bears this title.

species: ". . . where there arises the consciousness of the
species as a species, the idea of humanity as a whole, Christ
disappears, without, however, his true nature disappearing"
(Feuerbach, p. 269).

Feuerbach's creed combined many of the elements that
George Eliot had encountered elsewhere: his "idea of
humanity as a whole," for example, was quite similar to
that of the Comteans; his deep awareness of suffering resembled that of T. H. Huxley; his assumption that faith
and salvation could be found in the love of the species was
analogous to that of Charles Bray. On the other hand,
Feuerbach's ideas were presented without the dogmatism of
Comte, the cold logicality of Huxley, or the pseudoscientific
garb of Bray's phrenology. What is more, his was the "homiletic theology" that Strauss had demanded. George Eliot not
only agreed with the theology itself, but also was strongly
attracted to the emotional homilies through which it was
presented. Feuerbach's revaluation of the main ceremonies of
the Christian religion appealed to her vehement desire to
retain the poetry of the old faith. Her symbolism in *Adam
Bede* skillfully exploits Feuerbach's own humanist adaptation
of the sacraments of the church.

In *The Essence of Christianity* Feuerbach regarded the
sacraments as the semiconscious expression of man's worship
of natural forces. Contrasting Baptism to the Lord's Supper,
he expounded the "moral and intellectual" significance of
water, bread, and wine, and unabashedly invited the reader
to participate in the "essential" rites he claimed to have re-
discovered:

> Water, as a universal element of life, reminds us of our
> origin from Nature, an origin which we have in common
> with plants and animals. In Baptism we bow to the power

of a pure Nature-force; water is the element of natural equality and freedom, the mirror of the golden age. But we men are distinguished from the plants and animals, which together with the inorganic kingdom we comprehend under the common name of Nature;—we are distinguished from Nature. Hence we must celebrate our distinction, our specific difference. The symbols of this our difference are bread and wine. Bread and wine are, as to their materials, products of Nature; as to their form, products of man. If in water we declare: Man can do nothing without Nature; by bread and wine we declare: Nature needs man, as man needs Nature. In water, human mental activity is nullified; in bread and wine it attains self-satisfaction. . . . Hence this sacrament is only for man matured into consciousness; while baptism is imparted to infants. [pp. 276-277]

Feuerbach concluded his unorthodox "homily" with this final exhortation:

Hunger and thirst destroy not only the physical but also the mental and moral powers of man; they rob him of his humanity—of understanding, of consciousness. Oh! if thou shouldst ever experience such want, how wouldst thou bless and praise the natural qualities of bread and wine, which restore to thee thy humanity, thy intellect! It needs only that the ordinary course of things be interrupted in order to vindicate to common things an uncommon significance, *to life, as such, a religious import.* Therefore let bread be sacred for us, let wine be sacred, and also let water be sacred! Amen. [*ibid.*, pp. 277-278]

In *Adam Bede* George Eliot depicts the "mental and moral" education of her protagonist through a series of symbolic suppers which ultimately lead to his conversion to a

Feuerbachian "religion of suffering." The first of these suppers is designed to remind Adam of his "origin of Nature," an origin represented by Feuerbach through the symbol of water. The second scene, as ironical as the first, now stresses Adam's inability to see that man must also be "distinguished from nature." In the third scene, Adam finally learns how to celebrate this "distinction" in a manner which will give a truly "religious import" to life. This scene, the most important of the three, relies entirely on Feuerbach's allegorization of the sacraments.

In the first supper scene, the self-righteous Adam finishes a coffin that his father, the carpenter Thias Bede, has failed to deliver. He refuses to eat the food that his mother proffers to him, but patronizingly allows his hungry dog to eat: "Adam noticed Gyp's mental conflict, and though his anger had made him less tender than usual to his mother, it did not prevent him from caring as much as usual for his dog" (ch. 4, p. 59). But Adam is still unaware that men, like animals, "can do nothing without Nature," a truth conveyed, according to Feuerbach's homily, by the symbol of water. Soon, Adam calls for "light and a draught of water (beer was a thing only to be drunk on holidays)," accepts a second "drop of water," and admits that he is getting "very thirsty." He works on, unaware that the intoxicated father to whom he feels so superior, has died of a "watery death" in a nearby creek. His tentative acceptance of the two sips of water foreshadows the "flood of relenting and pity" that dissolves his earlier harshness (ch. 4, p. 76), on discovering Thias' body. The symbol of water, like the parallel between man and dog, is designed to remind Adam of man's subservience to the cycle of extinction and preservation which governs all of life: "Nature, that great tragic dramatist, knits us together by bone and muscle" (ch. 4, p. 55).

But if man, according to George Eliot and Feuerbach, must "bow" to the forces of Nature, he must also know how to rise above them. Adam's ignorance of this second rule manifests itself at the supper which takes place during the birthday feast for Arthur Donnithorne, the young Squire. Sundered once again from his kin, Adam sits "upstairs" at the Squire's own table, no longer drinking water, but the rich Loamshire ale. He accepts a toast in which Arthur, the seducer of his beloved, wishes him to have "sons as faithful and clever as himself" (ch. 24, p. 404). With a slightly arrogant tone, Adam thanks Arthur for his appointment as keeper of the woods: "I believe he's one o' those gentlemen as wishes to do the right thing, and to leave the world a bit better than he found it" (ch. 24, p. 406). The irony is evident. Adam must still learn that his full "humanity" can only be celebrated through his "distinction" from the two "natural" creatures he will surprise in the woods he keeps. Arthur and Hetty will force upon him that suffering which, to George Eliot as to Feuerbach, can elevate man above the merely organic. For Hetty's "naturalness" is as deceptive as the beauty of Loamshire itself, a landscape which lacks those man-made images of the cross found in "foreign countries" as a visual reminder that man's religion can never be a mere worship of the impersonal forces of Nature: "No wonder man's religion has so much sorrow in it: no wonder he needs a suffering God" (ch. 35, p. 112).

The third and most significant supper in this symbolic sequence marks the attainment of Adam's matured "consciousness." Sitting "upstairs" again, but now in a bleak lodging in Stoniton,[59] Adam has become "powerless to contemplate irremediable evil and suffering" at the time of

[59] For an interpretation of the place names in the novel, see George Creeger, "An Interpretation of *Adam Bede*," *ELH*, XXIII (September 1956), 218-238.

Hetty's trial (ch. 42, p. 208). Unshaven, brooding, half-starved, he resembles David mourning the ugly beauty of Absalom. At this point, Bartle Massey, the crippled schoolmaster, enters the room. Bartle tells Adam about the trial he has witnessed, while pressing on him "a bit of the loaf, and some of that wine Mr. Irwine sent" (ch. 42, p. 210). But Adam pushes the cup aside. It is not until Bartle describes the pain of Hetty's uncle that Adam is willing to drink "a little." He asks about Hetty herself, and on hearing about her suffering and the Rector's gentle actions he is provoked into an exclamation: "God bless him, and you too, Mr. Massey." The involuntary blessing reverses Adam's earlier exclamation about Hetty: "God bless her for loving me" (ch. 35, p. 117). For Adam can now signify his "distinction" from Nature through an act which George Eliot, resorting to an explication quite similar to Feuerbach's own, describes as "a baptism, a regeneration, the initiation into a new state" (ch. 42, p. 209). Adam promises to "stand by" Hetty at court. Immediately, the schoolmaster asks him to eat a "bit" and to drink "another sup, Adam, for the love of me." Adam is now ready to become a celebrant: "Nerved by an active resolution, Adam took a morsel of bread, and drank some wine. He was haggard and unshaven, as he had been yesterday, but he stood upright again, and looked more like the Adam Bede of former days" (ch. 42, p. 214). It seems hardly necessary to elaborate on the symbolic parallel of this third supper taken by Adam, the bearded son of a carpenter, who "stood upright again." George Eliot's subtle use of the supper scenes is derived from Feuerbach's conclusion: "Bread and wine typify to us the truth that Man is the true God and Saviour of man" (p. 277).[60]

---

[60] Adam's supper in Stoniton is not designed as a "last" supper. The Harvest Feast at the Poyser farm is a true fertility ritual which

3. George Eliot, Matthew Arnold, and Tradition

George Eliot's adoption of a Feuerbachian creed of sympathy allowed her to retain an "essence" of Christianity amidst the evolutionary world of Darwin and Huxley. With consummate skill, she incorporated this "essence," as well as her belief in the laws of natural evolution, into her own world of fiction. Her novels reflect some of the inconsistencies of the new creed. Humanism minimized the existence of sin and evil. Thus, paradoxically enough, George Eliot was forced to disregard her own sense of human depravity and to distort character in order to remain faithful to the profound idealism on which her "realism" was built.[61] Humanism also denied all absolutes, and yet compelled her to abstract a fanciful relativism which would invalidate the abstractionism of religion. Above all, George Eliot's humanism con-

---

is accentuated by the Dickensian antics of Tom Saft (the German word for plant-juice). It sets the stage for Adam's marriage to the absent Dinah.

[61] Discussions such as William J. Hyde's "George Eliot and the Climate of Realism," *PMLA*, LXXII (March 1957), 147-164, tend to ignore the philosophic foundations of her curiously idealistic "realism." George Eliot's chromatic range is devoid of the black used by Hawthorne or Dickens. Those characters in her novels who come closest to the role of archetypal villains, such as the brutal Lawyer Dempster in "Janet's Repentance," Tito Melema in *Romola*, or Bulstrode and Raffles in *Middlemarch*, are rationally explained in terms of their background and psychological make-up. Their apparent evil is mitigated by an often sentimental insistence that they too are potentially capable of higher emotions. As a potential Feuerbachian "Man-God," the animalistic Lawyer is shown to possess tender feelings for his aged mother, although his repulsive nature is all too evident. George Eliot is thus forced to distort in order to remain tolerant. Significantly enough, only Grandcourt in *Daniel Deronda* and the Lamia-like wife in "The Lifted Veil" approximate pure evil: in both works George Eliot grants the existence of supernatural cosmic forces.

tended that the "essential" ethos of Christianity could live on in the "idea of humanity as a whole," but it failed to present her with an actual vehicle for this positive, and Positivist, morality.

George Eliot was fully aware of this last dilemma. Strauss had insisted that the Church develop its own "homiletic" theology of the future; Feuerbach had provided this theology, but he had failed to produce, with it, an authority that would validate and perpetuate his ethic. Like Matthew Arnold, George Eliot recognized the need for such an authority—an authority which would not only have to be concrete and positive, but also would have to be as compelling as the God the "Higher Criticism" had displaced. To be sure, there was Nature, Huxley's schoolmistress, and, in her rural novels, George Eliot appealed to its grim authority to imply the necessity for a "natural" humanist ethic. But her depiction of the rigorous "consequences" unleashed by Adam's or Maggie's actions was negative; her idealism demanded a positive instrumentation as well. In the rural novels, her "homilies" on tolerance were largely confined to the beliefs of clergymen like Rector Irwine or Dr. Kenn, to the virtues and wisdom of her rustics, or to the sagacity of her own editorial comments. After *Silas Marner*, George Eliot turned away from the pastoralism of her early fiction and sought a more compelling vehicle for her ideals. In *Romola* and *Felix Holt* she examined vast historical forces and tested their impact on her characters. But these forces—the cultural conflicts of Renaissance Florence and the political conflicts of the England of the 1830's—were hardly positive; George Eliot fell back on her earlier Feuerbachian stereotypes, an earthly "Madonna" and a working-man "Saviour," to carry her now undisguised ethic. New ground was broken in *Middlemarch* and *Daniel Deronda*, where she was able to portray, first negatively and then positively, the workings of history and to present, at the same time, a convincing and authoritative vehicle for her morality. This vehicle was tradition, or what, after the manner of Goethe and Coleridge, George Eliot and Matthew Arnold chose to call "culture."

Critics seldom connect the novels of George Eliot with the theological essays of Matthew Arnold. Yet, it is by no means an exaggeration to say that, at least in its final phase, George Eliot's ethical humanism finds its most immediate counterpart in the religious thought of Matthew Arnold. Basic for this similarity is their identical redefinition of "culture." At the end of 1867, George Eliot sent Frederic Harrison a sharp appraisal of his satire, "Culture: A Dialogue." A prolonged ridicule of Arnold's "cant about culture," the essay was to provoke Arnold's ironic retaliation and to lead to Harrison's enshrinement as one of "culture's enemies" in *Culture and Anarchy*. George Eliot was more cautious but just as firm with her young Comtean friend. She professed to "appreciate" the "force" of Harrison's criticism, but remarked that only "in one point I am unable to see as you do"; this one point of divergence, she delicately implied, was nothing less than Harrison's entire argument: "I don't know how far my impressions have been warped by reading German, but I have regarded the word 'culture' as a verbal equivalent for the highest results of past and present influences."[62]

Four years before, in response to R. H. Hutton's perceptive criticism of her artistic failure in *Romola*, George Eliot had already represented herself as the propagator of this same type of "culture":

The psychological causes which prompted me to give such details of Florentine life and history as I have given, are

[62] *GEL*, IV, 395.

precisely the same as those which determined me in giving
the details of English village life in "Silas Marner," or the
"Dodson" life, out of which were developed the destinies
of poor Tom and Maggie. . . . But . . . my predominant
feeling is,—not that I have achieved anything, but—that
great, great facts have struggled to find a voice through
me, and have only been able to speak brokenly. That
consciousness makes me cherish the more any proof that
my work has been seen to have some true significance by
minds prepared not simply by instruction, but by that
*religious and moral sympathy with the historical life of
man which is the larger half of culture* [italics added].[63]

"Culture," then, or "the highest results of past and present
influences," is identified with the "religious and moral sympathy with the historical life of man" which George Eliot
herself intends to elicit through her novels. Significantly,
Arnold's *Literature and Dogma* (1873), the most ambitious
of his theological essays, is based on very similar premises.
In his Preface to the work, Arnold echoes George Eliot's
earlier opinion about the insufficiency of the German
"Higher Criticism" by implying that a specifically English
"culture" is needed to go beyond the "historic method" of
"Dr. Strauss": ". . . to deal with the reality which is still
left in the New Testament, requires a larger, richer, deeper,
more imaginative mind than his."[64] This imaginative mind,
at least in *Literature and Dogma*, is to be that of Matthew
Arnold himself. But its richness, he implies, is definitely
derived from the English tradition of regarding the Bible
as a vehicle for moral experience.[65]

[63] *GEL*, IV, 97.
[64] *Literature and Dogma: An Essay Towards a Better Apprehension of the Bible* (London, 1873), p. xxv.
[65] *Ibid.*, pp. xxv-xxviii.

Literature and Dogma, like *Daniel Deronda,* which appeared less than three years later, is an undisguised attempt to provide England with a religion. Despite their discrepant media, Arnold and George Eliot saw themselves in strikingly similar roles as the disseminators of "culture"— *"the best that has been thought and said in the world."*[66] Even more remarkable than their joint belief in "culture," is the parallel evolution of their ideas about where this "culture" is to be found. Throughout their literary careers George Eliot and Matthew Arnold moved toward a common position. Their skeptical oscillation between agnosticism and faith, conservatism and progressivism, science and religion, finally found a common resting ground in their belief in a moral tradition which could embody an authoritative "power not ourselves." Regarding the religious dilemmas of their time as being inextricably linked with the sociopolitical ones, both writers moved away from their earlier conception of "culture" as a quasi-religious, but essentially social and secular force, and came to consider it instead as a predominantly spiritual force rooted in history. Arnold thus shifts from the political implications of *Culture and Anarchy* (1869) to the religious questions posed in *St. Paul and Protestantism* (1870); George Eliot moves from her 1868 "Address to Working Men, by Felix Holt"[67] to *Middlemarch* (1871-1872), where she examines a wider spectrum of creeds and modes of "religion" than that contained in any of her previous novels. Distracted by the bugbear of Nonconformism in *St. Paul and Protestantism,* Arnold abruptly becomes the advocate of a tradition based on the Bible in *Literature and Dogma* (1873) and in

[66] *Ibid.,* p. xxxiii.

[67] The essay was inspired by the same political upheavals Arnold had described in *Culture and Anarchy;* like his work, it was written in the spirit of Disraeli.

its lesser sequel, *God and the Bible* (1875). Dissatisfied with the Pyrrhic victory depicted in *Middlemarch*, George Eliot breaks sharply with some of her Positivist assumptions in *Daniel Deronda* (1876), where she endows Dorothea Brooke's "Hebraism" with an entire historical tradition which, like Arnold's Bible, is valued for its resistance to time and evolution. The later works of both writers, Arnold's last essays on religion and George Eliot's sketches in *Theophrastus Such*, only accentuate their fears for the future of a materialistic England deprived of its Bible.

Thus, both writers ultimately regard themselves as the enlightened spokesmen for an emphatically religious "culture." This "culture" is envisioned as the concrete embodiment of a deeply engrained sense of moral righteousness, a Hebraism which both Arnold and George Eliot had at one time rejected. For both, Hebraism and Hellenism are no longer held in equipoise. In *Literature and Dogma*, as well as in *Middlemarch* and *Daniel Deronda*, art and science, the product of "the best of the Aryan races," must bow to conduct, "the best of the Semitic."[68] Almost as if defining the climate of George Eliot's novels, Arnold writes: "Compare a Methodist day-labourer with some dissolute, gifted, brilliant grandee, who thinks nothing of him!—but the first deals successfully with nearly the whole of life, while the second is all abroad in it. Compare some simple and pious monk, at Rome, with one of those frivolous men of taste whom we have all seen there!—each knows nothing of what interests the other; but which is the more vital concern for a

---

[68] *Literature and Dogma*, p. 386. This is precisely the point in George Eliot's characterization of Tito Melema in *Romola* as the recipient of a brilliant but corrupt Hellenic tradition or of her subordination of Lydgate and Ladislaw, scientist and artist, to Dorothea Brooke in *Middlemarch*.

man: conduct, or arts and antiquities?"[69] To Arnold, as to George Eliot, the answer is conduct. In his "Conclusion" to *Literature and Dogma*, Arnold admits that, though attacking Hebraism elsewhere, he has upheld it here. The apparent inconsistency is shrewdly reasoned away: "In praising culture, we have never denied that conduct, not culture, is three-fourths of human life."[70] Thus, "culture" must now be enlisted to serve morality; the "man of culture" must employ his knowledge and his art to ensure the preservation of the "three-fourths of life" which is conduct. Ideally, Hellenism and Hebraism should merge; but their union of interests is now laid in the future: "for all this, however, man is hardly yet ripe."[71] For the time being, "culture" and literature must prepare a prosaic *Zeitgeist* for an era in which the "sweetness" of the Bible will again be undisturbed by the "light" of reason.

This act of preparation requires a consciousness of history and an awareness of prophetic destiny, a dual method of looking backward and forward, that only the critic who is also a "man of culture" can supply. In Arnold's program, "the idea of humanity, of intelligence, of looking before and after, of raising oneself out of the flux of things," produces what he calls "ethics heightened";[72] in George Eliot's scheme of values, this same process becomes "the divine gift of a memory which inspires the moments with a past, a present, and a future, and gives the sense of corporate existence."[73] Memory is enclosed in tradition, which sorts out

[69] *Ibid.*, p. 235.   [70] *Ibid.*, p. 381.

[71] *Ibid.*, p. 386. In *Daniel Deronda*, a prophetic novel, the "Aryan" education and "Semitic" heritage of Deronda are also envisioned as the ideal combination for the future.

[72] *Ibid.*, pp. 24, 21.

[73] "The Modern Hep! Hep! Hep!" in *Impressions of Theophrastus Such*, Cabinet Edition (Edinburgh, n.d.), p. 261.

those values which can withstand the mutability of time. In her long epic poem, *The Spanish Gypsy*, George Eliot identified "memory" or "tradition" as an "angel" guiding the "path of man".:

> We had not walked
> But for Tradition; we walk evermore
> To higher paths, by brightening Reason's lamp.
> Still we are purblind, tottering.[74]

In *Literature and Dogma* Arnold specifies that the "cultured" advocate of tradition must provide "a very wide experience from comparative observation in many directions, and a very slowly acquired habit of mind."[75] Though at variance in their presentation of these "observations," Arnold and George Eliot bring the same tools, the same "experience," to bear on their work. Arnold hopes that an artfully arranged array of "comparative" pairings and juxtapositions (of Newman facing Mill, Disraeli confronting Gladstone, Hellenism opposing Hebraism) will—if supported by key "touchstones" from Shakespeare, Goethe, Homer, and, of course, the Bible itself—yield the all-inclusive wisdom he has in mind. George Eliot's design also is preconceived, but she tries to furnish her "wide experience" in the more impersonal mode of her novels. While Arnold's "disinterestedness" lies in playing two opposing factions against each other, George Eliot adopts the role of a contemplative narrator who offers the reader the products of a collective human experience through the gradual unfolding of a self-inclusive irony, "a very slowly acquired habit of mind." Like Arnold, she resorts to "touchstones" and cross references through spatial allusions and chapter epigraphs. Analogy and juxtaposition

[74] *The Spanish Gypsy*, Cabinet Edition (Edinburgh, n.d.), Book II, pp. 215-216.
[75] P. 283.

are as essential to the art of *Middlemarch* and *Daniel Deronda*, as they are to that of Arnold's polemical essays.

Even the *literary* "culture" of both writers is similar. Though Arnold is influenced by Renan, and George Eliot is indebted to Feuerbach, both look to Wordsworth, Goethe, and Spinoza as "humanist" prototypes. Both admire but distrust the romantic effusions of a Shelley or Keats; both are careful students of the classics; both espouse the work of Heinrich Heine as a desirable *via media* between Hebraic morality and Hellenic wit.[76] They resort to similar models and adhere to similar aesthetic principles in their own creative writing. Many of their metaphors have common origins: Arnold's poetry and George Eliot's fiction abound in water imagery, which is employed to symbolize the flow of time, but also is endowed with religious associations.

Arnold rejected the writing of verse because he believed that poetry was dependent on religious faith. In her later years, George Eliot painstakingly composed poetry for precisely the same reason: she regarded it as the ideal vehicle to elevate her humanist ethic into "ethics heightened." Four years before her death, Arnold wrote to his sister with apparent satisfaction: "George Eliot says, a lady tells me, that of all modern poetry mine is that which keeps continually growing upon her."[77] Arnold's views on her art, or, for that matter, on the novel as a vehicle for the religious "culture" both she and he demanded, are unknown. Apparently he regarded her as spokesman for the very doubts he had

[76] See Sol Liptzin, "Heine: The Continuator of Goethe—A Mid-Victorian Legend," *Journal of English and Germanic Philology*, XLIII (July 1944), 317-325.

[77] *The Letters of Matthew Arnold*, ed. George W. E. Russell (New York, 1896), II, 146. Reviewing Arnold's *Poems, Second Series*, much earlier in her career, George Eliot had praised their emotional and cerebral appeal and singled out "Resignation" as her own favorite.

characterized so well: "Our trouble has . . . been with the doubts whether things which people assured us really existed or had really happened, but of which we had no experience ourselves and could not satisfy ourselves that any one had had any experience either, were really as people told us."[78] Arnold's idealistic attempts to overcome these doubts were to affect the thinking of future writers; yet, it was George Eliot's concrete novelistic conversion of ideas highly similar to his own which stimulated the development of a next generation of novelists which included, among others, Mrs. Humphry Ward, Arnold's niece; Walter Pater, Arnold's successor as apostle of "culture"; and Henry James, Arnold's steadfast admirer.

For, unlike George Eliot, Arnold was thrown upon the "critical" essay as an outlet for his imagination. In a famous passage in *Culture and Anarchy,* as notable for its power and elegance as for the questionableness of its facts, Arnold announced the imminent resurgence of "culture" in his own time by going back in history to the era of the 1832 Reform Bill. Resorting to the metaphor of the stream, Arnold asserted that the "currents of feeling" of the Oxford movement were, in 1832, broken by the rise of a prosaic and materialized "middle-class liberalism." Yet, though defeated and faulty, "Dr. Newman's movement" was a genuine expression of the idealism of "culture," which in its "keen desire for beauty and sweetness" only "swelled the tide of secret dissatisfaction" with the "hardness and vulgarity of middle-class liberalism" and the "grotesque illusions of middle-class Protestantism." Wishfully, Arnold climaxed his dubious history with a dubious prophecy by asserting that

[78] *God and the Bible: A Review of Objections to "Literature and Dogma"* (Boston, 1876), p. 87. George Eliot is the only contemporary novelist quoted in Arnold's *Note-books.*

the same stream "which has mined the ground under the self-confident liberalism" of the last thirty years would now bring about the triumph of his own humanist "culture."[79]

The passage bears comparison to *Middlemarch*, where George Eliot, exercising the same imaginative gift of "memory," also looks at the England of 1832 in order to examine the "origins" of the developments that both she and Arnold dislike. In her "study of provincial life," George Eliot likewise contrasts an ardent "desire for beauty and sweetness" to the prosaic reality of history. Unlike Arnold, however, she does not have to fasten her own idealistic yearning on an actual historical figure. Ironically enough, her imaginary Dorothea Brooke is far more credible than Arnold's semifictional recreation of "Dr. Newman." For the young woman's apostolic "sweetness" is juxtaposed, not to the "grotesque illusions of middle-class Protestantism" and to the "vulgarity of middle-class Liberalism," but rather to the distinct illusions of Mr. Bulstrode, the fanatical banker who regards himself as the executor of God's "will," and to the equally palpable vulgarity of Dorothea's uncle, the Liberal candidate devoid of ideas. Still, George Eliot's heroine and Arnold's "Dr. Newman" are the vehicles of identical implications. At the end of *Middlemarch*, the former Miss Brooke is likened to a river broken into "channels" of "no great name," which, like the underground "currents" described by Arnold, may one day guide the forward flow of history.

The intrusiveness of Arnold's imagination tends to alienate those who misread *Culture and Anarchy* as factual history and to distress even those who are fully aware of the significance of his ideas. But, transplanted to the realm of

[79] *Culture and Anarchy: An Essay in Political and Social Criticism* (London, 1869), pp. 35-39.

pure imagination and handled by a moralist craftsman of George Eliot's stature, these same ideas are truly raised "out of the flux of things" and given the ultimate permanence of art. Arnold scorned his age for denying him the substance for poetry; George Eliot turned to verse in the mistaken belief that it would heighten the substance of her humanist creed. But it was the prosaic *"architectonicè"* of the novel which, by transforming ideology into fiction, yielded that "allegory" which Arnold had rejected as an aim for poetry. And it was the intricate allegory of *Middlemarch* which best embodied the religious concerns both writers had shared in their essays and poems.

III

Middlemarch:
The Balance of Progress

*Truth, in the great practical concerns of life, is so much
a question of the reconciling and combining of opposites,
that very few have minds sufficiently capacious and impartial to make the adjustments with an approach to
correctness.* —J. S. MILL

*It is a narrow mind which cannot look at a subject
from various points of view.* —*Middlemarch*

Middlemarch is the most organic of George Eliot's novels.
Its Carlylean plot-"filaments" are so skillfully woven together that the critic who wants to unravel them is almost
forced to echo Tertius Lydgate's complaint: "I find myself
that it's uncommonly difficult to make the right thing work:
there are so many strings pulling at once."[1] The novel's
"strings" interlace into a three-dimensional web. Its scope,
which produces the inevitable comparison with *War and
Peace*, is achieved through the controlled motions of an
unusually large number of characters, linked either by gene-
alogical ties or by those intricate causal "relations" George
Eliot calls "the irony of events."[2] Its depth, however, is
produced through the creation of three concentric orbits or
spheres of action. In the innermost sphere, four separate, yet

[1] George Eliot, *Middlemarch*, 3 vols., Cabinet Edition (Edinburgh,
n.d.), chap. 50, p. 337. All future references to this edition are given
in the text.

[2] The links between the characters are outlined in George Eliot's
Quarry for Middlemarch, ed. Anna Theresa Kitchel (Berkeley,
1950), which contains a section called "Relations to be developed"
(p. 45).

complementary, plots are set in motion (the stories of Dorothea Brooke, of Tertius Lydgate, of the Garth family, and of the banker Bulstrode). In the next sphere the movement of these four plots is connected with the more slack "provincial life" of the Middlemarch community. In the outermost sphere, the progression of the Middlemarchers is related to the advancement of the English nation as a whole through allusions to the social, religious, and scientific reforms of the period,[3] and associated with the history of Western civilization through references to past events and discoveries, as well as to figures of tradition and myth. The theme of the novel then, in its vastest sense, is that of human progress; its object is to validate an ethic based on a "religious and moral sympathy with the historical life of man."[4] *Middlemarch* is also a prophetic or apocalyptic novel. Though fixed in the 1830's, the period it covers is only a "middle march" in the forward thrust of humanity as envisioned by the "Development theory" so familiar to George Eliot's thought. Its dynamic framework makes full use of that dual process of looking forward and backward advocated by Arnold and George Eliot, and described by the latter as the "divine gift of a memory which inspires the moments with a past, a present, and a future, and gives the sense of corporate existence."[5]

If the over-all structure of *Middlemarch* is in itself an illustration of the dynamics of historical evolution, this structure must be broken down in order to isolate the novel's

---

[3] See Jerome Beaty, "History of Indirection: The Era of Reform in *Middlemarch*," *Victorian Studies*, I (December 1957), 173-179, for a study of George Eliot's dramatic use of the reform background.

[4] *GEL*, IV, 97.

[5] "The Modern Hep! Hep! Hep!" in *Impressions of Theophrastus Such*, Cabinet Edition (Edinburgh, n.d.), p. 261.

main ideological issues. Here, however, the student who is concerned with "ideas" as well as with "form" must exercise extreme caution. In *Middlemarch* the "pulling strings," which even baffle the morphological expert Lydgate, are woven into a construct of which the final texture is different from and weightier than the mere sum of its parts. To isolate *Middlemarch*'s component strains is to lose the impact of their joint effect. Still, an approach combining literary perception with an awareness of George Eliot's intellectual preparation seems the most viable method of analysis for a novel of the nature of *Middlemarch*. Nor does a selective approach to the novel altogether mar a sense of its structure. George Eliot facilitates selectivity by her very definite weighing and proportioning of certain elements within her work. Her emphasis on the stories of Dorothea Brooke and Lydgate clearly subordinates the other two plots. Her religious vocabulary and her insistent identification of all characters with ranging modes of religious practice certainly convert *Middlemarch* into what Mark Schorer has called "a novel of religious yearning without a religious object."[6] It is as such a novel that *Middlemarch* is examined in the sections which follow.

[6] "Fiction and the 'Matrix of Analogy,'" *Kenyon Review*, XI (Autumn 1949), 539-560. Professor Schorer's brief section on *Middlemarch* is still one of the best appreciations of the novel. On the whole, George Eliot's accepted masterpiece lacks a body of critical interpretations as satisfactory as that pertaining to other Victorian novels or even to her lesser novels. Among the more valuable assessments of the novel in recent years, see Gordon S. Haight's Introduction to the Riverside edition; David R. Carroll, "Unity through Analogy: An Interpretation of *Middlemarch*," *VS*, II (June 1959), 305-316; W. J. Harvey, "The Omniscient Author Convention," in *The Art of George Eliot's Novels* (London, 1961), pp. 64-89; and Neil D. Isaacs' "*Middlemarch*: Crescendo of Obligatory Drama," *Nineteenth Century Fiction*, XVIII (June 1963) 21-34.

1. "HEART" AND "MIND": TWO FORMS OF PROGRESS

George Eliot described "Miss Brooke," the *novella* she eventually incorporated into *Middlemarch*, as dealing with "a subject which has been recorded among my possible themes ever since I began to write fiction, but will probably take new shapes in the development."[7] Actually, she had already exploited the story's theme—the "natural" education of a spiritually minded heroine—in *Adam Bede*, *The Mill on the Floss*, and *Romola*. In the "development" of *Middlemarch*, however, the story acquired a new "shape." Dorothea's education is utterly different from that of the rebellious Maggie Tulliver; its treatment and outcome are sharply in contrast with Dinah Morris's abrupt marriage to the redeemed Adam Bede or with the Feuerbachian worship of a widowed Romola crowned by a halo of "sun-rays." In *Middlemarch*, instead of a Romola canonized into a living Madonna, George Eliot depicts a "later-born Theresa" who, though endowed with "a heart large enough for the Virgin Mary," can only imperfectly emulate the saint who, according to Matthew Arnold as well as George Eliot, best embodied the "sweetness" of Jesus.[8]

The story of Dorothea Brooke, a "foundress of nothing," lies at the core of *Middlemarch*'s superstructure. What is more, it also circumscribes the entire novel. In the opening "Prelude," Dorothea's imminent tale is ironically likened to the "child-pilgrimage" of the infant Saint Theresa by a narrator who "cares much to know the history of man, and how the mysterious mixture behaves under the varying experiments of Time" (p. 1). Thus, at the very outset,

[7] *GEL*, v, 124.

[8] *Literature and Dogma: An Essay Towards a Better Apprehension of the Bible* (London, 1873), p. 294.

"Time" dissociates Dorothea from the "Spanish woman who lived three hundred years ago" (p. 2). In the main body of the novel, its inescapability converts Dorothea's evolution into the book's prime parable about that forward struggle against determining conditions "in which great feelings will often take the aspect of error, and great faith the aspect of illusion" ("Finale," p. 464). In the novel's "Finale," Dorothea's in-between "march" is assessed once again. Though not a new Theresa nor a new Antigone, though partially defeated by her initial unawareness of an increasingly complex world, Dorothea is now seen to have contributed to the forward flow of human progress: "Her full nature, like that river of which Cyrus broke the strength, spent itself in channels which had no great name on the earth. But the effect of her being on those around her was incalculably diffusive" (p. 465). In a novel which studies the "effects" of human actions like rippling chain reactions, Dorothea Brooke's rivulet is allowed to augment the maelstrom of social evolution. The "theoretic" enthusiast of the first half of the novel becomes an active healer who mends disrupted human relationships. This, and her marriage to the mercurial Will Ladislaw, a Victorian "second best," is the *via media*, the "middle march" between her soaring aspirations and the grounding force of a prosaic reality.

Yet of equal importance to the structure of *Middlemarch* is the parallel story of the young doctor Tertius Lydgate. Lydgate also is a would-be reformer, a healer "struggling for Medical Reform against Middlemarch" (ch. 46, p. 282). But if Dorothea's archetype is Saint Theresa, a believer in invisible truths, Lydgate's model is the anatomist Andreas Vesalius, a fighter for empirical truth. Lydgate's identification with the Flemish physician is made by himself: "No wonder the medical fogies in Middlemarch are jealous, when some of the greatest doctors living were fierce upon Vesalius because they had believed in Galen, and he showed that Galen was wrong. They called him a liar and a poisonous monster. But the facts of the human frame were on his side; and so he got the better of them" (ch. 45, pp. 279-280).

Lydgate's confident belief in "the facts of the human frame" is but an expression of his faith in scientific progress. Whereas Dorothea acts as if she were living in "the time of the Apostles," Lydgate is a "spirited young adventurer" driven into the "America" of anatomical studies. Both characters are equally eager for knowledge. But while Dorothea at first hopes to find this knowledge retrospectively in the outmoded dogmas of the past, Lydgate looks ahead with unflinching self-assurance. Dorothea believes that Mr. Casaubon's synoptical tabulations, "The Key to All Mythologies," may unlock a religious culture, "a binding theory which could bring her own life and doctrine into strict connection with that amazing past, and give the remotest sources of knowledge some bearing on her actions" (ch. 10, p. 128). Lydgate, on the other hand, longs to find a future "common basis" for all living organisms, a "primitive tissue" that will "demonstrate the more intimate relations of living structure, and help to define men's thoughts more accurately after the true order" (ch. 15, pp. 224-225). This "true order," like that upheld by T. H. Huxley, is grounded on a materialistic belief in "the physical basis of life."[9] Yet, at the novel's con-

[9] The identification between George Eliot's fictional physician and Huxley, the former surgeon of the H.M.S. *Rattlesnake*, is not purely arbitrary. In her *Quarry for Middlemarch*, George Eliot records a quotation from Huxley's 1853 essay on "Cell Theory" which provides the basis for Lydgate's belief. The two principles it enounces, already espoused by Bichat in the late eighteenth century and absorbed by Lydgate at the end of 1829, assert "that living beings may be resolved anatomically, into a comparatively small

clusion, Lydgate's ambitious desires to "define" the thoughts of others are shattered far more violently than Dorothea's personal illusions.

The stories of Dorothea and Lydgate are meticulously counterpointed. Both characters have been orphaned at an early age; both have received a Continental education; both try to challenge the provinciality of Middlemarch. But Dorothea's upbringing in Lausanne, the quiescent sister-city of Calvin's turbulent Geneva, only intensifies the "Hebraistic" strain of her Puritan ancestors: on her return to Middlemarch, the asceticism and "intensity of her religious disposition" lead her to accept the companionship of a blinking and shaggy-browed divine who merely takes the place of "Monk," her St. Bernard dog. On the other hand, Lydgate's sojourn in Paris, "the city of *l'homme sensuel moyen*" that Matthew Arnold was to hold out as a modern "Paradise of Ishmaels" opposed to Israel's (and England's) traditional concern with "righteousness," is even more detrimental to the doctor's intention to reform Middlemarch.[10] The laxity of a free-thinking Paris only accentuates Lydgate's tendency to disguise his innate sentimentality as "intellectual ardor": the same uncautious romanticism which makes him the dupe of the French actress Laure causes him, in Middlemarch, to abstract the vulgar and uneducated Rosamond Vincy into "an exquisite bird" able to teach him "a thousand things." Dorothea and Lydgate are equally wellborn, but both disregard their rank: the young woman, who has no "parcel-tying forefathers," rejects the suit of Sir James Chettam, a baronet; the physician, who "is one of the Lydgates of

---

number of structural elements" and "that these elementary parts possess vital properties" (*Quarry*, p. 31). For a further link between Lydgate and Huxley see Appendix I.

[10] *Literature and Dogma*, p. 358.

Northumberland, really well connected" (ch. 10, p. 136),
becomes alienated from Sir Godwin, his uncle. Dorothea thus
marries first a pedant who ponders over the origins of Dagon,
the Philistine god, and then weds his younger cousin, a man
of "alien blood, Jew, Corsican, or Gypsy," who turns out
to be related by marriage to Mr. Bulstrode, the arch-
Philistine. On the other hand, Lydgate's tie to the grand-
daughter of an innkeeper, his dependence on Bulstrode's
money, and his indulgence in gambling practices he had
condemned in others, make him "hardly distinguishable from
a Philistine under the same circumstances" (ch. 67, p. 221).

In their enthusiasm the two presumptive reformers are
comparable to that sympathetic, yet ironically presented,
pair in the opening of the novel, brother and sister toddling
"from rugged Avila, wide-eyed and helpless-looking as two
fawns, but with human hearts" ("Prelude," p. 1). Ideally,
Lydgate and Dorothea ought to walk "hand-in-hand" like
the two tiny pilgrims of a lost age of faith. The moral fervor
of Dorothea should supplement the young doctor's "distinction of mind"; his faith in a future built by science ought
to be allied to her reverence for the guidelines of the past.
Yet, as Matthew Arnold had lamented in his poems and
essays, the *Zeitgeist* or "Time" has sundered mystery and
dogma from reason and experience. Arnold had coupled the
two semantically in speaking of the "sweet reasonableness"
of the Bible; in *Middlemarch*, however, heart and mind remain irrevocably apart. In one of the most striking metaphoric ironies of the novel, Dorothea's "loving heart-beats"
lead her to marry an unaffectionate, but highly affected,
cardiac scholar suffering from an "affection of the heart,"
which is correctly diagnosed by Dr. Lydgate, "a loving-
hearted man." Yet the physician discovers in turn that "the
facts of the human frame" are insufficient to ensure him

against a "future without affection." The "intellectual passion" which leads him to regard human nature as a mere compound of separable organs—"brain, heart, lungs, and so on"—also acts as a justification for his "scientific view of woman" and leads to the fragmentation of his own heart and mind. Ironically enough, this "passion" stems from his childhood perusal of an encyclopaedia containing a description of the "valves of the *heart*" under "the *head* of Anatomy" (ch. 15, p. 217; italics added).

Lydgate and Dorothea complement each other both in their surfeits and in their defects. Dorothea's religious fervor incorrectly demands that her emotionalism be chastened by Mr. Casaubon's intellectual lucubrations, which are composed of the same dull "formulae of past thinkings" that Mark Pattison, George Eliot's friend, had deplored in his contribution to the *Essays and Reviews*.[11] But if Dorothea yields to a debased rationalism, Lydgate errs in the opposite direction. It is impetuousness, not reflection, which leads him to choose medicine as a career "presenting the most perfect interchange between science and art; offering the most direct alliance between intellectual conquest and the social good" (ch. 15, p. 219); his "scientific view of woman" merely gives a semblance of rationality to his own brand of emotionalism. Cheap sentimentality and sensualism are the "spots of commonness" which cause the young naturalist to

[11] "Tendencies of Religious Thought in England, 1688-1750," quoted by Basil Willey in *More Nineteenth Century Studies: A Group of Honest Doubters* (New York, 1956), p. 153. Pattison's attack on the "reasonable" creeds of the eighteenth century was echoed in the same volume by Rowland Williams whose denunciation of "that dulness which turns symbol and poetry into materialism" sounds like a point-by-point description of Mr. Casaubon. In apparent agreement, George Eliot makes Casaubon a caricature of the Age of Reason throughout the novel.

mistake Miss Rosy, "the flower of Mrs. Lemon's school," for an exotic plant requiring a "much-needed transplantation." His "native warm-heartedness" thus precipitates his one sentimental indulgence, his submission to Rosamond's tearful vulgarity: "There was no help for this in science" (ch. 27, p. 407). The cerebral physician who is able to warn Mr. Casaubon that "diseases of the heart are eminently difficult to found predictions on" (ch. 42, p. 228), soon finds that his own heart has yoked him to an unpredictable "animal of another and feebler species" (ch. 65, p. 205). The tame, musical "bird of paradise," whose "language" he was so willing to learn, suddenly evolves into a reptilian creature whose "flute-like tones" and scorpion-like "pincers" force Lydgate to seek refuge in opium dreams and in the gambling room of "The Green Dragon." Andreas Vesalius was slandered as "a liar" and "a poisonous monster," but Lydgate, his emulator, actually betrays his scientific standards and turns into "an animal with fierce eyes and retractile claws" (ch. 66, p. 213).[12]

Dorothea and Lydgate, "heart" and "mind," race against each other in the forward "march" of the novel. Dorothea's meliorism is momentarily arrested by Mr. Casaubon's static scholarship: "crawling a little way after men of the last century" (ch. 22, p. 339), the elderly scholar is hardly aware that he is pitted against nimble Germans whose progress has been accelerated by the new development theories. Lydgate, on the other hand, in tune with ideas "vibrating along many currents of the European mind," is fully conscious of competitors "still strutting or shambling along the old paths" (ch. 15, pp. 225, 224), and just as confident in his own ability to spurt ahead of "some 'plodding fellow of a German'" (ch. 36, p. 115). Nonetheless, he is stopped

[12] See Appendix I.

as decisively as Mr. Casaubon. Able to diagnose the "fatty degeneration of the heart" of Dorothea's husband, the physician himself succumbs to a "sense of mental degeneracy." His commitment to science, his Huxleian belief in "the supremacy of the intellectual life," founders because of his inability to understand the fallibility of his own heart. He abstracts his wife into a mythical creature emerging out of "some gigantic flower," "an accomplished mermaid" or "water-nixie," whose singing is to provide "the relaxation of his adored wisdom." But Rosamond's siren song, utterly devoid of "the 'little language' of affection," induces a fatal relaxation. Lydgate's yearning for "the sweet furtherance of satisfying affections—beauty—repose" ends in a state of hypnotic torpor. The experimenter is drugged by the swamp-like exhalations of Rosy Vincy, a common "garden-flower" he has unintentionally transformed into a poisonous flower of evil. At the novel's end, Lydgate sarcastically calls Rosamond "his basil plant; and when she asked for an explanation, said that basil was a plant which had flourished wonderfully on a murdered man's brains" ("Finale," p. 460). Thus, in the general "march" of the novel, Lydgate's progress is blocked.[13] Dorothea's stream of influence, albeit a mere "brook" or "channel of no great name," is allowed to flow on, "incalculably diffusive."

Lydgate's materialist faith in the future becomes as sterile as Mr. Casaubon's cogitations over a static past or as foolish as Mr. Brooke's blundering enslavement to a present that only provides him with an unruly parade of "ideas." For,

[13] In his article Professor Schorer suggests that Lydgate's very name implies a double process of blocking (through the connotation of a shutting "lid" and "gate"); to be sure, Lydgate's first view of the heart comes through an illustration of valves he believes to be "folding doors."

in her over-all balance, George Eliot very definitely favors the "heart" over the "mind." But this preference does not in itself determine the downfall of Lydgate, whose genuine "distinction of mind" is stressed again and again, and who, in the "ardent kindness of his heart" is as fully sympathetic a character as Dorothea herself. Why then, despite this apparent equilibrium, is Lydgate's brand of idealism degraded while Dorothea's is upheld? Why must her "Hebraism" be united to the "Hellenism" of a Will Ladislaw rather than to that of the doctor? The answer is simple: Lydgate is amoral; his physical science is impotent against moral disease. George Eliot's choice of a medical man to bring home this truth coincides with Matthew Arnold's remarks on moral illness in *Literature and Dogma*: "Medical science has never gauged,—never, perhaps, enough set itself to gauge,—the intimate connexion between moral fault and disease."[14] Dorothea's emotion can touch and translate her inbred morality into meaningful actions; her "consciousness of Christian centuries" can be enlisted as a motive power. Lydgate's "heart" is wasted on the cheap romanticism which converts his wife into "an accomplished mermaid."

Lacking the Hebraic sense of "righteousness" defined by Arnold in *Literature and Dogma*, Lydgate must learn that in George Eliot's (or Arnold's) humanist religion of experience, "happiness" can only belong "to conduct."[15] It is here that the subordinated plots of the Garth family and of the banker Bulstrode, and the ranging "modes of religion" of all other characters, are brought into full play to sharpen the novel's basic oppositions of heart and mind, experience and dogma, reaction and progress, duty and free will. Arnold's conclusion to his essay can well stand as a summary of *Middlemarch*'s basic moral axiom: "For the whole series

[14] P. 143.   [15] P. 360.

of experiences, of which the survey is thus completed, rests, primarily, upon one fundamental fact,—itself, also, a fact of experience: *the necessity of righteousness.*"[16] The "series of experiences" depicted in George Eliot's novel are designed to illustrate this "fundamental fact." Its truth is tested by the main sets of oppositions and analogies she creates; its validity is upheld by the relationship of Dorothea and Lydgate to each other and to practically every character in the novel.

2. "Modes of Religion"

a. Dorothea and Farebrother vs. Lydgate and Bulstrode

Tertius Lydgate's first encounter with Dorothea Brooke takes place at the dinner given as a preliminary to her wedding. It is noteworthy that the young woman's yearning for a life "filled with action at once rational and ardent" has already produced her irrational engagement to Dr. Casaubon, the Philistine of the mind (ch. 10, p. 129); thus, Lydgate who also desires "the most direct alliance between intellectual conquest and the social good" arrives too late for such an alliance to take place. What is more, the intellectual physician completely underestimates Dorothea. There is a double irony in his disparagement of her moral earnestness: " 'She is a good creature—that fine girl—but a little too earnest,' he thought. 'It is troublesome to talk to such women. They are always wanting *reasons*, yet they are too ignorant to understand the merits of any question, and usually fall back on their *moral sense* to settle things after their own taste' " (ch. 10, p. 139; italics added). Lydgate is to discover that his patronizing tone is misplaced. His own lack of a "moral sense" not only is to produce his downfall, but will also make him increasingly indebted to the "good creature" before him.

[16] P. 380.

"MODES OF RELIGION" (a)

The second meeting between the two characters occurs after intervening events have illuminated their respective blind spots. Dorothea's Roman honeymoon and, with it, her confrontation with a grim historical process, grasped neither by her "toy-box history of the world" nor by her husband's "stock of false antiquities," have given her a different sense of past and present:

> She did not really see the streak of sunlight on the floor more than she saw the statues: she was inwardly seeing the light of years to come in her own home and over the English fields and elms and hedge-bordered highroads; and feeling that the way in which they might be filled with joyful devotedness was not so clear to her as it had been. But in Dorothea's mind there was a current into which all thought and feeling were apt sooner or later to flow—the reaching forward of the whole consciousness towards the fullest truth, the least partial good. There was clearly something better than anger and despondency.
> [ch. 20, p. 311]

Once hoping to receive a "nearer introduction to the Stoics and Alexandrians" through the "guiding visions" projected by Mr. Casaubon's lamp of knowledge, Dorothea now learns how to apply the failure and suffering of antecedent generations to the immediate reality of her own present. Schooled by experience, her "consciousness" can now begin to flow.

But while Dorothea begins to expand her Puritanic notions through her contact with the cosmopolitan past of Rome, Lydgate, though as ambitious as ever of a "wider effect," finds that his "notions in science" are contracting more and more. Increasingly dependent on the pettier aspects of Middlemarch life, the young crusader is about to become ensnared by George Eliot's "strings." In the novel's careful counterpointing, Dorothea gains by exercising pity for her husband's wasteful illusions and by allowing her sympathy for Casaubon's plight to overrule her physical attraction to Ladislaw. Lydgate, on the other hand, loses when he decides to overrule the dictates of his conscience in the name of scientific progress; despite his actual sympathy for the Reverend Mr. Farebrother, he rationalizes himself into voting for Mr. Bulstrode's candidate, the Reverend Mr. Tyke. Lydgate has vowed to exclude all moral considerations or "clerical disputes" from his pursuit of empirical truth, but his decision to be governed only by the goals of his "profession" leads to unexpected results. Though scornful of his patron's demands that the New Hospital administer more than the "cure of mortal diseases," Lydgate soon discovers that the "religious tone" given to the clinic by Mr. Bulstrode and Mr. Tyke alienates other donors. Paradoxically enough, his destiny has become entangled with that of the one character whose religious fanaticism and hypocrisy are anathema to any sense of empirical truth.[17]

Thus, when Lydgate and Dorothea meet for the second time, the "irony of events" has already modified their respective creeds. Presumably, the young physician, who has been called by Dorothea to treat her husband's heart-attack, still has the upper hand. Dorothea is still his debtor, the recipient of his superior knowledge. In a flash, however, the author intimates that their roles are to be reversed. Dorothea's inviolable dedication rises above that of the doctor. Even the

---

[17] Bulstrode's pietistic religion is a replica of that attacked by George Eliot in "Evangelical Teaching: Dr. Cumming," *Westminster Review*, LXIV (October 1855), 436-462, where her wrath is directed against an insistence on salvation "as a scheme rather than as an experience" (p. 439).

gestural "stage-directions" of the scene convey the superiority of her spirit:

> Lydgate rose, and Dorothea mechanically rose at the
> same time, unclasping her cloak and throwing it off as if it
> stifled her. He was bowing and quitting her, when an im-
> pulse which if she had been alone would have turned into
> a prayer, made her say with a sob in her voice—
> "Oh, you are a wise man, are you not? You know all
> about life and death. Advise me. Think what I can do. He
> has been labouring all his life and looking forward. He
> minds about nothing else. And I mind about nothing
> else—"
> For years after Lydgate remembered the impression
> produced in him by this involuntary appeal—this cry from
> soul to soul, without other consciousness than their moving
> with kindred natures in the same embroiled medium, the
> same troublous fitfully-illuminated life. But what could he
> say now except that he should see Mr. Casaubon again
> to-morrow? [ch. 30, pp. 26-27]

The "kindred natures" of both characters, their joint motion
in "the same embroiled medium," their respective isolation,
and the limitations of Lydgate's knowledge are superbly
compressed in this short scene.

Lydgate's gradual fall and Dorothea's gradual ascendancy
are punctuated through a progression of further meetings
which culminates in the "Sunset and Sunrise" of the last
book.[18] Their relationship is now expressed through a mutual
process of ministration. Lydgate's help is limited by his science; Dorothea's becomes spiritually transcendent. In chapter
44, although Dorothea ostensibly asks Lydgate's advice about

---

[18] "Sunset and Sunrise," the title of Book Eight, also refers to
the rise of the Garth family and the fall of Bulstrode.

her husband's "bodily condition," she volunteers her own assistance on discovering that Lydgate's hospital is suffering from the unpopularity engendered by the "religious tone" of its chief patron, Mr. Bulstrode.

In chapter 48, Lydgate relieves a Dorothea whose delirious "brain" has become dangerously "excited" upon the discovery of her "motionless" husband. Lydgate prescribes "perfect freedom" for the young widow, since he believes her to be suffering from "self-repression." But Dorothea's freedom is to be of another sort. No longer bound by its pity for the "living, suffering man," her heart undergoes its first test. Dorothea disengages herself from the grasp of Casaubon's "Dead Hand" by rejecting the provisions of his last will and by refusing to be tied to the "fragments of a tradition which was itself a mosaic wrought from crushed ruins." She turns instead to a more active creed. In chapter 50, she repairs Lydgate's moral mistake by granting his request that Farebrother be given Casaubon's living. Once mystically removed in "the time of the Apostles," Dorothea now has gained enough experience to realize that the beliefs of a worldly clergyman who is also proficient in entomology may embody traditional Christian virtues better than the "crushed ruins" of religious dogma. Her vacillations are soon overcome:

> "My uncle says that Mr. Tyke is spoken of as an apostolic man," said Dorothea, meditatively. She was wishing it were possible to restore the times of primitive zeal, and yet thinking of Mr. Farebrother with a strong desire to rescue him from his chance-gotten money.
>
> "I don't pretend to say that Farebrother is apostolic," said Lydgate. "His position is not quite like that of the Apostles: he is only a parson among parishioners whose lives he has to try and make better. Practically I find that

what is called being apostolic now, is an impatience of
everything in which the parson doesn't cut the principal
figure. I see something of that in Mr. Tyke at the Hospital: a good deal of his doctrine is a sort of pinching hard
to make people uncomfortably aware of him. Besides, an
apostolic man at Lowick!—he ought to think, as St.
Francis did, that it is needful to preach to the birds." [ch.
50, pp. 337-338]

"Dodo" Brooke, who as a child "believed in the gratitude
of wasps and the honourable susceptibility of sparrows" (ch.
22, p. 329), agrees that Lydgate's advice is practical; she
is of course unaware of the futility of his own sermons to his
domestic bird of paradise. Dorothea's Christianity has altered
considerably. The "later-born Theresa" has come to understand that an "apostolic" preacher, addressing his parishioners
as if they belonged to the age of St. Francis, can no longer
fulfill the spiritual needs of the present.[19] Having learned to
shun Mr. Casaubon's abstractions, she is ready to uphold
Mr. Farebrother's lax but pragmatic religion of experience,
a relativist creed based on his awareness of his personal foibles
and on his more comprehensive view of "man the object."
Dorothea's attitude toward the dogmatism of Mr. Tyke,
Bulstrode's protégé, and thus toward Bulstrode's own "spiritual religion" as well, shows the extent to which her own
religious views have become modified:

[19] In his "Religion in the Novels of George Eliot," *Journal of
English and Germanic Philology*, LIII (April 1954), 145-159, Mr.
Martin J. Svaglic glosses this passage by pointing out that in 1833
there was an open conflict between the "apostolical" Tractarians and
Evangelicals. This suggestion loses its force, however, if one reflects
that, though spoken of as an "apostolic man," Mr. Tyke quite ob-
viously is an Evangelical himself—a curate at St. Peter's under
Rector Thesiger, "a moderate Evangelical" (p. 137).

"True," said Dorothea. "It is hard to imagine what sort of notions our farmers and labourers get from their teaching. I have been looking into a volume of sermons by Mr. Tyke: such sermons would be of no use at Lowick— I mean, about imputed righteousness and the prophecies in the Apocalypse. I have always been thinking of the different ways in which Christianity is taught, and whenever I find one way that makes it a wider blessing than any other, I cling to that as the truest—I mean that which takes in the most good of all kinds, and brings in the most people as sharers in it. It is surely better to pardon too much, than to condemn too much. But I should like to see Mr. Farebrother and hear him preach."

"Do," said Lydgate; "I trust to the effect of that." [ch. 50, p. 338]

But if Dorothea's personal religion becomes identified with that of Mr. Farebrother, the "irony of events" associates Lydgate's empiricism with the dogma of Nicholas Bulstrode. The next and final meeting with Dorothea occurs after Bulstrode's crime has dragged Lydgate along, forever ruining his expectations of becoming "the Middlemarch doctor and immortal discoverer" he had once hoped to be. Scorned by all Middlemarchers, shunned by his wife, disbelieved in even by Mr. Farebrother, Lydgate discovers that his dedication to scientific truth has become flawed by the very same inconsistencies he had detected in Bulstrode's evangelicalism. Lydgate's standards are open to the same criticism applied by the author to the false "reasoning" underlying Bulstrode's religion: "There is no general doctrine which is not capable of eating out our morality if unchecked by the deep-seated habit of direct fellow-feeling with individual fellow-men" (ch. 61, p. 133). Bulstrode has hypocritically rationalized his egotism into a "serviceable-ness to God's cause";[20] Lydgate has allowed his "spots of commonness" to tarnish his Hippocratic oath. By precipitating the death of Raffles, Bulstrode is untrue to his God; by declaring this death to be accidental after he has accepted the banker's money, Lydgate not only violates the ethics of his profession, but also becomes false to his highest ideal: the detachment of empirical truth. Significantly enough, the dilemma which ravages Lydgate's mind, though of a moral nature, is presented in purely scientific terms as the doctor is forced to retrace his own actions to their psychological origins:

> But then came the question whether he should have acted in precisely the same way if he had not taken the money? Certainly, if Raffles had continued alive and susceptible of further treatment when he arrived, and he had then imagined any disobedience to his orders on the part of Bulstrode, he would have made a strict inquiry, and if his conjecture had been verified he would have thrown up the case, in spite of his recent heavy obligation. But if he had not received any money—if Bulstrode had never revoked his cold recommendation of bankruptcy—would he, Lydgate, have abstained from all inquiry even on finding the man dead? [ch. 73, p. 316]

Lydgate's mental inquiry forces him to admit that Bulstrode's loan has corrupted his allegiance to scientific truth. For the first time he realizes that science, far from being self-sufficient, can become as unsound as the banker's dogmatism:

[20] Cf. "Evangelical Teaching: Dr. Cumming," p. 461: "It is in vain for Dr. Cumming to say that we are to love man for God's sake: with the conception of God which his teaching presents, the love of man for God's sake involves, as his writings abundantly show, a strong principle of hatred."

That was the uneasy corner of Lydgate's consciousness while he was reviewing the facts and resisting all reproach. If he had been independent, this matter of a patient's treatment and the distinct rule that he must do or see done that which he believed best for the life committed to him, would have been the point on which he would have been the sturdiest. As it was, he had rested in the consideration that disobedience to his orders, however it might have arisen, could not be considered a crime, that in the dominant opinion obedience to his orders was just as likely to be fatal, and that the affair was simply one of etiquette. Whereas, again and again, in his time of freedom, he had denounced the perversion of pathological doubt into moral doubt and had said—"the purest experiment in treatment may still be conscientious: my business is to take care of life, and to do the best I can think of for it. Science is properly more scrupulous than dogma. Dogma gives a charter to mistake, but the very breath of science is a contest with mistake, and must keep the conscience alive." Alas! the scientific conscience had got into the debasing company of money obligation and selfish respects. [ch. 73, pp. 316-317]

Lydgate thus finds himself chained to Bulstrode against his will. He attends the "sanitary meeting" in the Town Hall and witnesses the banker's self-righteous defense against his enemies and former friends. When Bulstrode is exiled by men who act in his own self-righteous spirit, it is Lydgate who leads him away from his accusers, "morally forced" into this act of help. But Lydgate regards this help only as painful evidence of his complicity: ". . . this act, which might have been one of gentle duty and pure compassion, was at this moment unspeakably bitter to him. It seemed as if he were putting his sign-manual to that association of himself with Bulstrode, of which he now saw the full meaning as it must have presented itself to other minds" (ch. 71, p. 301). The doctor's desolation surpasses Bulstrode's; for, unlike the banker, he must bear his ostracism alone.

The scene in which Bulstrode receives his wife's support is followed by that in which Rosamond denies all understanding to Lydgate. Ready to share her husband's "shame and isolation" with "one leap of her heart," Mrs. Bulstrode adopts the drab attire of an "early Methodist" in order to express her "new compassion and old tenderness." Her symbolic act captures the emotionalism of a more primitive religion: Mrs. Bulstrode is able to sustain her husband's faltering belief by suggesting the traditional loyalty of Ruth the Moabitess. Rosamond Lydgate, who thrives on the bombast of *Lalla Rookh*, not only has no such tradition to back her, but also lacks her aunt's power of sympathy. Her central creed is one of aimlessness: "There is really nothing to care for much." At the time of Lydgate's fall, she yields to wishful fantasies featuring a new prince: "Will Ladislaw was always to be a bachelor and live near her" (ch. 75, p. 338). Rosamond is the standard egoist of Victorian fiction, but she is neither a melodramatic *femme fatale* nor a Becky Sharp. She remains a secondary character manipulated only to define the larger issues at hand and to accentuate her husband's need for ministrations of the "good creature" he had once disparaged.

Of all Middlemarchers, only Dorothea Brooke is willing to espouse Lydgate's cause. Here, her "impetuous generosity" even rises above Mr. Farebrother's benevolent but evasive moral relativism. Though he owes Casaubon's living to Lydgate, the Rector's "keen perception of human weakness" makes him all too ready to believe in his friend's guilt.

Dorothea's instinctive faith soars above that of the clergyman: rather "discontented with Mr. Farebrother," she dislikes his "cautious weighing of consequences, instead of an
ardent faith in efforts of justice and mercy, which would
conquer by their emotional force" (ch. 72, p. 308). Her
reproof of the Rector conveys George Eliot's own partial
dissatisfaction with the creed of moral "realism" she had
preached since the publication of "Amos Barton"—a dissatisfaction that was to come to the fore in *Daniel Deronda*:

> "But, my dear Mrs. Casaubon," said Mr. Farebrother,
> smiling gently at her ardour, "character is not cut in
> marble—it is not something solid and unalterable. It is
> something living and changing, and may become diseased
> as our bodies do."
> "Then it may be rescued and healed," said Dorothea.
> [ch. 72, p. 310]

Middlemarch's reversal of roles, its Aristotelian *peripateia*,
is thus completed. Dorothea has become the healer; Lydgate
the patient. In their final encounter in chapter 76, the
"heart" subdues the "mind." Appropriately enough, the
chapter's epigraph is taken from Blake's poem "The Divine
Image":

> For Mercy has a human heart,
>   Pity a human face;
> And Love, the human form divine;
>   And Peace, the human dress.

Dorothea's "full heart" and "sweet trustful gravity" over-
power the young anatomist who had once regarded the
cardiacal valves in such an analytical fashion. Gratefully,
Lydgate yields to Dorothea's faith in humanity: "Lydgate
did not stay to think that she was Quixotic: he gave himself

up, for the first time in his life, to the exquisite sense of leaning entirely on a generous sympathy, without any check of proud reserve. And he told her everything, from the time when, under the pressure of his difficulties, he unwillingly made his first application to Bulstrode" (ch. 76, p. 353). After Lydgate's confession, the young priestess promises absolution. She will vindicate him before Rosamond and "in a few other minds." In George Eliot's religion of humanity, man's exoneration can only come from his fellow men:

> As Lydgate rode away, he thought, "This young creature has a heart large enough for the Virgin Mary. She evidently thinks nothing of her own future, and would pledge away half her income at once, as if she wanted nothing for herself but a chair to sit in from which she can look down with those clear eyes at the poor mortals who pray to her. She seems to have what I never saw in any woman before—a fountain of friendship towards men—a man can make a friend of her. Casaubon must have raised some heroic hallucination in her. I wonder if she could have any other sort of passion for a man? Ladislaw?—there was certainly an unusual feeling between them. And Casaubon must have had a notion of it. Well—her love might help a man more than her money." [ch. 76, pp. 361-362]

Lydgate's invocation of Dorothea as a secular madonna completes the metamorphosis of their relation to each other. Once mocked by him as being "a little too earnest," Dorothea has now become a symbol for the true disinterestedness that was lacking in his own idealism. But the balance is still there. Unlike Romola, Dorothea does not remain a widowed "Saint of Humanity." Lydgate's speculation about the physical needs of his nunlike confessor is clinically shrewd.

And, unknown to him, it is his own wife who, aided by the "irony of events," manages to connect Dorothea to Will Ladislaw.

3. "Modes of Religion"

b. Ladislaw and Dorothea; the Morality of Experience

Will Ladislaw has always disturbed those readers of *Middle-march* who, after the manner of Leslie Stephen, find the "young gentleman" to be "conspicuously unworthy of the affections of a Saint Theresa."[21] But Dorothea is *not* a Saint Theresa, nor is her second marriage meant to be an ideal union of the "heart" and the "mind." If Ladislaw's unsatisfactoriness persists, this is so, not because of his unsuitability as Dorothea's husband, but because, as a character, he serves too many different roles in the novel's ideological scheme. As a physical foil to the weak-legged Casaubon, Ladislaw is portrayed as being young, vital, "a spirited horse"; as the intellectual foil to the blind "Bat of erudition" of Lowick, he is depicted as a "sunny" Ariel who can interpret history imaginatively and who can, above all, "read the idealistic in the real." Although Will can thus see in Dorothea an "ideal" perceived neither by Casaubon nor by Lydgate, he is by no means an idealized figure himself.[22]

---

[21] "George Eliot," *Hours in a Library* (London, 1907), IV, 179. Stephen's opinion is partly echoed by as recent a critic as Professor Jerome Thale who would like to see Ladislaw "grow" more worthy of Dorothea before sanctioning their match: "Had Ladislaw been more fully realized, we might accept him as an eligible husband," *The Novels of George Eliot* (New York, 1959), p. 119, n.2.

[22] In *The Great Tradition* (London, 1948), F. R. Leavis, apparently as unaware of George Eliot's irony as Leslie Stephen, is convinced that Ladislaw is "not to be distinguished from the novelist" who uses him as a mouthpiece for her "idealizing" view of Dorothea (p. 179).

Mr. Casaubon is a ludicrous latter-day reincarnation of great divines, such as Hooker and Milton, who is mocked for his willingness to pose for a portrait of the "angelical doctor," Thomas Aquinas. Will's identification with Shelley, Byron, Chatterton, and Churchill is almost as uncomplimentary. The association is greatly qualified by the fact that it is made by Mr. Brooke, Ladislaw's absurd patron, whose view of Ladislaw changes from "a kind of Shelley, you know" to the more conservative estimate of "Burke with a leaven of Shelley." What is more, it is undermined by George Eliot's own reservations about the figure of the Romantic rebel—reservations which prompt her to ascribe "petulance" and a "tone of almost boyish complaint" to her creation. After Will exposes Casaubon's ignorance of the German developmental theories to his wife, George Eliot glosses Will's revelation caustically: "Young Mr. Ladislaw was not at all deep himself in German writers; but very little achievement is required in order to pity another man's shortcomings" (ch. 21, p. 319).[23]

Will's opposition to Casaubon is of course subordinated to his role as Dorothea's admirer; as such, he is also contrasted to Lydgate. In the novel's general scheme, Ladislaw is the poet, artist, and radical who stands for "feeling itself." His emotionality causes him to magnify Dorothea in a way open neither to Casaubon nor to Lydgate, the avowed rationalists. He worships at Dorothea's feet long before Lydgate soberly concludes that the young matron has "a heart large enough for the Virgin Mary." Will's quick recognition of Dorothea's

[23] George Eliot spoofs Will throughout the novel. The most extended ridicule of his unpredictable temperament comes in chapter 47 which opens with Will walking briskly to the Lowick church full of enthusiasm and love-hymns, and ends with his despondent return.

qualities is based on a "truth" of feeling which is unlike Lydgate's perversion of feeling and truth into his "spots of commonness." Yet, taken by itself, Ladislaw's impulsiveness is hardly superior to Lydgate's steadfast devotion to scientific truth; his carefree "Hellenism," contrasted with Dorothea's early Puritanism, is even less attractive than her rigorous religious zeal.

Though in love, Ladislaw is by no means uncritical of the woman described by his German painter friend as "a sort of Christian Antigone" who combines "sensuous force" with "spiritual passion." He reprimands Dorothea for her self-enforced asceticism, but his overenthusiastic "Defense of Poetry" ("to be a poet is to have a soul . . . in which knowledge passes instantaneously into feeling, and feeling flashes back as a new organ of knowledge") is undercut by Dorothea who points out innocently that poems are "wanted to complete the poet" (ch. 22, pp. 341-342). Resorting to her favorite method of looking "at a subject from various points of view," George Eliot juxtaposes Ladislaw's aesthetic cult of feeling to Dorothea's spiritual self-negation. The result, superbly ironical, is rather to the detriment of Will:

"I fear you are a heretic about art generally. How is that? I should have expected you to be very sensitive to the beautiful everywhere."

"I suppose I am dull about many things," said Dorothea, simply. "I should like to make life beautiful—I mean everybody's life. And then all this immense expense of art, that seems somehow to lie outside life and make it no better for the world, pains one. It spoils my enjoyment of anything when I am made to think that most people are shut out from it."

"I call that the fanaticism of sympathy," said Will, impetuously. "You might say the same of landscape, of poetry, of all refinement. If you carried it out you ought to be miserable in your own goodness, and turn evil that you might have no advantage over others. The best piety is to enjoy—when you can. You are doing the most then to save the earth's character as an agreeable planet. And enjoyment radiates. It is of no use to try and take care of all the world; that is being taken care of when you feel delight—in art or in anything else." [ch. 22, pp. 335-336]

Despite this frank "invitation to learning," however, Ladislaw is not a mere hedonist. Bolstered with qualities opposed to his epicureanism, he emerges in the second third of the novel as a selfless reformer and a believer in social change. Here his Continental "Hellenism," like Lydgate's own variety, clashes against the provincialism of Middlemarch.

To George Eliot, Will's cosmopolitanism is an asset. It is a vehicle for "culture." Ladislaw is hardly admired by the reactionary Middlemarchers: he is repeatedly ridiculed as an "Italian with white mice" by the sharp-tongued Mrs. Cadwallader, despised as a "quill-driving alien" by Sir James Chettam, and distrusted for his "Whiggish twist" by lawyer Hawley: "He'll begin with flourishing about the Rights of Man and end with murdering a wench. That's the style" (ch. 37, p. 129). He is defamed as the "grandson of a Jew pawnbroker" by the town's rank and file, and even mildly disparaged for his "queer genealogy" by the Reverend Mr. Farebrother.[24] But it is Lydgate's characterization of Will as

[24] In "The Forgotten Past of Will Ladislaw," *NCF*, XIII (September 1958), 159-163, Mr. Jerome Beaty provides a helpful outline of Will's complicated genealogy, although he uses this outline to indulge in speculations which have since been refuted.

"a sort of gypsy, rather enjoying the sense of belonging to no class" which perhaps comes closest to George Eliot's own meaning (ch. 46, p. 286). Young Ladislaw is a Victorian version of Shelley's "unacknowledged legislator of the world." Bound by no single tradition, not too "ecclesiastical," he is receptive to impulses of all sorts. He incites Dorothea against Casaubon's demands, yet at the time is himself bound by his cousin's pecuniary help. He supports the new Reform Bill and the fumbling Mr. Brooke with the same zest with which he espouses a utopian settlement in the American Far West.[25] He refuses to be fettered under obligations of any kind. Even his name assumes a special significance in a novel which pits "will" against the duties engendered by causal "laws."[26] It is not surprising that the novelist's efforts to reduce this abstracted and multi-form spirit into a concrete figure should not be altogether successful.

George Eliot contrasts Ladislaw's brand of "Hellenism" with Lydgate's by their parallel relationships to Dorothea, Rosamond, and Bulstrode. The opposition of "poet" to "physician" goes back to Plato's contrast of Homer to Asclepius, a contrast elaborated on by Sir Philip Sidney: "How often, thinke you, doe the Phisitians lye, when they aver things. . . . Now, for the Poet, he nothing affirmes, and therefore never lyeth."[27] George Eliot, likewise, contrasts the inflexibility which leads Lydgate to his one perversion of truth to Ladislaw's malleability. As usual, the irony works both ways:

[25] In the *Quarry* George Eliot laconically glosses Will's return to Middlemarch to procure funds for this settlement: "Means to go to Utopia."

[26] See section 4 of this chapter.

[27] "An Apologie for Poetrie," *Criticism: The Foundations of Modern Literary Judgment*, eds. Josephine Miles, Mark Schorer, Gordon McKenzie (New York, 1948), p. 421.

"That is the way with you political writers, Ladislaw—crying up a measure as if it were a universal cure, and crying up men who are a part of the very disease that wants curing."

"Why not? Men may help to cure themselves off the face of the land without knowing it," said Will, who could find reasons impromptu, when he had not thought of a question beforehand. [ch. 46, p. 292]

Ladislaw is a more independent figure than Lydgate. He renounces all claims on Dorothea upon hearing of Casaubon's prohibitive testament. His melodramatic rejection of Bulstrode's "ill-gotten money" and his casual association with Mr. Brooke compare favorably with Lydgate's increasing dependence on his patron's wealth. To be sure, Will's sensitivity barely rescues him from the romantic overtures of Lydgate's wife, when his sensationalism proves almost as weak as the doctor's "science." Yet, his artistic temperament, open to all influences yet yielding to none, is less vulnerable than Lydgate's dogged faith in scientific progress.

On the whole, however, Dorothea's second suitor is a compromise, a Victorian "second-best." Lydgate's story and Dorothea's sympathy for Lydgate are of greater importance to George Eliot than Ladislaw's displacement of "poor Tertius" from the two triangles that form around Dorothea and Rosamond. Lacking the physician's singleness of purpose and knowledge, Will is correctly described as a "sciolist" by his vindictive cousin, Mr. Casaubon. He is a phantasist, a would-be poet, and amateur painter with only a surface knowledge in a variety of fields. George Eliot's frequent disparagements of his irrationality and aimlessness are too forceful to counteract her attempt to endow him with a "heart" as ardent as Dorothea's or Lydgate's.[28] The author's

[28] One of the main sentimental devices used to elevate Will is

own stern "Hebraism" is unsympathetic to her "Hellenic"
creation. George Eliot's treatment of Ladislaw echoes
Arnold's ambivalence toward Shelley or Byron, or his apologetic subordination of "culture and of Hellenism" to the
"conduct or righteousness" which is "three-fourths of life."[29]

Ladislaw's "Hellenism," then, must merely act as a channel for Dorothea's developing "religion of humanity." In
chapter 39, George Eliot redefines the "modes of religion"
of the young couple:

> "Oh, my life is very simple," said Dorothea, her lips
> curling with an exquisite smile, which irradiated her
> melancholy. "I am always at Lowick."
>
> "That is a dreadful imprisonment," said Will, impetu-
> ously.
>
> "No, don't think that," said Dorothea. "I have no
> longings."
>
> He did not speak, but she replied to some change in
> his expression. "I mean, for myself. Except that I should
> like not to have so much more than my share without
> doing anything for others. But I have a belief of my
> own, and it comforts me."
>
> "What is that?" said Will, rather jealous of the belief.
>
> "That by desiring what is perfectly good, even when
> we don't know what it is and cannot do what we would,
> we are part of the divine power against evil—widening
> the skirts of light and making the struggle with darkness
> narrower."
>
> "That is a beautiful mysticism—it is a—" [ch. 39,
> p. 179]

---

his reiterated kindness to Mr. Farebrother's maiden aunt, Miss
Noble, who becomes Ladislaw's advocate before Dorothea.

[29] *Literature and Dogma*, p. 381.

"MODES OF RELIGION" (b)

But Dorothea interrupts Ladislaw. Fresh from Mr. Casaubon's etymological tabulations she has become distrustful of pigeonholes of any sort and fears even the poet, Emerson's "Namer or Language-maker."

"Please not to call it by any name," said Dorothea, putting out her hands entreatingly. "You will say that it is Persian, or something else geographical. It is my life. I have found it out, and cannot part with it. I have always been finding out my religion since I was a little girl. I used to pray so much—now I hardly ever pray. I try not to have desires merely for myself, because they may not be good for others, and I have too much already. I only told you, that you might know quite well how my days go at Lowick."

"God bless you for telling me!" said Will, ardently, and rather wondering at himself. They were looking at each other like two fond children who are talking confidentially of birds.

"What is *your* religion?" said Dorothea. "I mean—not what you know about religion, but the belief that helps you most?"

"To love what is good and beautiful when I see it,"[30] said Will. "But I am a rebel: I don't feel bound, as you do, to submit to what I don't like."

"But if you like what is good, that comes to the same thing," said Dorothea, smiling.

"Now you are subtle," said Will. [ch. 39, p. 180]

[30] Cf. Shelley's "A Defence of Poetry," *English Romantic Poetry and Prose*, ed. Russell Noyes (New York, 1956), p. 1098: "But poets . . . draw into . . . a certain propinquity with the beautiful and true, that partial apprehension of the agencies of the invisible world which is called religion."

Schooled by Mr. Casaubon's erudition by hearsay, Dorothea has become distrustful of knowledge *"about* religion." She has become a pragmatist willing to accept "the belief that helps you most" as a substitute for faith and to regard any concrete act of fellow-feeling as an adequate belief: even Will's qualified love of the "good" is acceptable to her. No longer able to pray to an "other-worldly" Power, Dorothea, like George Eliot herself, must do the next best thing and abstract Christianity into "ethics heightened."[31]

It is in this ethical domain that the "modes of religion" of all other characters coalesce into meaning. It is here that the didactic story of Fred Vincy's schooling by experience, the contrast of Mary Garth to Peter Featherstone, and the opposition of Caleb Garth's probity to Bulstrode's cant are to be located. In *Middlemarch* "righteousness" is confirmed by experience. And, in George Eliot's pulling of the strings, experience is tantamount to a refutation of all unnatural abstractions. Despite the differences among them, the Casaubons, Lydgates, and Bulstrodes are abstractionists. Mr. Brooke is a living parody of the man of "ideas"; Dorothea must abandon her "theoretic" inclinations. Even Celia Chettam's jejune cult of her husband and child is more practicable than her sister's high-minded denial of her sexuality.

[31] *Literature and Dogma*, p. 21. In his excellent study, "George Eliot as Author," *Essays in Some of the Modern Guides of Thought in Matters of Faith* (London, 1887), pp. 147-258, R. H. Hutton argued that George Eliot's resolution of her own personal doubts into a "noble" but bleak humanism is directly applied to Dorothea without an adequate documentation of the byways leading to her ultimate agnostic position. Hutton's criticism is only partly valid, for he demands an actual presentation of "deep speculative doubts" and seems unsympathetic to George Eliot's artistic method of indirection (p. 223). Hutton's essay, as perceptive a contemporary appraisal of George Eliot's fiction as that of Henry James, is taken up again in the next chapter.

Mary Garth's illusionless skepticism is less susceptible to disappointments than Dorothea's high hopes or the lesser aspirations of the "Christian Carnivora" gathered to feast on the carcass of Featherstone's fortune. In turn, old Featherstone's hate-inspired superstition that "God A'mighty" will "stick to the land," rather than to Bulstrode's city-fortunes, provides the dying man with a greater relief than the abstract spiritual beliefs of a Mr. Casaubon who, "with some private scholarly reservations," holds himself to be "a believing Christian, as to estimates of the present and hopes of the future" (ch. 42, p. 230). The private ritual of his wife, an "imperfectly-taught woman," is far more soothing to Nicholas Bulstrode than the "pressure of retribution" he expects from his Calvinist God.

In George Eliot's humanist religion of experience the best Christians are those who possess a remnant of the stiff "Hebraic" righteousness of the past. Caleb Garth practices "a religion without the aid of theology." His "virtual divinities" are secular: "his prince of darkness was a slack workman." Mary, his daughter, professes to have a "dreadfully secular mind." She refuses to marry Fred Vincy if he persists in his intentions to become a clergyman. At the novel's end, Caleb once more administers the lands of the Chettams, Brookes, and Bulstrodes. Fred Vincy, whose "good heart" is unlike that of his sister, has responded to Caleb's schooling and becomes an "ideal craftsman" and Mary's husband. The Reverend Mr. Farebrother, Mary's disappointed lover, has taken over Casaubon's living. His maiden aunt, Miss Noble, can practice her charity undisturbed. Thus, in *Middlemarch* as well as in *Literature and Dogma*, "happiness belongs to conduct." Chief among all Middlemarchers, Dorothea is wedded to a new Ladislaw converted into "an ardent public man, working well in those times when reforms were begun with a young hopefulness of immediate good which has been much checked in our days" ("Finale," p. 461). Time and experience have altered the "later-born Theresa": "Many who knew her, thought it a pity that so substantive and rare a creature should have been absorbed into the life of another, and be only known in a certain circle as a wife and mother. But no one stated exactly what else that was in her power she ought rather to have done—not even Sir James Chettam, who went no further than the negative prescription that she ought not to have married Will Ladislaw" ("Finale," pp. 461-462).

Through her "reconciling and combining" of the incomplete "opposites" of materialism and idealism, science and morality, thought and feeling, and abstraction and experience, George Eliot hoped "to make the adjustments" necessary for a creed based on imperishable truths. The drabness of this "religion" is deliberate. It too is a "middle march" between the discarded beliefs of the past and the longed-for faith of the future. Its essence consists, in the words of Caleb Garth, in the stoical ability to "make the best of it." George Eliot went beyond this bleak creed in *Daniel Deronda*. But the "religious yearning" of *Middlemarch*, which is a result of her compromise between the actual and the ideal, is not only evident through the incomplete "modes of religion" of its multiple characters; it is also expressed through the unresolved clash of determinism and "will" within the novel's own system of causality.

4. The "Metaphysics" of *Middlemarch*

The Victorian clash of science and religion rekindled the age-old dispute over man's free will. Natural science pointed to a uniformity of cause and effect and questioned the spontaneity of human will in a world seemingly dominated by the mechanistic processes of evolution. Plagued by theories which regarded man as a new Adam limited by the "natural" laws of development, Victorian thinkers could no longer echo Dr. Johnson's forceful assertion, "Sir, we *know* our will is free, and *there's* an end on't."[32] Instead, they were forced into painstaking reassessments. One of the first acts of the newly founded Metaphysical Society was to poll its members on their individual definitions of "Will." The lines thus drawn, theologians and intuitionists could battle scientists and empiricists over a redefinition of the Libertarian doctrine.[33] To the one camp, Will remained synonymous with conscious choice; to the extremists in the other, it became a function of matter and thus wholly resolvable into physiological phenomena.

Summing up this conflict from his own empiricist standpoint, George Henry Lewes argued in his *Study of Psychology* that Dr. Johnson's statement no longer had the same validity for an age imbued with evolutionary thought. To Lewes, the exercise of choice is not equivalent to free will, for an "inexorable subjection to conditions" rules all our choices: "actions, sensations, emotions, and thoughts are subject to causal determination no less rigorously than the movements of the planets or the fluctuations of the waves."[34] And yet, though the individual organism is "swept along in the great current of natural forces" that operate within and

[32] *Boswell's Life of Johnson*, ed. R. W. Chapman (Oxford, 1953), p. 411.

[33] Cf. Alan Willard Brown, *The Metaphysical Society: Victorian Minds in Crisis, 1869-1880* (New York, 1947), pp. 47-54, 68, *et passim*.

[34] George Henry Lewes, *The Study of Psychology* (London, 1879), p. 102. Subsequent page references to this work are given in the text.

without it, man is nonetheless conscious of a Will based on his power of choice (p. 103). To resolve this apparent paradox, Lewes cites the "individual movement" of sailors on the deck of a ship "swept onwards by the waves": "Each sailor knows that he moves with the vessel, but knows also that he is free to move to and fro on deck" (p. 103). A consciousness of freedom can prevent man from yielding completely to the external and internal forces which propel him; in the realm of ethics, man's volition may overcome his desires, themselves the result of the "conditions" to which he is subjected. Human volition can thus become "the abstract expression of the product of Experience, it is educable, and becomes amenable to the Moral Law" (p. 109).

Lewes's rather wishful compromise allows him to escape the implications of a purely mechanistic view of life, such as T. H. Huxley's belief that all human activities, including man's will, are rooted in the protoplasm which makes up the "physical basis of life." To Lewes, the mind is not a "function of the Organism" but an "entity operating on and through the Organism"; this "Organism" is, in turn, "to a great extent self-regulatively variable" (pp. 110, 111). But Lewes is unwilling to venture beyond this qualified statement; his empirical standards do not permit him to go much further. Man is free only in "the sense that we have a range of motives surveyed by a Personality which is the incorporation of our past experience, and carries the prevision of alternative futures" (p. 111). Lewes is silent as to the nature of this "Personality"; he does not say whether he regards it, like Samuel Butler after him, as a vital power extending beyond the span of an individual life. Instead, he insists that, as a psychologist, he is bent only on a scientific interpretation of the "conditions" which make up human conduct. Like Freud, decades later, he reduces theology into "science" by quitting, as he says, "the metaphysical for the biological point of view" (p. 102). "The only question therefore is, What are the conditions? It is the task of the psychologist to specify them" (p. 111).

The *Study of Psychology* was the last part of Lewes's incomplete *chef-d'oeuvre,* the ambitious *Problems of Life and Mind* (1873-1879). It was published by George Eliot in the year after his death. George Eliot's own *Middlemarch* —and in a different way, her *Daniel Deronda*—must be placed against Lewes's inquiries, as well as against those of other contemporaries concerned with the Libertarian controversy. As a novelist, George Eliot assumes a "task" analogous to that which Lewes prescribed for his "psychologist." She surveys the "range of motives" of her characters with an eye to "past experience" and, in doing so, cautiously assesses "the prevision of alternative futures." The choices offered to the novel's individual characters are examined not only from the "biological point of view" demanded by Lewes, but also from that of a moralist and fabulist employing a very similar scientific idiom in order to determine and verify the existence of higher ethical truths. As we shall see in the next chapter, George Eliot eventually abandoned the analytical manner of *Middlemarch* in order to turn to a more elevated form of presenting these truths in *Daniel Deronda,* her final novel, where she deliberately flaunts the causal and "inexorable subjection of conditions" which, according to Lewes, governs all our action. In *Middlemarch,* however, she sets up a complex deterministic system governed by what she alternately calls "the train of causes" (ch. 61, p. 129), "the force of circumstances" (ch. 36, p. 109), the "rush of unintended consequences" (ch. 57, p. 64), or, perhaps most appropriately, "the irony of events" (ch. 46, p. 289).

In the scheme of *Middlemarch* this "irony of events" affects the individual wills of all the characters who are, like Lewes's sailors, swept along by the inexorable stream of human progress. As we have seen already, Dorothea— the story of whose "errant will" provides the main line of action—and her fellow-seekers for perfection, Lydgate and Ladislaw, are all desirous of higher "effects." Fred and Rosamond Vincy likewise want to make an "impression" on the world. That revengeful pair, Featherstone and Casaubon, hope to affect the lives of their survivors through the provisions made in their last "wills." The banker Bulstrode's own desire to control human destiny is masked by his sanctimonious deference to the mandate of a "Divine Will." And yet, without exception, the wills of all these characters are blunted.

Bulstrode succumbs to the pressures of past actions he has tried to ignore (and which, according to Lewes's psychological determinism, are an integral part of his "personality"). Lydgate, Bulstrode's unwilling associate, is similarly caught in a causal web, paralyzed by his yoke to a feebler being capable of seeing "causes and effects which lay within the track of her own tastes and interests" (ch. 58, p. 80). Featherstone's dying wish to alter his last will is countered by Mary Garth, who by her choice and "without a will of her own" thereby alters the lot of Fred Vincy, her fiancé. Similarly, Casaubon's posthumous demands are defied by a matured Dorothea, who chooses to marry young "Will" the Radical (who is in turn tamed by her influence, just as Lewes's "Will" becomes "educable" and "amenable to Moral Law"). Thus, on the whole, the volition of all characters is checked by "the irony of events" and must be tempered by experience or, what amounts to the same thing, by a conformity to prosaic "conditions" of existence. Caleb

Garth, the very voice for this conformity, concludes sadly at one point: "For my part, I wish there was no such thing as a will." Although, in context, Caleb's words merely refer to the stipulations in Featherstone's testament, they are misinterpreted by an indignant listener: "That's a strange sentiment to come from a Christian man, by God! . . . I should like to know how you will back that up, Garth!" (ch. 35, p. 98). Caleb remains silent, but the answer is obvious. Backed up by experience, Caleb, his daughter Mary, and his son-in-law and disciple, Fred Vincy, as well as the matured Dorothea and her second husband, abandon all "great expectations." The effects of their being can become "diffusive" only upon their recognition and acceptance of the "conditions" established by a power greater than themselves.

In *Middlemarch* this power is not supernatural. It is merely the summation of human actions, the cumulative wills of past and present which make George Eliot's "irony of events" quite similar to the World-Will of Schopenhauer or to the evolutionary "current of natural forces" postulated by Lewes.[35] The novel's intricate network of causal connections approaches the mechanism of these "natural forces." Characters and events are linked within the realm of probability. Their interaction and the effects of this interaction are

[35] According to Antonio Aliotta, *The Idealistic Reaction Against Science* (London, 1914), the voluntarism of Schopenhauer seemed to supply "the metaphysical view best suited to explain the process of evolution" and to provide "that which was lacking in a mechanical theory" (p. 29). Lewes rejected Schopenhauer's all-encompassing definition of Will, although there are several correspondences between their thought. George Eliot recommended an 1853 article by John Oxenford as "one of the best" on Schopenhauer (*GEL*, II, 95); it is said to have secured the philosopher's reputation in England and to have stimulated his belated recognition in Germany.

examined by an ironic, but sympathetic novelist-observer and by her reader, both of whom can momentarily detach themselves from their own submission to similar laws or "conditions." George Eliot likens her fictional chains of reaction to those of the experimental scientist: "In watching effects, if only of an electric battery, it is often necessary to change our place and examine a particular mixture . . ." (ch. 40, p. 190). Yet, unlike Thomas Hardy, she is unwilling to aggrandize the deterministic sequences she portrays into a pattern conforming to an invariable cosmic order or into a monumental vision of the "World as Evil."[36] Nor does her determinism lead her to worship at the foot of an abstraction such as Auguste Comte's "Grand Être," which, like her own concept of tradition and culture, combines a cumulative past with the needs of the present.[37] Instead, George Eliot answers as an artist and moralist the question that Lewes poses as a psychologist: "What are the conditions?"

In *Middlemarch* the conditions created by the "irony of events" stress man's dependence on the actions of his fellow man. To George Eliot, as to Matthew Arnold, a "consciousness of the not ourselves," of powers beyond the scope of the individual will, makes for "righteousness." God, immor-

[36] Lewes, like George Eliot, rejects any mechanical view based on a "rigorous invariableness of sequence, irrespective of any variations in the conditions," an invariableness which well applies to the fatalistic world of Hardy's novels (*The Study of Psychology*, p. 110).

[37] Comte classified human progress according to three "states" or stages: the theological or imaginative, the metaphysical or abstract, and the scientific or positive. It is noteworthy that George Eliot inverts the order in *Middlemarch* by giving supremacy to the nonscientific, but imaginative, Dorothea. The young widow's escape from the grasp of Casaubon's "Dead Hand" is also in defiance of Comte's favorite aphorism that "the living are governed by the dead."

tality, providence may not exist: yet man must therefore act as if they do. The believing skeptics of Middlemarch, the Garths and the Farebrothers, are didactically rewarded by the same deterministic sequences they recognize and obey. On the other hand, the "irony of events" is enlisted to shatter the scientific *hybris* of Lydgate or the fanaticism of Bulstrode. *Middlemarch* tests the efficacy of ethical conduct. But it separates conduct from faith in a God and reduces mystery to a verifiable experience. Although George Eliot was to reintroduce "mystery" in *Daniel Deronda,* in *Middlemarch* she can be accused of the same inconsistencies evident in the work of those Victorian thinkers who likewise confused the unknowable with the unknown. As if aware of the possibility of such an imputation, she defends herself in chapter 61 of the novel by taking her epigraph from Johnson's *Rasselas*: " 'Inconsistencies,' answered Imlac, 'cannot both be right, but imputed to man they may both be true.' " Though hailed as the most "philosophic" of novelists by her contemporaries, George Eliot reminds the reader that she is concerned with an artistic interpretation of "truth" and not with the resolution of metaphysical inconsistencies. Transplanted to the medium of fiction, her world-picture can create a greater semblance of truth than its numerous counterparts in the philosophical and critical essays of her contemporaries. Lewes's speculations have been superseded by the advent of Freudianism; the anti-mechanist doctrines of Spencer and Butler have been dismissed by stricter thinkers. Even the heated debates of the Metaphysical Society ended in a lame stalemate by an acceptance of the conclusion that "if free will does not exist, we must and do act as if it did."[38] Though unsatisfactory from a philosophical standpoint, this

[38] Brown, *The Metaphysical Society*, p. 103.

same conclusion carries an air of authenticity when borne out by the intricate "irony of events" which governs in *Middlemarch*.

Like the work of so many a Victorian "truth-seeker," *Middlemarch* thrives on paradox. It is a mystic's rejection of religion and a rationalist's plea for irrationality. It contains a scrupulous "scientific" dissection of character by a writer hostile to the aims of science. Part of the novel's success in its emulation of "truth" lies in George Eliot's ability to recreate in its poetic *architectonicè* the very same tension that Matthew Arnold had regarded as being inimical to poetry. No other novel by George Eliot approaches the detachment of *Middlemarch*; no other novel before *The Ambassadors* uses complementary points of view to a greater effect. The endless oppositions of *Middlemarch* define, modify, and redefine characters and actions alike. Even the titles of the various parts of the book are carefully counterpointed. As Mr. Brooke so helpfully volunteers, "Everything is symbolical, you know" (ch. 34, p. 86).

Balance is all in *Middlemarch*. George Eliot the rationalist corrects George Eliot the enthusiast; Dorothea the enthusiast corrects Lydgate the rationalist. Although this balance is occasionally broken, the author qualifies her "gushiness" through a steady sense of humor; she softens her satiric denunciations by an all-inclusive sympathy. She becomes a "Bat of erudition" in the creation of Mr. Casaubon; she spouts lusty provincialisms in portraying her "Philistine" louts. At times George Eliot speaks through the witty Mrs. Cadwallader, at times through Dorothea and through Tertius Lydgate. But she is closest perhaps to Mary Garth, the homely observer without illusions. Of all the characters, Mary alone is able to laugh at the human scene: ". . . people were so ridiculous with their illusions, carrying their fool's caps unawares, thinking their own lies opaque while everybody else's were transparent . . ." (ch. 33, p. 65).

Middlemarch carries the imprint of Mary Garth's observation. Despite the novel's "high seriousness" and despite the starkness of its description of Lydgate's fall and Dorothea's Pyrrhic victory, the world it reproduces is only potentially tragic. *Middlemarch* does portray a relentless and gloomy evolutionary process; it laments for a lost age of faith and exhibits its makeshift "modes of religion" with wistfulness and reluctance. But in its over-all compromise, its "middle" march between religious despair and religious affirmation, George Eliot's masterpiece implies a confidence in man's ability to surmount his enslavement to time and change. It finds in time present and time past a possibility of future redemption. *Middlemarch* is neither tragedy nor comedy. It is the tragicomedy of human progress.

IV

Daniel Deronda:
Tradition as Synthesis and Salvation

So if the real is the object of knowledge, the object of belief must be something other than the real.
—The Republic

"Imagination is often truer than fact," said Gwendolen, decisively, though she could no more have explained these glib words than if they had been Coptic or Etruscan.
—Daniel Deronda

Middlemarch ILLUMINATEs the past for the benefit of the present; it is analytical, prosaic, and, for the most part, detached. *Daniel Deronda*, written only five years later, examines the present, but ardently longs for the future; it is prophetic, quasi-poetical, exhortatory, and rigidly moralistic; its emphasis and tone reveal the author's deep involvement with her subject matter. *Middlemarch* yearns for the ideal, but brands it as an illusion: Dorothea Brooke is prevented from becoming another St. Theresa as her "heart," though incalculably "diffusive," must spend itself in a commonplace age. In *Daniel Deronda*, however, the ideal acts both as guide and as utopia: brought up as an English aristocrat, Deronda suddenly finds himself converted into an exotic Jewish patrician who, as a member of the "heart of mankind," Israel,[1] can assume the role of national leader, lawgiver, and returned Messiah as an overidealized reminder of the simple fact that "Christ was a Jew."[2]

[1] George Eliot, *Daniel Deronda*, 3 vols., Cabinet Edition (Edinburgh, n.d.), chap. 42, pp. 384-385; all subsequent references are given in the text.
[2] *GEL*, VI, 302.

TRADITION AS SYNTHESIS AND SALVATION

It has by now become a commonplace to regard *Daniel Deronda* as a work of extremely uneven qualities. The semi-mystical quality of the book's "Jewish" half jars with the psychological realism prevailing in George Eliot's previous fiction, as well as in the superb "English" half of the novel. But the detailed psychological study of Gwendolen Harleth and her England is clearly subordinated to what George Eliot's editor called "the Tale of Deronda's goodness and that of the stray Jewish Maid."[3] While many a reader has been tempted to dismiss this "Tale" as a mere sentimental excrescence, stricter critics have examined it in the light of the themes and conventions of George Eliot's earlier work;[4] others have linked it to the realistic half of the novel and have thus become engaged in a controversy over the supposed unity or lack of unity of the two plots.[5] The novel's curious

---

[3] *GEL*, VI, 145.

[4] Besides Dr. Leavis's classical chapter on "*Daniel Deronda* and *The Portrait of A Lady*" in *The Great Tradition* (London, 1949), pp. 79-125, there are three interesting studies: Jerome Thale, "*Daniel Deronda*: The Darkened World," *Modern Fiction Studies*, III (Summer 1957), 119-126, reprinted in *The Novels of George Eliot* (New York, 1959); Barbara Hardy, "Imagery in George Eliot's Last Novels," *Modern Language Review*, L (January 1955), 6-14, reprinted in *The Novels of George Eliot* (London, 1959); and Robert Preyer, "Beyond the Liberal Imagination: Vision and Unreality in *Daniel Deronda*," *Victorian Studies*, IV (September 1960), 33-54. The most thorough study in this category is Professor Richard M. Eastman's unpublished dissertation, "George Eliot's *Daniel Deronda*: Its Place in the Development of her Fiction" (University of Illinois, 1952).

[5] Although this controversy dates back to George Eliot's days, it was revived by F. R. Leavis's remark that the "Jewish" half of the novel could easily be cut away. Although Dr. Leavis has revised his opinion in "George Eliot's Zionist Novel," *Commentary*, XXX (October 1960), 317-325, an essay reprinted as the Introduction to the Harper Torchbook edition of the novel, two excellent refutations of his view are Maurice Beebe, " 'Visions Are Creators': The

mixture of modes has also invited attempts at classification: throughout eighty years of criticism, *Daniel Deronda* has been labeled as a pre-Zionist *Tendenzroman*, a utopian romance, a satire, a novel of manners, and a Goethean *Bildungsroman*; it has also been viewed as the work which cosmopolitanized English fiction by allowing the American Henry James, a "Derondist of Derondists," to leap gracefully into the "great tradition" of the British novel.[6] Although most of these estimates are helpful and many of them are quite correct, surprisingly few have established what *Daniel Deronda*—regardless of its importance, its unity or disunity, and its *genre*—is really "all about."

A recent critic of the novel, Mr. Robert Preyer, is correct when he points out that the artistic departures of the novel must be examined hand in hand with George Eliot's revision of some of the humanist standards which led to the creed of "realism" exemplified in the earlier novels. Still, Mr. Preyer does not quite establish where and why and how George Eliot's last novel differs so markedly from her earlier work.[7] The ensuing interpretation tries to provide this

---

Unity of *Daniel Deronda*," *Boston University Studies in English*, (Autumn 1955), 166-177, and D. R. Carroll, "The Unity of *Daniel Deronda*," *Essays in Criticism*, IX (October 1959), 369-380. Arguing against the book's unity is Jerome Beaty, "*Daniel Deronda* and the Question of Unity in Fiction," *Victorian Newsletter*, 15 (Spring 1959), pp. 16-19.

[6] By restoring Henry James's excellent essay on *Daniel Deronda* in his book, Dr. Leavis did a great service.

[7] Mr. Preyer's suggested reading of the novel as a partial critique of a "liberal failure" seems sound and convincing, and is marred only by his failure to produce the critical evidence necessary to support his interpretation. By equating nineteenth-century liberalism with Romanticism, laissez faire, scientism, historicism, and a series of other "isms," Mr. Preyer's manifold use of the term "liberal imagination" acquires a vagueness unsuited to the scope of his short essay.

answer. Neither a condemnation nor an apology for the artistic demerits of *Daniel Deronda,* it attempts to furnish a much-needed gloss of the book's intentions and of their execution. The study of the novel falls into three sections. The first dwells on the characteristics which distinguish *Daniel Deronda* from *Middlemarch.* The second section, a brief consideration of the English half of the novel, is followed by a more detailed inspection of the meaning of the book as a whole and of the Jewish half in particular.

Daniel Deronda is a novel about belief and disbelief. That only the latter has been extended to the book itself is unfortunate, but logical. Unlike the Shakespeare whom she so consciously imitated, George Eliot was unable to mingle actuality and phantasy or to combine the prosaic with the heroic. She finally demanded a heightened belief which would rise above the quasi-idealistic "realism" displayed in her earlier work, but she also remained a skeptic at heart. It is her skepticism which obtrudes in *Daniel Deronda* and thus contributes to a disbelief in her own creation. George Eliot's deliberate superimposition of a religious purpose on her last novel provides it with a unifying principle, albeit an unsuccessful one. Still, Mr. Preyer does not exaggerate when he calls the work her "most ambitious book."[8] As a magnificent failure, *Daniel Deronda* deserves to be studied with closer attention than has hitherto been accorded it.

I. *Middlemarch* AND THE TWO "WORLDS" OF *Daniel Deronda*

Middlemarch depicts an implacable evolutionary process. The stories of Lydgate and Dorothea Brooke are emblematic of the pains inherent in the forward march of human progress; the ultimate triumph of Dorothea's "heart" is enlisted to

---

[8] Preyer, "Beyond the Liberal Imagination," p. 39.

stress the need for a disembodied belief in "righteousness," a humanist faith vaguely based on an awareness of the religions of the past. Yet Dorothea's victory is at best a Pyrrhic one. The enthusiastic girl who used to fall suddenly on the brick floors of cottages to pray becomes Dorothea Ladislaw, a sobered matron who must annul herself in order to contribute to the channels of social progress. R. H. Hutton, one of George Eliot's most perceptive Victorian critics, pointed out long ago that there is a small, but telling, inconsistency in the novelist's treatment of Dorothea's story, an inconsistency George Eliot herself seems to have been aware of when she toned down the concluding paragraphs of the novel.

In the first version of her "Finale," George Eliot abandoned the sympathetic, but detached and impartial, role she had tried to maintain throughout the novel and acidly attacked the "prosaic conditions" of a society blind to the aspirations of her late-born Theresa.[9] Blaming society for "smiling" at Dorothea's marital "mistakes," she forgot that it was the young woman's own self-willed idealism which had magnified a pedantic clergyman into a "Hooker or a Milton," and that therefore Dorothea, and not a faulty society, was responsible for her initial failure.[10] George Eliot's lapse is significant. It illustrates the unresolved clash between her own idealism and her belief in the deterministic sequences she had portrayed through the "irony of events." Her inconsistency demonstrates that while preaching a submission to the "prosaic conditions" of life itself, she could not quite bring herself to accept the barrenness of the conditions she had created. As Hutton puts it: "This little inconsistency is important only as showing that George Eliot had uncon-

[9] *Middlemarch*, ed. Gordon S. Haight (Boston, 1956), p. 612, n.1.
[10] *Ibid.*

sciously, in the course of her story, aggravated the faults of the society against which she brought her indictment both at the beginning and the close—a tendency which attaches more or less to her very negative spiritual philosophy. Faith is wanted to make people perfectly candid about the blots in human ideals. A frequent tendency may be noted in those who find no anchor for faith, to throw upon some abstract offender like 'society' the faults they see in those who most satisfy their longing for perfection."[11]

In *Daniel Deronda* George Eliot "aggravates the faults of society" to an even larger extent. Gwendolen Harleth— a Rosamond Vincy expanded into a tainted Eve "tempted by a serpent"—is aggrandized so as to stand for an entire insular society become incurably sterile and purposeless, an England dead to history and hopelessly enmeshed in the pursuit of material goals. Yet the novel also departs from *Middlemarch* by magnifying the idealism of Dorothea, the would-be Theresa and would-be Antigone, into something very much like Hutton's hoped-for "anchor for faith." With *Daniel Deronda,* George Eliot moves from the conditional to the categorical. While the elaborate causal network of *Middlemarch* is enlisted to verify the need for ethical conduct, *Daniel Deronda* merely asserts this need. In her last novel George Eliot refuses to disguise her blatant use of the coincidental, the improbable, and even the supernatural. "It is part of probability that many improbable things will happen," she argues defiantly by citing Aristotle's *Poetics* in the first chapter of a part of the book that she entitles, significantly enough, "Revelations."[12]

[11] *Essays on Some of the Modern Guides to English Thought in Matters of Faith* (London, 1891), p. 220.

[12] George Eliot takes Aristotle's quotation as the epigraph for chapter 41 which opens Book Six, "Revelations."

It is this new kind of probability that may cause "improbable things to happen," which, more than anything else, separates *Daniel Deronda* from *Middlemarch*. The world of *Middlemarch* is one of infinite gradations; *Daniel Deronda* offers only a choice between black and white. The contrast between the worlds of Deronda and of Gwendolen is expressed through the alternation of "high" and "low," of the idealistic and the satirical, in a manner skillfully recreated by Maurice Beebe.[13] This alternation resembles in intent, though by no means in execution, the counterpointing of a double plot in a Shakespearean drama.[14] Deronda's sphere of action is to envelop a positive "prophetic vision"; accordingly, it is to be treated poetically. Gwendolen's negative world is one of "blind visions"; as a consequence, it is examined with a social satirist's critical eye.

Initially, however, Deronda is a "yearning disembodied spirit" very much like Maggie Tulliver, Romola, or Dorothea Brooke, a character who very definitely belongs to Gwendolen's narrow world. Only providence, a force totally outside that "irony of events" which rules in the world of *Middlemarch* or *Adam Bede,* can allow Deronda to disengage himself from the aimless society of which he is a part. The drifter on the Thames must be submerged into the waters of faith in order to be converted into a patriarch of epic proportions, a new Moses with that "sense of the universal" which Gwendolen's England no longer can provide (ch. 5, p. 68). At first the ultra-earnest Deronda is not quite sure whether he wants "to be an ancestor" (ch. 15, p. 242), but he becomes one anyway when he finds in his

[13] Cf. note 5, above.

[14] See the present writer's, *"Daniel Deronda* and William Shakespeare," *VNL,* 19 (Spring 1961), 27-28, for an analysis of George Eliot's deliberate "use" of Shakespeare in her novel.

Hebraic tradition both a faith and a missionary purpose. Gwendolen, however, must remain chained to a "puerile state of culture" (ch. 5, p. 67). She regards the world her husband describes as a "great bore," as being eminently comical, and protests with the gusto of an Oscar Wilde or Samuel Butler: "It is very nice to come after ancestors and monks, but they should know their places and keep underground" (ch. 35, p. 200). In the semicomical world of *Middlemarch* such irreverence would have been permissible. It has no place in *Daniel Deronda,* where "high seriousness" is the rule and where a disregard for tradition is tantamount to blasphemy.

In *Middlemarch* George Eliot employs her own acceptance of the "Development theory" as she forces Lydgate and Dorothea to fall in step with the fitful "march" of human progress. In *Daniel Deronda,* however, evolutionism is enlisted to proclaim the existence of a unique spiritual tradition, lodged in the development of a chosen race.[15] Dorothea's "heart," now provided with the authority of an entire Hebraic tradition, becomes "the core of affection which binds a race and its families in dutiful love, and the reverence

---

[15] According to L. E. Elliott-Binns, *English Thought 1860-1900: The Theological Aspect* (London, 1956), many theologians of the time argued that religion had already illustrated the theory of natural selection by holding that the Jewish people had "evolved" a "unique aptitude for apprehending spiritual realities" and that science, therefore, according to A. J. Balfour, merely "'adopted an idea which has always been an essential Christian view of the Divine economy'" (p. 31). The link to Balfour is significant because of George Eliot's acquaintance with the author of *A Defence of Philosophic Doubt* (1897) and promulgator of the 1917 Balfour Declaration. George Eliot's belief in the Jews as a chosen race was, incidentally, a sharp reversal of her earlier belittlement of "everything *specifically* Jewish" and her ridicule of any "assumption of superiority in the Jews" (*GEL,* I, 247, 246).

for the human body which lifts the needs of our animal life into religion" (ch. 42, p. 385). In *Middlemarch* Dorothea's fervor is partially balanced by the scientific dedication of Lydgate, whose devotion to his profession, though more fallible than her faith, is nonetheless as praiseworthy and as idealistic. In *Daniel Deronda,* however, the magnitude of Deronda's mission admits no such foil. His selfless devotion to the tradition he recovers is sharply contrasted to the personal egotism of Gwendolen, a Rosamond Vincy expanded into a fuller creation, but a Rosamond Vincy still. The difference between these two oppositions is appreciable. Lydgate's gradual fall is treated with the ironic sympathy accorded to a flawed but princely nature; Gwendolen's debasement is carried out by a novelist indignant at the "queenly" ways of a character who dares to aggrandize herself into a "princess in exile" or "fallen royalty." The reason is all too clear. Gwendolen stands in the way of the exotic "Prince Camaralzaman," who turns out to be the son of an actual princess; of Mirah, his bride, who is likened to a "king's daughter"; and of the historical destiny of the Jews.

In *Middlemarch* a sober acceptance of the "conditions" of life is exemplified by Caleb Garth, the ideal craftsman who perpetuates his devotion to the land through his disciple and son-in-law, Fred Vincy. In *Daniel Deronda* the transcendence of temporal "conditions" is exemplified by Mordecai, a visionary prophet who can foretell "in thought" the ideals which Deronda, his pupil and brother-in-law, will fulfill "in action." Mordecai can live on "as an idea" even after his premature death. For Deronda assumes both the identity of his teacher and that of his own grandfather, Daniel Charisi, who, as a physician and a religious enthusiast, is a Lydgate and Dorothea rolled into one, and thus represents the "marriage" of "head" and "heart" which cannot come about in the scheme of *Middlemarch*. Charisi, we are told, is far more concerned "with what had been before and what would come after" (ch. 60, p. 274) than with the temporal bounds of his own life, that demarcation treated in the earlier novel as the "middle march" that lies between the past and the future. There, the prosaic conditions of the 1830's were best represented by Mr. Brooke, the defeated Whig candidate. In *Daniel Deronda*, however, the conditions of the 1860's, though "aggravated," are imaginatively transcended.

The mediocrity of the Middlemarchers has spread, in the later novel, to an entire land whose hierarchy is headed by the benign but totally incompetent Sir Hugo Mallinger, a Mr. Brooke come into power. Lacking "a son to inherit the lands," Sir Hugo reverts his property and his last name to Gwendolen's husband, Henley Mallinger Grandcourt, although he affectionately regards Daniel Deronda as his personal "substitute for a son." But England as a whole cannot deter the future "Deliverer" who is harbored in the Mallinger mansion as Moses was harbored in the palace of the Pharaoh. Losing his "enthusiastic belief in Sir Hugo's writings as a standard, and in the Whigs as the chosen race among politicians" (ch. 16, p. 265), the young man soon comes to believe in his new tutor, Mordecai, and to accept his membership among the elect, "the heart of mankind."

Deronda is contrasted to Gwendolen's husband who, by inheriting the baronet's lands, hopes to become a "peer of the realm." Grandcourt, the "remnant of a human being" and the owner of a "withered heart," represents the reward of Gwendolen's genteel aspirations. A superb embodiment of decadence and perversion, he provides her with a much-needed understanding of evil, suffering, and, ultimately, death. In the Jewish half of the novel his role is adopted by the actor Lapidoth, the villainous father of Mordecai and Mirah, who stands for the cursed "lot of Israel." A far more theatrical figure of malignity than Grandcourt, he presumably endows his children with an "experience of evil" and an awareness of their "tragic" race. Gwendolen cannot share this consciousness. Unable to "believe in sorrow," she is a figure of mirth. While Mirah puritanically dislikes "comic things on the stage" (ch. 37, p. 286), Gwendolen has to be dissuaded from becoming an actress of light comedy and farce.[16]

Although George Eliot's portrayal of Mordecai, Mirah, and Lapidoth is highly stylized, the contrast of their world to that of Sir Hugo, Gwendolen, and Grandcourt is quite acceptable. Nor, as we shall see, is the author's blatant use of the improbable and the coincidental at all detrimental to her purpose. Instead, what is so ruinous to the book's artistic integrity is the deliberate interlocking of both worlds through the character of Deronda, whose "entanglement" with Gwendolen's "horoscope" even mystifies the unimaginative Sir Hugo. George Eliot refuses to keep the actual and the ideal in suspension. She insists on exalting Deronda at Gwendolen's expense: the proud girl must "wince" under his stern gaze and open herself to his endless admonitions. Aloof and unbending even under Grandcourt's sexual enslavement, Gwendolen somehow abounds in humiliating self-excoriations whenever she faces Deronda. For Deronda, who

[16] Gwendolen is prevented from becoming a comic actress by Herr Klesmer, the artist, who assures her that her frivolity is not matched by talent. One cannot but help thinking that he (and thereby George Eliot) was wrong.

has been called "a lay father-confessor"[17] or the "English gentleman as Alyosha,"[18] is above all meant to be a "part of her conscience." As such, he must necessarily be a lamentable failure. For he cannot function as a semi-allegorical figure and act at the same time as the dandyfied "young swell" mocked by the little Jacob Cohen. Nor can he possibly entertain the romantic notions about Gwendolen which are first ascribed to him and then quickly withdrawn as being beneath his dignity. Deronda's revelation to Gwendolen of his high mission, though intended as the book's culmination, is painfully ludicrous. The scene stresses the utter impossibility of blending the novel's two halves into a credible whole. The vista of Deronda and Mirah sailing off to the East as the proud possessors of a prophetic destiny and a useful "Eastern" travel-outfit donated by the Mallingers as a wedding gift, brings to mind the famous photograph of William Holman Hunt equipped with palette, gun, and leggings while painting his allegorical portrait of "The Scapegoat" on locale at the Dead Sea.[19]

Gwendolen and her society remain basically unchanged. The subtle dispensation of rewards and punishments which makes *Middlemarch* so ingenious and so delightful a creation, is totally absent in *Daniel Deronda*. To be sure, there is a return to the land as Sir Hugo adopts the role delegated to Caleb Garth and Fred Vincy in the earlier novel and decides to "regain and strengthen his personal influence in the neighborhood" (ch. 64, p. 334). But his conviction as a Whig that the "notion of reproducing the old is a mistake"

[17] Henry James, "*Daniel Deronda*: A Conversation," in *The Great Tradition*, p. 262.

[18] Thale, *The Novels of George Eliot*, p. 123.

[19] Hunt returned to Palestine around the time of Deronda's presumed pilgrimage, imbued with a new religious fervor.

(ch. 35, p. 212), when handled by a traditionalist author, does not augur much improvement. Sir Hugo's lands will presumably fall to his timid daughters; Grandcourt's vacant estate is inherited by his bastard son. With Deronda in the Promised Land, it seems to matter very little.

Neither has Gwendolen Harleth profited by her debasement. She has become sadder and wiser; widowed and childless, the "spoiled child" of the earlier portions of the book finally manages to lose her frivolity and sense of humor. But she is still adrift, as purposeless as ever. Her self-chosen exile with a platitudinous mother as her constant companion can at best produce a mortification of the flesh. As Henry James shrewdly reasoned: "The very chance to embrace what the author is so fond of calling a 'larger life' seems refused to her. She is punished for being narrow, and she is not allowed a chance to expand."[20] James gallantly gave George Eliot the benefit of the doubt. In *The Middle Years* he even retracted his own misgivings about her use of the novel as a "philosophic" allegory and praised her for the richness of her thought. Still, with his keen knowledge of a transatlantic "Hebraism" of a similar sort, he must have realized that George Eliot broke her equipoise both as a thinker and as an artist when she converted the coquettish Miss Harleth, a Jane Austen creation, into the fabled harlot of Puritan myth.

2. HEBRAISM AS NATIONALITY

Daniel Deronda's recovery of an ancestral tradition provides him with a "fixed local habitation to render fellowship real" and makes him "an organic part of social life" (ch. 32, p. 133). Gwendolen Harleth, on the other hand, is doomed by her environment. The England of the Mallingers has become

[20] P. 264.

depleted and sick. The "cloisters" of Sir Hugo's "abbey"—an estate given to the family by Henry the Eighth, the spoiler of monasteries—have been converted into stables for stud horses: hay hangs from the racks "where the saints once looked down." "Diplow," the country estate bespoken by Grandcourt, "lay in another county, and was a comparatively landless place which had come into the family from a rich lawyer on the female side who wore the perruque of the Restoration" (ch. 16, p. 246). It is located near Quetcham, whose owners, the Arrowpoints, are the new rich who engage in culture only as "a privilege of wealth." Lord Brackenham and the neighboring gentry engage in fox-hunts and participate in an archery contest which is a travesty of England's heroic past. Mrs. Glasher, Grandcourt's former mistress; Lush, "a half-caste among gentlemen," who acts as Grandcourt's menial instrument; Lord Slogan, "an unexceptionable Irish peer," courted by Miss Arrowpoint's parents; Mr. Bult, a "political platitudinarian" passing as "English gentleman"; and Mr. Vandernoodt, a rumor-monger who profits from "contemporary gossip, not antediluvian," round out the picture of a society in which only "a variety of *ennui*" can furnish a form of escape.

The English half of *Daniel Deronda* thus depicts a nation which has become totally purposeless. It has no Adam Bedes or Caleb Garths, the master craftsmen of a past age. Philistinism and mediocrity are the rule. George Eliot has Gwendolen complain wittily to Grandcourt about the limitations of the male society of which he is a part: ". . . I can't eat *pâté de foie gras* to make me sleepy, and I can't smoke, and I can't go to the club to make me like to come away again" (ch. 48, p. 64). It is no coincidence that George Eliot should have turned from Deronda to the more undisguised satire of *Impressions of Theophrastus Such*. "There are some things in it which I want to get said," she remarked about her book of essays.[21]

In *Daniel Deronda,* however, what George Eliot wants "to get said" is subsumed by what she hopes for: Gwendolen clings to her faith in Deronda with an "anxious tenacity, as a Protestant of old kept his Bible hidden or a Catholic his crucifix" (ch. 48, p. 74). For if Deronda represents a challenge to the "puerile state of culture" of Gwendolen's world, his treatment as a part of Gwendolen's "conscience" is too idealized to allow him to become a social critic. Although his training is intended as an ironical counterpart of the standard education of the English gentleman, his function is not that of an Arnoldian heckler of Barbarians and Philistines. Since Deronda must be reserved for the role of spiritual adviser, a secondary figure is needed to remind Gwendolen that her world represents "the passion and thought of people without any breadth of horizon" (ch. 5, p. 67). This critic is Herr Klesmer, the artist, a new rendition of Will Ladislaw. Klesmer is a lofty, though slightly ludicrous, idealist, described as a "felicitous combination of the German, the Sclave [*sic*], and the Semite, with grand features, brown hair floating in artistic fashion, and brown eyes in spectacles" (ch. 5, p. 65). The musician's ostentatious self-introduction as "the Wandering Jew" shocks the proper Mr. Bult; his oratory and gesticulations all but startle the "impassive" Grandcourt. Klesmer is pointedly contrasted to Grandcourt's minion, Thomas Cranmer Lush, who "passed for a scholar once" and who is rebuked by his master for playing the violoncello in his presence. For, unlike his English counterpart, Klesmer devotes himself only to the "dignity of a high purpose": he refuses to prostitute the standards of his profession. Culture is to him classless and cosmopolitan; it

[21] *GEL,* VII, 126.

knows no limits but those of artistic excellence. Klesmer rebukes Gwendolen for her grandiose aspirations, praises Mirah for the narrowness of her artistic pretensions, and loves the heiress, Catherine Arrowpoint, not for her fortune, but for her understanding. Like Will Ladislaw, his prototype, he is amply rewarded. Although the bluestocking Mrs. Arrowpoint deprecates him as "a gypsy, a Jew, a mere bubble of the earth," her daughter is willing to share the artist's lot by defying "ideas that I don't believe in and customs I have no respect for" (ch. 12, p. 369). Reminding her parents that, "The land of England has often passed into the hands of foreigners" and benefited from it (ch. 12, p. 371), Catherine defies convention and marries Klesmer. Though not a Dorothea Brooke, she nonetheless demonstrates a way open to Gwendolen Harleth. In her defiance of provincialism and her identification with a Continental culture, she anticipates E. M. Forster's Schlegel sisters or the heroines of D. H. Lawrence.

In order to give Klesmer's cosmopolitanism a definite "Hebraic" flavor, George Eliot sprinkles her novel with allusions to Meyerbeer, Mendelssohn, the actress Rachel, Spinoza, and other Jewish figures of fact and fiction. What is more, she suggests also that the learning of Gentile Europe "is fed and fattened by Jewish brains—though they keep not always their Jewish hearts" (ch. 60, p. 272). Still, she balances the picture through her portrayal of a more "Hellenic" artist, the painter Hans Meyrick, Deronda's friend and protégé. Hans is the son of a dead engraver whose Calvinistic widow, "half French, half Scotch," provides a suitably "quakerish" home for the destitute Mirah. But the young painter has inherited little of his mother's temperament. Seeing all things aesthetically, ruled by his romantic impressionability, he represents that half of Will

Ladislaw which is treated so unsympathetically in *Middle-march*. Meyrick regards people as potential portraits: Gwendolen is a "Vandyke duchess" and Mirah is Berenice, a "king's daughter." "Hans's egotism" disturbs Deronda, for it distorts reality in an irresponsible fashion, converting the puritanical Mirah into the mistress of Titus. But Meyrick's enthusiasm knows no limits. Vowing that he is in love with Mirah, he professes himself willing to renege upon his own religion in order to further the "amalgamation of races" (ch. 37, p. 283).

Meyrick's "Hellenic" aestheticism is employed to exalt Klesmer's more "Hebraic" type of culture, but it is also employed to question the validity of any creed based on the self-sufficiency of the artist. For Meyrick's excesses also undermine Klesmer's credo: "We help to rule the nations and make the age as much as any other public men. We count ourselves on level benches with legislators" (ch. 22, p. 363). If, according to Klesmer and to Shelley, the artist is the unacknowledged legislator of the world, then George Eliot is clearly distrustful of the possible effects of his legislation. Something more than a brotherhood of art is needed. For a lack of culture "lies very close to the worst kind of irreligion."[22] Neither the national laws of Sir Hugo nor the international decrees of Klesmer or Meyrick can be expected to restore to England the spiritual vitality it once possessed. Thus, it is through the Jewish half of her novel that George Eliot reminds her readers that the nation's desiccated tradition can be replenished only by an essentially religious form of "culture," a spiritual force which must have both a national location, as well as an international authority. In defining the aims of Mordecai the Prophet, George Eliot looked hopefully at her public and asked them

[22] *GEL*, VI, 302.

to remember that their "religion is chiefly a Hebrew religion" (ch. 32, p. 148). By trying to promote a movement for the Jews, she also wanted to "awaken a movement in other minds" (ch. 69, p. 398). Daniel Deronda, Jew and Englishman, is given this dual task. Stirred by Mordecai into action on behalf of the aspirations of his race, Deronda also becomes the recipient of a tradition which transcends the boundaries of race or nationality.

Deronda's first contact with Mordecai's ideas comes when both attend the meeting of the artisan club at the *Hand and Banner*. The club, called "The Philosophers," is a forum composed of different races and creeds. Significantly enough, the debate opens with a discussion of evolution and progress, but veers off to a consideration of the question of nationality and race. The three Jews are split on a question which affects them closely. Gideon, who belongs to a type "easily passing for Englishmen," believes in the merging of races into nationalities: "There's no reason now why we shouldn't melt gradually into the populations we live among. That's the order of the day in point of progress" (ch. 42, p. 379). Pash, the skeptic with pronounced Semitic features, is indignant. He believes in race. The Jews, he argues, are the product of natural selection: "What I thank our fathers for is that there are fewer blockheads among us than among other races" (ch. 42, p. 381). As for religion, he asserts, there is no difference between Jewish "rubbish" or that of "Brahmanism or Bouddhism." Progress has done away with all such superstitions. It is at this point that Mordecai, excited by Deronda's presence, enters the discussion. To him Judaism must be both race and nation in order to fulfill its historic function: the preservation of ethical laws. As a fount of moral conscience, Judaism can thus appeal to other nations and other races as well.

Attacking the "genial and rational" Gideon as well as the sardonic Pash, Mordecai makes it clear that he is not defending Jewish theology as such: "I praise no superstition, I praise the living fountains of enlarging belief. What is growth, completion, development? You began with that question, I apply it to the history of our people. I say that the effect of our separateness will not be completed and have its highest transformation unless our race takes on again the character of a nationality" (ch. 42, p. 390). As a nation, Mordecai argues, Judaism would once again have an "organic centre, a heart and brain to watch and guide and execute" (ch. 42, p. 391). A "new Judaea" could function as a "covenant of reconciliation," by revivifying the "brightness of Western freedom" and maintaining a "new brotherhood with the nations of the Gentiles." Such a nation would not allow the shrinking of its ancestral memories into "withered relics"; nor would it, he implies, model itself entirely on the England whose "relics" have already been observed by Deronda. Instead, Mordecai points to the example set by the Puritan settlers of New England whose "memories of Europe, corrected by the vision of the better," gave rise to "the great North American nation" (ch. 42, p. 395).

There is no reason to doubt the sincerity of George Eliot's advocacy of a Jewish state twenty-one years before the first international Zionist Congress convened at Basel in 1897. What is more, her belief that a nation of European Jews would provide Christian Europe with a valuable "neutral ground" in the Middle East is eminently sensible when seen from the vantage point of British political history.[23] Indeed, Mordecai's arguments are far more practical and plausible than those advanced by Pash or Gideon, the rationalists.

[23] See Appendix II.

Why then does George Eliot present these arguments through the shrill fanaticism of Mordecai and base his plea for "nationality" on "feeling" rather than on thought? The prophet's speech is not even directed at his sparring-partners of the artisan club: "His extraordinary excitement was certainly due to Deronda's presence: it was to Deronda he was speaking, and the moment had a testamentary solemnity for him which rallied all his powers" (ch. 42, p. 388). Mordecai addresses himself exclusively to Deronda because, in a vision, he has come to realize that the young man before him is the "Deliverer" who alone can execute his most ardent wishes.

Were George Eliot merely writing a "Zionist novel," as *Daniel Deronda* has so often been called, this added improbability would seem gratuitous and incomprehensible. She had once protested against Disraeli's characterization of Sidonia and now was painfully aware of the resemblances between Coningsby's exotic tutor and Mordecai, the mentor of Deronda: "I thought it likely that your impressions about Mordecai would be doubtful," she wrote to John Blackwood, her editor. "Perhaps when the work is finished you will see its bearings better. . . . Doubtless the wider public of novel-readers must feel more interest in Sidonia than in Mordecai. But then, I was not born to paint a Sidonia."[24] The Mordecai-Deronda relationship and, with it, the entire "prophetic" cast of the novel were uppermost in George Eliot's mind. They suggest that her main purpose was something more than a plea for toleration of the Jews and the establishment of a Jewish nation. For if the exalted treatment of Deronda's mission is intended as a social corrective for the England he leaves behind, it also conveys George Eliot's attempt to define a new climate for religious belief.

[24] *GEL*, VI, 223.

3. Hebraism as Religious Belief

Middlemarch is a "novel of religious yearning without a religious object"; *Daniel Deronda* tries to provide this object. The Jewish half of the novel is designed as asylum and escape from an England displaying "the worst kind of irreligion." It is to illustrate the validity of a poetic faith and the possibility of a "prophetic consciousness." *Middlemarch* had cautiously verified the existence of a separable ethical truth through its intricate, scientifically plausible causal network —the "irony of events." *Daniel Deronda* does no such thing. It authoritatively asserts the need for righteousness and flaunts the causality of the "real" world by questioning the very meaning of its reality.

What is the cause for this marked difference between *Deronda* and George Eliot's earlier work? The answer lies in part, as Mr. Preyer has suggested, in George Eliot's increasing disbelief in her scientific humanism and in her ultimate realization that her era's acceptance of the new progressive theories had brought with it a paradoxical weakening of values and convictions. In the earlier novels, figures such as the Reverend Mr. Tryan of "Janet's Repentance" or Rector Irwine of *Adam Bede* were hailed as "natural" ministers by a writer who had previously denounced the religions of Dr. Cumming and the poet Young as sham and demagoguery. The relativist gospels of George Eliot's pastors were opposed to dogmatism. This-worldly, rather than other-worldly, they were adaptable to the advances of a future age. This perspective alters in George Eliot's later novels. The Reverend Mr. Lyon in *Felix Holt*, a new version of the same figure, is strikingly ineffectual. Almost subordinated to Felix Holt, Mr. Lyon anticipates his successor, the Reverend Mr. Farebrother, who is definitely eclipsed by Dorothea Brooke, the religious enthusiast. Mr. Farebrother is a scientific man able to converse with the learned Lydgate, as well as with his rustic parishioners. He is self-denying, sympathetic, and humane. But George Eliot's dissatisfaction creeps in as, in the final pages of the novel, she proves that the clergyman's moral relativism is definitely inferior to the young matron's passionate conviction about Lydgate's innocence. *Daniel Deronda* represents the culmination of this changed outlook. Mr. Gascoigne, a former military man, is of the same cast as his predecessors: his "tone of thinking" is "ecclesiastical rather than theological" (ch. 3, p. 40): he is intelligent, selfless, and by no means other-worldly. But his role has been completely taken over by Daniel Deronda, who asks Gwendolen at one point whether "the evil temptation has been resisted" (ch. 56, p. 225)! Gwendolen's uncle is all too practical: he misunderstands the extent of Grandcourt's degradation and the depth of his niece's predicament. His sincere desire that she be "religiously dutiful, and have warm domestic affections" clashes with his far more fervent wish that she have "an increasing power, both of rank and wealth" (ch. 13, p. 211). Gwendolen must be confronted with an entirely different world for true moral edification. Mr. Gascoigne is relegated to a secondary role; at the novel's conclusion the clergyman becomes associated with Sir Hugo Mallinger, an even blinder benevolist.

Daniel Deronda, then, carries George Eliot into a new territory. But the path is laid out by her preceding works. The book does not constitute a complete break with the philosophical outlook which had led George Eliot to her novelistic creed of "realism." Despite its allowance for the cognition of nonperceptual truths and its portrayal of an extrasensory world of prescience and providence, *Daniel Deronda* is by no means an agnostic's latter-day "retracta-

tion." There is merely a change in emphasis. Miss Evans, the
one-time "infidel *esprit*" of the *Westminster Review*, has
been partially displaced by her predecessor, the ardent Evangelical. "Mordecai is an enthusiast," Deronda warns us, "I
should like to keep that word for the highest order of minds
—those who care supremely for grand and general benefits
to mankind" (ch. 46, p. 34). There is little here of the
critic who demolished the religions of Dr. Cumming and the
poet Young; there is much of the creator of Dinah Morris
and Janet Dempster.

Despite her sincere defense of the aspirations of an actual,
contemporary Jewry, George Eliot is far more concerned
with depicting this Jewry as the recipient of a living tradition
which, though initially a "national faith," evolved and "pene-
trated the thinking of half the world" (ch. 33, p. 137).
By holding out this Hebraic tradition to an England in need
of "a national religion" and by presenting it in a heightened,
nonrealistic fashion, George Eliot hoped to replenish that
which she had neglected in her earlier work: the foundations
of religious belief as she conceived them to be.

Feeding "himself on visions," Mordecai the Prophet stands
on a bridge to await the arrival of the future "Deliverer"
he is to instruct. He identifies Deronda as his disciple. Although the young man protests that he is not a Jew, Mordecai
remains firm. George Eliot quickly anticipates a rationalist's
disparagement of Mordecai's belief in the validity of his
vision:

What, after all, had really happened? He [Deronda]
knew quite accurately the answer Sir Hugo would have
given: "A consumptive Jew, possessed by a fanaticism
which obstacles and hastening death intensified, had fixed
on Deronda as the antitype of some visionary image, the

offspring of wedded hope and despair: despair of his own life, irrepressible hope in the propagation of his fanatical beliefs. The instance was perhaps odd, exceptional in its form, but substantially it was not rare. Fanaticism was not so common as bankruptcy, but taken in all its aspects it was abundant enough. While Mordecai was waiting on the bridge for the fulfilment of his visions, another man was convinced that he had the mathematical key of the universe which would supersede Newton, and regarded all known physicists as conspiring to stifle his discovery and keep the universe locked; another, that he had the meta-physical key, with just that hair's-breadth of difference from the old wards which would make it fit exactly. . . ."

[ch. 41, pp. 352-353]

The passage bears close scrutiny. The "metaphysical key" alluded to recalls Mr. Casaubon's "Key to All Mythologies" which never unlocked the "binding theory" of the universe that Dorothea had hoped for on marrying the "old ward." The scientific key of the physicist is reminiscent of Lydgate's insistence that his impending discovery of a "common basis" for all living organisms would one day define men's thoughts "after the true order." In each instance, the presumptuous-ness of metaphysician and scientist are equally undermined. But while in *Middlemarch* a disparagement of this pre-sumptuousness is employed to assert the "irony of events," it is employed here to exalt the supremacy of vision. It is noteworthy that the rational objector to Mordecai's vision is none other than the blind Sir Hugo. In George Eliot's handling, "the answer Sir Hugo would have given" becomes self-refuting. The relativity of knowledge only suggests the possibility of the unexpected and the unknown. Soon, Deronda himself is forced to admit the existence of " 'The bare possibility.' He could not admit it to be more" (ch. 41, p. 361).

In *Daniel Deronda* events are determined not by the cumulative will of all characters, but by an omnipresent destiny: "all things are bound together in that Omnipresence" (ch. 63, p. 313). While George Eliot had skillfully disguised coincidences and improbabilities in *Middlemarch*, she only stresses their implausibility in *Daniel Deronda*. Deronda's messiahship and his redemption from a negative skepticism are purely "providential," based as they are on his coincidental rescue of the drowning Mirah and of his discovery of her lost brother Ezra, who lives in the house of another Ezra Cohen under the name of Mordecai. To belabor George Eliot for not being "organic" in her depiction of these coincidences, as some critics have unfortunately done,[25] is to miss her entire point. Nor can she be accused of a sudden conversion to a transcendental belief in supernatural signs and emblems. For George Eliot remains a sober rationalist even during her fits of enthusiasm. Unlike Hannah More before her, she does not insist on reading improbabilities as infallible signs of the workings of providence. Quite to the contrary, she holds that a trust in "outward signs" may well be deceiving (ch. 41, p. 357). But by questioning all signs, she enlists her relativism to reintroduce the possibility of nonverifiable and nonperceptual truths. She tries to hew belief out of disbelief, affirmation out of denial. Thus, the jovial Sir Hugo unsuspectingly supervises the schooling of a future Moses. The "real" Ezra Cohen, a placid and like-

[25] Cf. Jerome Beaty, *"Daniel Deronda* and the Question of Unity in Fiction." Mr. Beaty's *"Middlemarch" from Notebook to Novel, A Study of George Eliot's Creative Method* (Urbana, 1960), on the other hand, contains a most valuable analysis of the "organic" links that operate in *Middlemarch*.

able vulgarian, harbors the authentic or "ideal" Ezra Cohen, Mordecai the misunderstood prophet.

The first Ezra Cohen seems to Deronda "to be the most unpoetic Jew he had ever met with" (ch. 33, p. 174). But his household shelters a timeless figure, a suffering visionary with "the face of a man little above thirty, but with age upon it which belongs to time lengthened by suffering" (ch. 40, p. 332). The cheerful Cohen family, by way of contrast, have a "vulgarity of soul" identical to that of "a prosperous pink-and-white huckster of the purest English lineage" (ch. 33, p. 174); their tastes are mundane and their language is utterly unlike the Old Testament ejaculations of the scholarly Mordecai, who somewhat disdainfully regards England, his native land, "but as a breaking pot of earth around the fruit-bearing tree, whose seed might make the desert rejoice" (ch. 40, p. 335). And yet, for all their mediocrity, the Cohens are forced, almost despite themselves, into charity and fellow-feeling. Centuries of tradition assert their force. George Eliot's brief sketch of the Cohens is as successful as her more detailed portrayal of the Warwickshire rustics of her rural novels. It succeeds, in miniature, precisely where the over-all attempt to integrate the larger worlds of Gwendolen and Deronda fails so lamentably. For in the household of Ezra Cohen the "realistic" and the "ideal" *can* merge into the common tradition. The prosaic Cohens shelter Mordecai's visions and provide, in George Eliot's words, the "alphabet" for his "language." Their world envelops and supports the lonely prophet, just as in *Adam Bede*, the practical world of Mrs. Poyser buoys up another emaciated and bearded sufferer, Adam Bede, the carpenter's son.

Yet it is Deronda, and not Mordecai, who must bridge the gap between the real and the ideal, and the discovery of his own Jewish heritage is deliberately withheld from him until he has become capable of appreciating the full significance of his contact with Mirah and her brother. After his rescue of the young Jewess and before his first meeting with Mordecai, Deronda goes abroad. "In his anxiety about Mirah's relatives," he has become openly interested in Judaism and its ways, but he also thinks "of vulgar Jews, with a sort of personal alarm" (ch. 32, p. 135). Under George Eliot's schooling, Deronda must learn to distrust appearances. Trying to rid himself of "prejudice and ridiculous exaggeration," he enters a synagogue in Frankfort. To his surprise he finds himself yielding to the liturgy of the Sabbath service: "the chant of the *Chazan*'s or Reader's grand wide-ranging voice with its passage from monotony to sudden cries, the outburst of sweet boys' voices from the little quire, the devotional swaying of men's bodies backwards and forwards," blend for Deronda into an "expression of a binding history, tragic and yet glorious" (ch. 32, p. 137). Deronda's submission to the ritual he witnesses as an outsider is not unlike a similar scene in Pater's *Marius the Epicurean*. Yet, unlike Pater, George Eliot is not concerned with a semiconscious absorption of a hazy atmosphere of "sensations and ideas." Deronda dutifully scans his German translation of the Hebrew text, fully conscious of the fact that he is reading "Psalms and Old Testament passages or phrases." His historical imagination endows the service with a significance that transcends "the shabbiness of the scene" and causes him to wonder "at the strength of his feeling." But, "with the cessation of the devotional sounds," Deronda's disbelief is reawakened. Looking at the "many indifferent faces and vulgar figures" shuffling by him, he once again trusts only in external appearances; priggishly, he considers himself, the outsider, as "the only person in the congregation for whom the service was more than a dull routine" (ch. 32, pp. 137, 138). He shakes off a "white-bearded" Jew who asks him about his parentage, unaware that the questioner is none other than Joseph Kalonymos, his grandfather's old friend and associate.

Only after his encounters with the Cohen family and his realization that Mordecai is Mirah's brother, does the returned Deronda learn to distrust the external "conditions" of the present which enslave Gwendolen Harleth. He becomes irresistibly drawn to the tradition he will soon discover to be his very own. The discovery is withheld, however, by an act which Deronda himself later characterizes as nothing less than an act of providence. He must first become fired by Mordecai's teachings; he must engross himself in his Hebrew readings (at one point Gwendolen is even rebuked for failing to understand the momentous significance of the Hebrew grammar that Deronda carries under his arm); above all, Deronda must fall in love with Mordecai's spiritual sister. When Hans Meyrick ebulliently vows that he will "turn proselyte" if Mirah should wish so, Deronda frowns severely (ch. 37, p. 282). But he himself would now like to become a Jew.

Until his rescue of Mirah, Deronda had merely eluded "the pressure of that hard unaccommodating Actual," the actuality which dominates in *Middlemarch* (ch. 33, p. 156). Notwithstanding "all his sense of poetry in common things," he had been unable to translate his dreamy idealism into the reality of his surroundings, to "find poetry and romance among the events of everyday life" (ch. 33, p. 156; ch. 19, p. 305). Drifting on his boat in the Thames, he had taken refuge in a romantic denunciation of the irreconcilability between these two extremes, or, as in the Frankfort episode, had adopted a posture of detached aloofness. It is not until his schooling under Mordecai and his love for Mirah, that the "unaccommodating Actual" begins to assume the shape of the realizable Ideal. The chief poetic energy lies, George Eliot comments in a variation on Coleridge, "in the force of imagination that pierces or exalts the solid fact, instead of floating among cloud-pictures. To glory in a prophetic vision of knowledge covering the earth, is an easier exercise of believing imagination than to see its beginning in newspaper placards" (ch. 33, pp. 157-158). The "believing imagination," once lodged in the trustful Dorothea Brooke, is now provided with an entire historical tradition. *Middlemarch* probes for spatial associations with the past; *Daniel Deronda* finds these associations in Judaism's historical evolution. To George Eliot, Judaism contains a proportionate combination of the ideal and the actual, the spiritual and the material, the traditional and the progressive. Like the religion of the ministers of the earlier novels, its emphasis is on the secular rather than on the abstract; its sentiments are based on homely and ineradicable truths: " 'No man,' says a Rabbi, by way of indisputable instance, 'may turn the bones of his father and mother into spoons'—sure that his hearers felt the checks against that form of economy. The market for spoons has never expanded for anyone to say, 'Why not?' and to argue that human progress lies in such an application of material. The only check to be alleged is a sentiment, which will coerce none who do not hold that sentiments are the better part of the world's wealth" (ch. 33, p. 156). Compressed in this aphorism is George Eliot's commentary on a blind belief in material progress. She asserts here, as she had done in *Middlemarch*, that human progress must be aided by "sentiment," by the reasoning of a heart schooled by the head. Deronda's heart, like Dorothea's, is in need of schooling. But his schooling is not that of experience. It is providence that prepares him as the new Daniel by furnishing him with a ready-made tradition already tested by the experiences of history and heredity. Dorothea must live among the Middlemarchers, content with an ideal pared down by prosaic "conditions." Deronda can sail away on a messianic mission, as an exemplum of the attainable Ideal.

In what is designed as one of the novel's climactic scenes, Daniel meets the Princess, his mother, who restores to him the religion of her father in the form of documents contained in a precious casket. Tutored by Mordecai and by Mirah, Deronda now eagerly returns to the fold. The scene takes place in Genoa at the precise location and time in which Gwendolen's life is affected by an incident of a different nature. The young woman has been spirited off on a Mediterranean cruise by her husband. An accident occurs, and Gwendolen, paralyzed by her hatred, watches Grandcourt drown, in an obvious reversal of Deronda's earlier rescue of the drowning Mirah. Haunted by the vision of her husband's upturned face and now fully aware of her own evil, Gwendolen is soothed only by Deronda's mysterious hint that her own "momentary murderous will" could not have altered the "course of events" (ch. 58, p. 235). In what for George Eliot amounts to a religious experience, Gwendolen signifies her understanding of the reality of suffering and the finality of death. What is more, she has become aware of a force perceived by Mordecai, Mirah, and Deronda. At the book's conclusion she realizes that "the pressure of a vast mysterious movement" has dislodged her from her imagined "supremacy in her own world" and rewarded instead the virtuous Daniel and his bride.

In *Middlemarch* this "movement" is a causal World-Will which is merely the summation of the wills of all the characters. In *Daniel Deronda* it is very tentatively called "God" by Mirah and by Deronda. For it is the possibility of the "divine influx" felt by Deronda at the service in Frankfort which constitutes the prime purpose of the Jewish half of the novel and not its Zionist message. George Eliot deliberately creates a suspension of disbelief to make belief once again possible. In the realm of the unknowable, she enlists her skepticism to allow for a "bare possibility": probabilities are no longer rejected because of the hopelessness of absolute certainty. In the realm of the known, however, her humanism remains unaltered. Mordecai, we are told, is "not a strictly orthodox Jew" (ch. 46, p. 34); Mirah "does not half know her people's religion" (ch. 32, p. 128); Deronda makes it perfectly clear that in calling himself a Jew he will "not profess to believe exactly as my fathers have believed." For to him, as to George Eliot, Judaism is an evolutionary faith: "Our fathers themselves changed the horizons of their belief and learned of other races" (ch. 60, p. 275).

Daniel Deronda thus illustrates the recovery of "a bare possibility." Deronda's mother reluctantly restores a "Jewish heart" to her son. She had hoped to educate him as an English aristocrat; providence has decreed otherwise. The voice of Deronda's grandfather speaks through the Princess, who repeats his voice mechanically and almost "unwillingly": "I have after all been the instrument my father wanted," she concludes wearily (ch. 53, p. 179). It is tempting to read George Eliot's own voice into the Princess's self-justification: "Had I not a rightful claim to be something more than a mere daughter and mother? The voice and genius matched the face. Whatever else was wrong, acknowledge that I had a right to be an artist, though my father's will was against it. My nature gave me a charter" (ch. 53, p. 183). It is too one-sided to read *Daniel Deronda* only as a reparation for the lost faith of Robert Evans. Yet, even if it is much more, it is that as well.

The Deronda half of the novel is an undeniable failure. But to affirm this statement without further qualification as has so often been done, is after all merely to mouth the old truism that the artistic expression of a "positive" vision is more often than not inferior to its counterpart, that kind of religious art which, through satire or distortion, makes the lack of vision its prime target. The sermon told by the Parson is to us a less attractive moral vessel than the tale told by the Nun's Priest—but to Chaucer their value was no doubt inverse. The gargoyle at Amiens delights the modern cultist of the "grotesque," but the nearby medallion depicting the visitation to Zechariah was surely held to be artistically, because ideally, superior by the medieval artisan. In both cases belief in a positive vision made the idealization real by bringing the hopeful nearer to the actual. As Deronda himself remarks, "the exaggeration is a flash of fervour" (ch. 37, p. 289).

George Eliot's characterization of her protagonist demands, but unfortunately cannot receive, such a fervor. We are told that Daniel Deronda "puts in mind of [an] Italian painting," but he remains fleshless and ethereal. Resembling the idealized Pre-Raphaelite portraits of the same period, his characterization asks, as they do, for a receptiveness which can be accorded neither by the religious devotee nor the skeptical critic of art. Deronda's "belief in the validity of Mordecai's impressions" lights up his face: "Receptiveness," glosses George Eliot, "is a rare and massive power, like fortitude; and this state of mind now gave Deronda's face its utmost expression of calm benignant force" (ch. 40, pp. 332, 333). But George Eliot is unable to translate this force into her last work of fiction. She could not go far enough in voiding her unbelief. She was unwilling to destroy in order to rebuild: Gwendolen Harleth is not allowed to become the utopian superwoman of Butler, Shaw, or Lawrence, ready to discard the past for a revitalized future. George Eliot was even less willing to deny all "force": the pilgrimage of Daniel Deronda could never have become the static absorption of the multiple and conflicting religions encountered by Marius the Epicurean on his long quest for a faith.

It is thus that the reader is left only with Deronda's "calm benignant force," oscillating uneasily between the ideal and the real. By assuming the identity of Mordecai the Prophet, while ambling along the corridors of Sir Hugo's mansion or along the promenades of a fashionable European spa, Deronda cannot succeed as the awaited "Deliverer" and spokesman for a "Suffering Race." He is a queer mixture, half-clergyman and half-dandy, a cross between Theobald Pontifex and Disraeli's Coningsby. Unnatural for all his "naturalness," infallible and arrogant in his presumed fallibility and lack of pride, neither Jew nor Christian, he can hardly be held out as an exemplary figure to a Gentile England. There was a more credible way to depict this complex figure. As George Eliot's intelligent characterization of the "real" Ezra Cohen well demonstrates, Leopold Bloom was not completely out of her reach. Yet, seeking for "poetry" with genuine desperation, George Eliot felt compelled to reject the prosaic actuality she had so superbly depicted in her rural novels. Bloom, the Christlike vulgarian and city-dweller oppressed by time and flesh, was contained in the reality she rejected.

V

Walter Pater:
The Search for a Religious Atmosphere

Fundamental belief gone, in almost all of us, at least some relics of it remain—queries, echoes, after-thoughts; and they help to make an atmosphere, a mental atmosphere, hazy perhaps, yet with many secrets of soothing light and shade, associating more definite objects to each other by a perspective pleasant to the inward eye against a hopefully receding background of remoter and ever remoter possibilities.

—WALTER PATER

Life is not a series of gig lamps symmetrically arranged; but a luminous halo, a semi-transparent envelope surrounding us from the beginning of consciousness to the end. Is it not the task of the novelist to convey this varying, this unknown and uncircumscribed spirit, whatever aberration or complexity it may display, with as little mixture of the alien and external as possible?

—VIRGINIA WOOLF

IN MAY OF 1870 George Eliot recorded the high lights of a four-day visit to Oxford. Among the new acquaintances singled out in her diary for future attention were "Mr. Deutsch," who was to provide her with much of the inspiration for *Daniel Deronda*, and "Mr. Jowett," who would soon become her "particular friend." A certain "Mr. Pater, writer of articles on Leonardo da Vinci, Morris, etc.," also seems to have raised her expectations.[1] Three years later, however, George Eliot bestowed a very different recognition

[1] *GEL*, v, 100.

on the young art critic who had just published his *Studies in the History of the Renaissance*. "Mr. Pater's book," she declared, "seems to me quite poisonous in its false principles of criticism and false conceptions of life."[2] There is nothing to suggest that she ever reversed this estimate. When J. W. Cross published his biography of George Eliot in 1885, he reproduced the description of her 1870 excursion to Oxford, but very carefully deleted Pater's name from the list of notables she had encountered.

Cross's excision was undoubtedly stimulated by his reluctance to associate the dead novelist, then at the height of her posthumous fame, with a writer as controversial as "Mr. Pater" (ridiculed by many as "Mr. Rose") had become since the publication of *The Renaissance*. Yet, in the same year in which Cross's biography made its appearance, Walter Pater published a philosophical novel of his own, *Marius the Epicurean: His Sensations and Ideas*, as an expansion and reassessment of the views he had expressed in his earlier work. Hoping to clarify his position to others and to himself, Pater had spent seven painstaking years in the composition of his novel. His efforts were only moderately successful. For he remained the most misunderstood member of that band of Victorian prophets who addressed their age on matters of faith and culture. The misgivings which *The Renaissance* had created were never quite removed during Pater's lifetime. Even in our own times, there persists a widespread tendency to regard Pater as a withdrawn "decadent," the more scholarly, more fastidious, and therefore less dazzling counterpart of writers like Swinburne or Wilde.[3]

[2] *GEL*, v, 455.

[3] Paul Elmer More's attack on Pater in *The Drift of Romanticism* (New York, 1913) and T. S. Eliot's essay on "Arnold and Pater" in *Selected Essays* (London, 1932) have contributed to this identifi-

This misconception and, with it, the erroneous identification of Pater with the tenets of the "art for art's sake" movement, are at least partially attributable to Pater's own reticence and indefiniteness in spelling out his aims. What is more, decades of antipathy have obscured the man and made it virtually impossible to reconstruct the formation of his ideas.[4] Pater's contemporaries left no adequate biographical record of his activities. In what has been aptly called "one of the (unintentionally) comic masterpieces" of English literature,[5] Pater's main biographer, Thomas Wright, not only failed to employ material that is now irretrievably lost, but also obscured important facets of Pater's life in order to fashion a wishful portrait of a "dweller in Mesech" who was saved by a saintly childhood.[6] Despite Wright's efforts, however, even the reader of his *Life of Walter Pater* can obtain occasional glimpses of the mental conflict that Pater underwent during his undergraduate career at Oxford from 1858 to 1862, that crucial four-year period of ferment which saw the publication of the work of Darwin, of Bishop Colenso and of "The Seven Against Christ."

---

cation. Among recent evaluations of Pater which try to reverse this dictum, see: René Wellek, "Walter Pater's Literary Theory and Criticism," *Victorian Studies*, I (September 1957), 29-46; Iain Fletcher, *Walter Pater* (London, 1959); Philip Appleman, "Darwin, Pater, and a Crisis in Criticism," in *1859: Entering an Age of Crisis* (Bloomington, 1959), pp. 81-95; Ruth Z. Temple, "The Ivory Tower as Lighthouse," in *Edwardians and Late Victorians* (New York, 1960), pp. 28-49; Wolfgang Iser, *Walter Pater: Die Autonomie des Ästhetischen* (Tübingen, 1960); and R. V. Johnson, *Walter Pater: A Study of his Critical Outlook and Achievement* (Melbourne [1961]).

[4] See, however, Germain d'Hangest, *Walter Pater: L'Homme et l'Oeuvre*, 2 vols. (Paris, 1961).

[5] Fletcher, *Walter Pater*, p. 41.

[6] Wright, *The Life of Walter Pater* (London, 1907), I, xvi.

As an adolescent, Walter Pater had been emotionally drawn toward the ritualism of the High Church. He apparently was acquainted with the works of Newman and the chief Tractarians well before his arrival at Oxford. His early religious poetry, to judge from the few fragments reproduced by Wright, bears significant resemblances to the *Christian Year* of Keble, whom Pater met at the age of fifteen. A youthful "Essay on Justification," now lost, points to the certain influence of *The Tracts for the Times*. Once at Oxford, Pater was confronted with an entirely different atmosphere. He attended the lectures of Stanley, Arnold, and Jowett, alternately attracted to the Broad Church movement, the creed of "culture," and the study of classicism as foundations for a theory of life.[7] Despite Wright's blunt assertion that Pater never concerned himself with the scientific movements of his time, he unintentionally documents the young student's preoccupation with the implications of Darwin's ideas, when he quotes a fellow undergraduate as remembering how Pater "and another who had been reading Darwin's *Origin of Species* proved with remorseless logic that if God was everywhere—*we* could have no existence at all."[8] Somewhat cryptically, Pater's undergraduate colleagues also attributed his agnosticism to "his German friends."[9]

[7] One of the recurrent motifs in Mallock's *The New Republic* is the antagonism displayed by Mr. Jenkinson (Jowett) toward Mr. Rose (Pater). Pater was not one of Jowett's pupils at Balliol; he was up at Queen's from 1858 to 1862; nonetheless he attended Jowett's lectures and most likely read his contribution to *Essays and Reviews*. According to Wright, Pater's closest friend at Canterbury and at Oxford was J. R. McQueen, a Balliol man.

[8] Wright, I, 203.

[9] *Ibid.*, p. 169. The remark may apply either to the environment Pater encountered at Heidelberg during the Christmas vacation of 1858, or, more likely, to the German philosophers he was reading at the same time. Pater's tutor at Queen's told Wright that as a

The historicism of the Hegelians, whose ideas he absorbed at this time, undoubtedly did complete his awareness of "the entire modern theory of 'development,' in all its various phases."[10] Pater's acceptance of this theory, and his near despair over its presumed repercussions, affected all his subsequent writings.

Pater received a unique chance to assemble and solidify the discrepant strands which had made up his education when he was made a Probationary Fellow at Brasenose in 1864, the year of his earliest essay, "Diaphaneitè." But this cohesion was never to be achieved. His writings, fragmented and sporadic, fall into two distinct phases. The first of these, extending over nine years, begins with the circulation of "Diaphaneitè" and ends with the furor over *The Renaissance,* which, in its unabashed plea for a pagan tradition, a certain levity of tone, and, above all, the presumed hedonism of its "Conclusion," shocked even those readers who, like George Eliot, had shared many of the foundations of Pater's judgment. The second phase, a period spanning the twenty years from 1874 to Pater's death in 1894, involves a gradual amplification and revision of some of the "principles" that she and so many others had declared to be "false" and "poisonous."

In 1877, in the same year he became fixed as the hedonist "Mr. Rose" of W. H. Mallock's *The New Republic,* Pater removed the offending "Conclusion" from the second edition of *The Renaissance.*[11] Through thinly veiled "imaginary

---

student he "seemed more attracted by the thoroughness of German thought than by the clearness and precision of French style" (p. 156).

[10] *Plato and Platonism: A Series of Lectures,* Library Edition (London, 1910), p. 19. Subsequent references to this edition of Pater's works are given in the text.

[11] See Geoffrey Tillotson, "Pater, Mr. Rose, and the 'Conclusion'

portraits," he now proceeded to test out the assumptions which had gone into his book. Pater resigned his Brasenose tutorship in order to devote full time to the longest of these "portraits," *Marius*. He regarded the composition of his novel as nothing less than a "sort of duty."[12] Not until 1888, three years after the publication of *Marius*, did he dare to reintroduce his "Conclusion" with an explanatory note: "This brief 'Conclusion' was omitted in the second edition of this book, as I conceived it might possibly mislead some of those young men into whose hands it might fall. On the whole, I have thought it best to reprint it here, with some slight changes which bring it closer to my original meaning. I have dealt more fully in *Marius the Epicurean* with the thoughts suggested by it" (*Renaissance*, p. 233).

There is little doubt that the entire controversy over *The Renaissance* forced Pater into a more scrupulous reappraisal of what his "original meaning" had actually been. Was the aesthetic life, the cult of sensation "simply for those moments' sake," a truly valid pursuit? Was the Hellenism Pater believed in nothing more than finding "the end of all endeavour in the aspects of the human form"? Pater's years of reappraisal led him to a rejection of his earlier, somewhat facile enthusiasm for a "universal pagan sentiment." It led him, after the publication of *Marius*, to compose further "imaginary portraits" in which he sought, always through the same *persona* of a pensive young skeptic, to bridge the gap between his belief in the exclusive validity of the senses and his increasing awareness of the necessity for moral laws for which he could find no correlative in the visible world. It led him,

of *The Renaissance*," in *Essays and Studies by Members of the English Association*, XXXII (Oxford, 1947), 44-60.
[12] From a letter to Viola Paget written in July 1883, quoted by A. C. Benson, *Walter Pater* (London, 1906), p. 90.

finally, to collect his lectures on a highly imaginary "Platonic" tradition in order to attract a wider audience of "young students of philosophy" than that which had read his scattered essays and stories. The result, *Plato and Platonism*, most explicitly sums up Pater's matured thought. It was the favorite among his own works and merited even the praise of that archmoralist and fellow-classicist, Benjamin Jowett, George Eliot's own "particular friend."

Like George Eliot, Pater employed the novel as a vehicle for his religious ideas. But his fiction, addressed to a more exclusive audience and controlled by a more rigid ideological purpose, lacks the scope and variety of her own attempts to "trace the influence of religion upon human character." Most of Pater's stylized "imaginary portraits" are single-minded and schematic; they display a curious sameness of theme, form, and tone. The remainder of this chapter will be devoted to an appreciation of the features which distinguish his allegorical "portraits" and to a closer consideration of the developmental and sensationalist theories upon which they are predicated—theories which find their most coherent expression in *Plato and Platonism*. The next chapter will then examine Pater's longest and most ambitious work of fiction, *Marius the Epicurean*.

1. Pater's "Imaginary Portraits"

The corpus of Walter Pater's fiction comprises seven short stories or fictive essays, one philosophical novel, and seven chapters of the unfinished *Gaston de Latour*.[13] Small as this

---

[13] In order of their publication, these works are: "The Child in the House" (1878); *Marius the Epicurean* (1885); "A Prince of Court Painters" (1885); "Sebastian van Storck" (1886); "Denys L'Auxerrois" (1886); "Duke Carl of Rosenmold" (1887), separate chapters from *Gaston de Latour* (1887); "Emerald Uthwart"

group is, its make-up raises immediate reservations. The earliest of these nine works, "The Child in the House," a Proust-like evocation of the "environment of early childhood" (*Miscellaneous Studies*, p. 177), is totally devoid of any plot or relevant action.[14] What is more, many of Pater's "imaginary portraits" are almost indistinguishable from his presumably authentic portraits, such as those which make up the *Studies in the History of the Renaissance*. Thus, Pater's recreation of the genius of Watteau in "A Prince of Court Painters," the first of the *Imaginary Portraits*, differs from his equally fanciful interpretation of Michelangelo or Leonardo in *The Renaissance* only in that it is attributed to a fictitious character, the sister of one of the painter's disciples, Jean Baptiste Pater (whose surname is meticulously avoided). Again, the author's candid admission that another of his imaginary subjects, the Duke Carl of Rosenmold, is nothing but the "embodiment" of the "aspirations" of a pre-Goethean Hellenism (*Imaginary Portraits*, p. 152), although illustrative of the very narrow lines of demarcation that exist between his ideological fiction and essays such as "Winckel-

---

(1892); "Apollo in Picardy" (1893). The third, fourth, fifth, and sixth items were gathered in *Imaginary Portraits* (1887); the first and last two were incorporated in *Miscellaneous Studies* (1895), which, like *Gaston de Latour* (1896), was posthumously published. Few attempts have been made to examine the totality of Pater's fiction. Two exceptions are Eugene J. Brzenk, "The Unique Fictional World of Walter Pater," *Nineteenth Century Fiction*, XIII (December 1958), 217-226, and R. T. Lenaghan, "Pattern in Walter Pater's Fiction," *Studies in Philology*, LVIII (January 1961), 69-91.

[14] Mrs. Humphry Ward first suggested that "The Child in the House" was a fragment of a larger work abandoned in favor of *Marius*, which follows it in chronology ("Marius the Epicurean," *Macmillan's Magazine*, LII, June 1885, 132-139). If correct, this supposition would account for the story's sketchiness and for its resemblance to the opening chapters of *Marius*.

mann," hardly contributes to a belief in the verisimilitude of his creation.

Pater's peculiar philosophico-historical fiction can be traced to his private search for "diaphanous" models of the past, which began, years before the uproar over *The Renaissance*, with his first three essays, "Diaphaneitè" (1864), "Coleridge" (1866), and "Winckelmann" (1867). "Diaphaneitè," curiously un-Paterian in its crabbed style and poorly concealed self-examination, had posited the need for a transparent and simple "character" whose genius—though neither that of the philosopher, the artist, nor the religious saint—would rise above the "play of circumstances" created by heredity and environment (*Miscellaneous Studies*, pp. 247, 252). This character, "not disquieted by the desire for change" nor struggling against "conditions" like the figures depicted by "the author of Romola," would, after the manner of Carlyle's heroes, act as an inspiration to others and thus become "a basement type." "A majority of such would be the regeneration of the world" (p. 254). While "Diaphaneitè" merely postulated the need for elect figures, such as George Eliot herself was to invent, a decade later, in *Daniel Deronda*, Pater's next essay, "Coleridge," provided a negative amplification by expanding the vague anti-intellectualism of the first article into a sustained attack on Coleridge's idealistic philosophy. Associating Coleridge's morbidity with his presumed belief in an "absolute" spirit, Pater implied that the transcendence demanded in "Diaphaneitè" could not be effected through a belief in the abstractions of religion or philosophy. He deplored Coleridge's failure to take heed of the spirit of the "relative," which, he asserted, had been validated by the modern "sciences of observation" (*Appreciations*, pp. 66-67). In "Winckelmann," which was to provide the core for *The Renaissance*,

Pater carried these views to their fullest extension. He now seized on the German Hellenist as a "diaphanous" character who, unlike Coleridge, had rejected the abstractions of metaphysics and turned instead toward a concrete Greek ideal based on visual impressions produced by art and ritual. Abruptly, and without much logic, Pater then identified the feelings produced by these impressions with a permanent aesthetic religion available to all. He hailed Winckelmann for facilitating the progress of his superior disciple, Goethe, who presumably restored his master's Hellenism to its proper context in an age ruled by the "relative" spirit.

Pater's imaginative distortions in "Winckelmann" and the other essays of *The Renaissance*, even exceeded, in their looseness, Matthew Arnold's similar manipulations of history in *Culture and Anarchy*.[15] Made painfully conscious of the questionableness of his use of historical fact by the controversy over his book, Pater cautiously moved from the "real" sketches of *The Renaissance* to the "imaginary portraits" of his fiction. Most of his creations are transparently autobiographical. They are reiterations of a common theme: the search of a lonely individual for the "influence" of a meaningful "atmosphere," "background," "perspective," or "environment" (these five terms recur with an amazing frequency throughout Pater's stories and essays) to be found in, but more often to be denied by, the physical or intellectual milieu into which that individual is placed. By lining up his characters against the "perspectives" provided by the past, Pater attempted to rescue their "sensations and ideas" from the inexorable flux of historical circumstances created by heredity and environment that he had described in "Diaphaneitè": "Most of us are neutralised by the play of circumstances. To most of us only one chance is given in the life of the

---

[15] See pp. 69-71, above.

spirit and the intellect, and circumstances prevent our dexterously seizing that one chance" (*Miscellaneous Studies*,
p. 252).

Pater's fiction contains the same mixture of factual ac-
curacy and subjective distortion found in his critical essays.
In recovering the "play of circumstances" which molds the
temperament of his characters—historical events, the words
and actions of past thinkers, the physical environments provided by cathedrals, palaces, or villas—Pater turns into a
fastidious antiquarian concerned with reproducing details as
accurately as possible. Yet, in determining the *effects* of these
"circumstances," Pater becomes a visionary subjectivist who
superimposes a new and wholly imaginary design on the
realities he has so scrupulously recovered. The Cecilian villa
in *Marius the Epicurean* thus acts as much more than a mere
setting for the Christian mass observed by the young Pagan;
the utterances of Marcus Aurelius represent more than a
mélange of phrases culled from the *Méditations*. They are
meant to be read as influential "mental" atmospheres, Pater's
own interpretations of the elusive physical and ideological
components of a receding, but ever-meaningful past.

As a result, the quality of Pater's fiction is nondramatic,
derivative, almost static. It is the fiction of an art critic. Just
as Pater the critic of the *Mona Lisa* needs an "actual" painting which he may then transcend imaginatively through
his prose, so Pater the creative portraitist needs a fixed delin-
eation of a figure whose sensations and ideas he can then
interpret freely in relation to changing "environments" or
"atmospheres." Pater's imaginary portraits are as stationary
and immobile as pictures in a gallery; Gaston de Latour,
Florian Deleal, Emerald Uthwart, even Marius the Epicurean, differ from each other only by virtue of the different
perspectives against which they are placed. And, since each

of these perspectives gives the portrait its peculiar coloring and refraction, its basic features are deliberately kept simple. Pater's *personae* are always sketched as serious, introspective, and impressionable young men. Like their creator, they possess a "mystical appetite for sacred things," and share with him also "the fear of death intensified by the desire of beauty" (*Miscellaneous Studies*, pp. 193, 189-190). Their interaction with other characters is negligible; as a result, motivation, dialogue, even plot, are used sparingly. For Pater, as for George Eliot, truth can be found only by looking at a subject from various points of view. But whereas George Eliot's novels capitalize on the collision of the attitudes and motivations of a wide range of characters, in Pater's fiction it is the range of "environments" which act upon his single-minded protagonists that can truly be said to hold varying "points of view," a term used in this sense by the author himself.[16]

It is hardly a coincidence that all of Pater's fiction should be set in the past, a past remoter even than that "autumn haze" which he, like Henry James, admired in the rural novels of George Eliot.[17] Each of Pater's protagonists is

[16] Cf. *The Renaissance*, p. 236. Despite an occasional Arnoldian derogation of "an age of novelists," Pater's essays are studded with references to Balzac, Hugo, Zola, Flaubert, George Sand, Thackeray, and George Eliot. In his reviews of the fiction of Mérimée, Fabre, Filon, Feuillet, Mrs. Ward, and Oscar Wilde, Pater displays a familiarity with the standard techniques of the novel, but reveals a weakness for sentimental touches. He also welcomes the imprint of an author's personality and applauds Flaubert's failure to efface himself ("Mérimée," *Miscellaneous Studies*, p. 36).

[17] Significantly, it was *Romola*, George Eliot's "remotest" novel, set in the Italian Renaissance he cherished, that was his favorite among her novels (cf. Wright, II, 179-180). He seized on the defects inherent in his own methods of characterization when he accused George Eliot's characters of being "practically identical"

subjected to "influences" peculiar to a distinct historical period. Thus, although initially the identity of a Marius or Gaston de Latour or Emerald Uthwart might be alike, it is the particular sequel of historical atmospheres through which each of these "constitutionally impressible" young men is conducted which provides his quest with a definite character of its own (*Marius the Epicurean*, ch. 23, p. 132). Yet even here a homogeneity of sorts remains, for Pater selects his "atmospheres" with utmost care: all of his fictional recreations of the past are conditioned by the needs of his own present. The alert historical imagination given its fullest play in the philosophical reconstructions of *Plato and Platonism* is, in Pater's imaginary portraits, continually establishing relationships between the intellectual crosscurrents of his own age and those of previous periods. Pater's fiction abounds in spatial cross references. In *Gaston de Latour*, for example, the theories of the French Pléiade are regarded as a possible anticipation of "our modern idea, or platitude, of the *Zeitgeist*" (p. 70), while in *Marius* the senseless slaughter of the Roman arena is described with an eye toward a Darwinian age obsessed with " 'survivals' " (ch. 14, p. 237).

All of Pater's protagonists belong to transitional periods of history. They move in a Roman Empire yielding to a new faith; in a sixteenth-century France purging its medievalism through bloody religious wars; in a semifeudal Germany yearning at once for foreign enlightenment and for a native culture. Marius, Gaston, and Duke Carl are condemned to span two worlds, one dying, and the other, its antithesis, in the process of being reborn. With the exception of "Denys L'Auxerrois" and "Apollo in Picardy," where the mythic protagonists themselves represent the continuity of

---

one to another: "What . . . is Maggie Tulliver but Tito in petticoats?" (Benson, *Walter Pater*, p. 192).

history, all of Pater's stories are in the form of historical inter-
ludes which take a fixed stencil of a "portrait" (a sort of
master-character), hang it in a predetermined location in
the galleries of the past, examine it critically from the vantage
point of later history, and remove it once again to its original
position in a dubious and eclectic late-Victorian present.

This historicism informs all of Pater's stories; it shapes
their subject matter, their form, and their tone. Invariably,
each tale illustrates the basic opposition that Pater was to
describe in *Plato and Platonism*: the opposition of flux to
stasis, of motion to rest. Motion is identified with change
and those ideologies which have made change their stock.
Motion thus is Heracliteanism, Epicureanism, Hellenism;
in its broadest sense it is evolutionism, "the entire modern
theory of 'development'" itself. Rest, on the other hand, is
identified with the vain desire for spiritual permanence and
related to those systems which aspire towards the One. Rest
therefore is Stoicism, the medieval *contemptu mundi*, Christianity, as well as the "cold" transcendentalism of thinkers
like Spinoza or Coleridge. Eventually, Pater attempted to
blend these two extremes through the spatial scheme of
Plato and Platonism. His stories, written before this proposed
summa was undertaken, hunt for the circumstances which
would facilitate such a combination: the "lower" pantheism
of Giordano Bruno, Hellenic yet Christian, the faith of the
early Christians, Hebraic yet Roman, are examined as possible
fusions. Yet they too are questioned in the critical "spirit also
of the Platonic Socrates, with whom such dubitation had
been nothing less than a religious duty or service" (*Plato
and Platonism*, p. 195).

As a result of this skeptical spirit, most of Pater's "portraits" only accentuate the impossibility of effecting a combination of motion and rest under an inauspicious set of

historical circumstances. In what is no doubt the least successful of Pater's tales, "Sebastian van Storck," the hero's search for ideal absolutes is in direct defiance of the "quaint new Atticism" invading the Holland of his times (p. 84). The story begins with motion: a vision of the skating Sebastian "in lively motion" is falsely interpreted by a friendly observer as an evidence of the young man's adaptation to times full of "reverberation, and great movement" (*Imaginary Portraits*, p. 85). For Sebastian, paralyzed by the "lulling power" of the mystic Catholicism he has inherited, refuses "to be moved" by the controversies around him. Like his fellow-idealist, George Eliot's Dorothea Brooke, Pater's protagonist dismisses a worldly match and takes refuge instead in the abstractionism of sterile ideas. Just as Dorothea refuses Sir James Chettam's proposal in order to seek a binding ideal in Mr. Casaubon's "Key to All Mythologies," Sebastian rejects the hand of a nubile Dutch maiden in favor of Spinoza's doctrines which, he hopes, will enable him to transcend "the uncertainty of the individual human life" (p. 93). Also like George Eliot, Pater depicts the futility of such a search. But while the massive apparatus of *Middlemarch* is employed to chasten the aspirations of a late-born Theresa, Pater's slim philosophical parable ends abruptly with a Sebastian martyrized by the *Zeitgeist*.

For, after a long "interpretative" paraphrase of Sebastian's Spinozistic reflections, we are succinctly told that the lonely philosopher perished in the drowning-scene manner prescribed by the allegorical conventions of Victorian fiction.[18] In Pater's almost casual handling of Sebastian's death, the

---

[18] Edward Fowler in Froude's *Shadows of the Clouds* and Robert Elsmere in Mrs. Ward's novel die after rescuing a victim from drowning, just as, in the more imaginative scheme of *The Mill on the Floss*, Maggie and Tom Tulliver "rescue" their childhood while drowning.

drowning is employed neither as a melodramatic device nor as a moral agent, as it would have been in the hands of Charles Dickens or George Eliot. There is hardly any symbolic exploitation of the streaming waters that break the dikes surrounding the philosopher's isolated house; there is no appended moralization branding this house as an undesirable ivory tower or "palace of art." Death, at the center of all of Pater's stories, has a decisiveness, a finality of its own. It is the only viable fusion of motion and rest, an act of transcendence which confirms the futility of the philosopher's search for transcendence. In "Sebastian van Storck," as in *Marius the Epicurean*, death rounds out the "portrait," makes it immobile once again, and forces it back into its historical niche.

The antithesis of movement and stasis is treated more elaborately in Pater's longer works. Gaston de Latour, living in "a difficult age, certainly, for scrupulous spirits to move in," becomes attracted to the static quiescence of "Our Lady's Church," a Chartres isolated from the feuds of the times, only to be catapulted into "Modernity" and motion, "the intellectual *movement*" of Ronsard's Pléiade (*Gaston de Latour*, pp. 16, 70).[19] In the habitual fashion of Pater's impressionable heroes, Gaston yields to the "influences" of two opposed systems of thought: "two worlds, two antagonistic ideals, were in evidence before him. Could a third condition supervene, to mend their discord . . . ?" (p. 38) Gaston hopes to find some equipoise in the "suspended judgment" of Michel de Montaigne, a "two-sided thinker" who alternates between indolent inaction and "movement, rapid movement of some kind" (pp. 86, 113).[20] Like the Socrates of *Plato*

[19] "Our Lady's Church" and "Modernity" are the titles of chapters 2 and 3 of the novel.

[20] "Suspended Judgment" is the title of chapter 5 of the novel.

and Platonism to whom he is linked, Montaigne stands for a critical spirit of "delicate balances": the dialogue of the mind with itself (p. 104). Yet Gaston's new-gained relativism, though based on his awareness of the historical flux, does not make him immune from its mechanical operations.

Involuntarily drawn into the controversies of his time, Gaston becomes affected by the "shadows of events."[21] His marriage to a weak Huguenot, Colombe, frustrates his ambitions and shatters his ideals. At first glance, Pater's exploitation of the "shadows of events" resembles George Eliot's use of the marriage of Tertius Lydgate to Rosamond Vincy as a dramatic exemplum of the "irony of events." But Gaston's love for Colombe, its tragic outcome, and the repercussions on the young man's character are hardly touched on at all. They are sketched in ever so lightly as a mere prelude for the necessity of still another "atmosphere." For the spiritually maimed Gaston is now drawn to the "spell" of a third major figure of the times, Giordano Bruno, whose pantheism, unlike that of Spinoza, is a Hellenistic offspring of that "old pagan religion" known to Marius the Epicurean (p. 156). Bruno's faith is accommodated to motion and change; but it too is incomplete. Its flaw lies in a denial of "that so very ancient antagonism between good and evil" (p. 159). Gaston thus faces the dilemma broached in the conclusion of *Plato and Platonism*: "the distinction, namely, between the precious and the base, aesthetically; between what was right and wrong in the matter of art" (p. 161). The unfinished *Gaston de Latour* ends on a question mark. Presumably, Gaston's predicament would have been solved only by death,

---

For Montaigne's position in the "independent" Platonic tradition created by Pater, see p. 181, below.

[21] "Shadows of Events" is the title of chapter 6 of the novel.

with his final immolation to the *Zeitgeist* after the manner of Marius, Sebastian van Storck, or Emerald Uthwart.

Motion, then, accentuates Pater's acceptance of and despair at "the entire modern theory of 'development,' in all its phases," the evolutionary processes that George Eliot had illustrated so consummately in her own novels. Technically, Pater's concern with past and present, "environment" and psyche, causality and will, cries out for the kind of form adopted by the modern novel or at least for the spatial juxtapositions of *Middlemarch* or *Daniel Deronda*. Another of Pater's less satisfactory "portraits," Duke Carl of Rosenmold, seems to speak for the novelist when he asks to be propelled "out of space beyond the Alps or the Rhine, into future time" (*Imaginary Portraits*, p. 143). In the context of the story, the good Duke's despair is caused by his inability to further the labors of his successor, Goethe, by leaving a legacy similar to that of Winckelmann in *The Renaissance*. But his predicament also speaks for Pater's technical needs. One way to move "out of space" was to resort to myth, and Pater, the student of comparative mythology, understood this well enough. In "Denys L'Auxerrois" and "Apollo in Picardy," the contrast of pagan motion to religious or philosophical rest is achieved by Pater's transformation of his protagonists, Denys and Brother Apollyon, into Christian reincarnations of Dionysus and Apollo, the Greek gods in exile.[22]

Pater's treatment of the two Greek gods is hardly uncritical. For he no longer vindicates them, as in *The Renais-*

---

[22] See Lenaghan, "Pattern in Walter Pater's Fiction," and John Smith Harrison, "Pater, Heine, and the Old Gods of Greece," *Publications of the Modern Language Association*, XXXIX (September 1924), 655-686, for a study of these two stories in the light of Pater's *Greek Studies*, as well as of the ideas of Hegel, Nietzsche, and Heine. Mr. Lenaghan gives the name of "Apollonian" and "Dionysiac" to the two forces I have preferred to call "rest" and "motion."

sance, where he had pictured them as creatures of light defamed by Christianity as "malignant spirits, the defeated but still living centres of the religion of darkness" (p. 30). Though regarded as the supple exponents of a self-renovating tradition, adjusted to change and motion, Denys and Apollyon are far from flawless. Contrasted to the static medieval world which they infect with a new and beneficent regard for the physical verities, their paganism is at the same time harmful and destructive. Apollyon, whose very name has a sulphurous, Bunyanesque connotation, kills the lay brother Hyacinth with a negligent throw of his discus in a re-enactment of the old Greek myth—Hyacinth being none other than Hyacinthus, who, together with Adonis and Adrastus, is elsewhere depicted as one of the "fated" ones who must die (*Greek Studies*, p. 109). Apollyon is also responsible for the end of the aged Prior Saint-Jean, driven to despair by his inability to reconcile the Greek fertility god with the Good Shepherd of Christianity. Only in death does the Prior perceive a cyclical unity between the two traditions, as he realizes that the blue hyacinths on which Hyacinthus was slain are also of the color of "Holy Mary's gown on the illuminated page, the colour of hope, of merciful omnipresent deity" (*Miscellaneous Studies*, pp. 170-171).

While Apollyon's actions injure all but himself, the Dionysiac fury of the followers of Denys even turns against the god's own reincarnation. The young man is literally torn to shreds by a frenzied mob. In both stories, the sober medieval world is tolerated as the logical outgrowth of a freer, but more irresponsible, Hellenism. Temperance or discipline is the contribution of the Christian Middle Ages. The "gay, wild" sculptures of Denys acquire a "well-assured seriousness" in the hands of the medieval artisan; his pastoral pipe is put to "sweeter purposes" in the building of a harmonious church organ: "It was as if the gay old pagan world had been *blessed* in some way" (*Imaginary Portraits*, pp. 70-71). The historical continuity which provides the intellectual structure for *Marius the Epicurean* also becomes the theme of Pater's two mythical parables.

Despite its depiction of this historical flux, however, Pater's fiction has a curiously static quality. Particularly in the longer pieces, his heroes pass from influence to influence, from the environment fixed by their childhood impressions to the unsatisfactory philosophies to which they are forever yielding, but which they continually feel compelled to reject. Inevitably, they return to their childhood haunts, exhausted and weary, and die, in an ultimate refinement of their experience. Pater's belief that this experience was "mechanically" determinable by "the influences of the sensible things which are tossed and fall and lie about us"—even by minutiae such as "little shapes, voices, accidents" which interweave themselves through the fabric of "all our thoughts and passions"—is responsible for his own static portrayal of the succession of separate "atmospheres" which mold the mind and will of his characters (*Miscellaneous Studies*, pp. 177, 178).

Pater's determinism has a freezing effect on his fiction. Unlike George Eliot or even Hardy, Pater cannot dramatize its operations by pitting the will of his creations against that of their environment. To him the "environment" is all. Complete reflections of their atmospheres, his characters lack any spark of volition. Thus, "lodged in Abelard's quarter," Gaston de Latour can but "repeat" the "typical *experience*" of his famous predecessor, an experience undergone almost five centuries before his own lifetime (*Gaston de Latour*, p. 124). In the individual illumination of an "atmosphere," however, Pater displays an often unrivaled power of suggestion. Believing that "indefectible certitude" can only happen by "a *summary* act of intuition upon the entire perspective" (*Plato and Platonism*, p. 181) he punctuates his fiction with moments of imaginative vision which unite, albeit for an instant, the random impressions of his characters. Rendered through an exquisite attunement of symbol and tone, these moments of vision are highly reminiscent of the Joycean "epiphany."

In the opening pages of *Gaston de Latour*, the sunlit corn-fields of La Beauce—a physical world of material mutability and continuity—are skillfully juxtaposed to the rites con-ducted inside the "incense-laden sanctuary" through which the "quivering" landscape is dimly seen by an aged and "visionary company" about to consecrate Gaston (p. 10). The momentary fusion of both atmospheres is attained by the young novice, ready to begin his pilgrimage, solely "by the privilege of youth" (p. 10). Ironically enough, he is never to recover this instant. The loss becomes evident when, later in the novel, Gaston attends his dying grandfather, the scion of a past age of belief, and "watches as the light creeps over the silent cornfields, the last sense of it in those aged eyes now ebbing softly away" (p. 128). Unbeknown to Gas-ton, at the very same moment the "far away" Massacre of St. Bartholomew sets a new era into motion and precipitates his own unsuspecting downfall.

Such effects are best sustained in Pater's longest and most unified work of fiction, *Marius the Epicurean*. But even there, Pater's most successful evocations of atmospheres, such as the one which permeates the impressions of the dying Marius, seem somehow separated from the character whose psyche they presumably affect. Nor can Pater's belief in the disjointed nature of human experience be wholly credited with this failure. Unlike Virginia Woolf after him, a writer

who shared and illustrated this belief, Pater lacked the power
to breathe life into his characters and the craftsmanship
necessary to endow his vision with a credibility and cohesion
of its own. Fitful and capricious, he sacrificed substance for
impression and scope for intensity. Yet he brings to English
fiction elements new and alien. Pater's stories fall into a twi-
light zone between parable and essay, romance and theory,
autobiography and criticism. But in their persistent hunt for
meaningful "atmospheres," they stake out many of the pre-
occupations and techniques of the novel of the future. Paradoxically enough, it is of Stephen Daedalus and of the motive
power of *Ulysses* that one thinks when confronted with the
odyssey of the immutable young outcast who recurs in all
of Pater's frozen stories, the exile searching through time and
space for the inheritance denied to him by his own present.

2. Pater's "Religion of Sanity"

In the first of his "imaginary portraits," "The Child in the
House," Pater outlined the predicament that his creation,
Florian Deleal, was to bequeath to Marius the Epicurean
and to the protagonists of his later tales:

In later years he came upon philosophies which occupied
him much in the estimate of the proportion of the sensuous
and the ideal elements in human knowledge, the relative
parts they bear in it; and, in his intellectual scheme, was
led to assign very little to the abstract thought, and much
to its sensible vehicle or occasion . . . and he remembered
gratefully how the Christian religion, hardly less than the
religion of the ancient Greeks, translating so much of its
spiritual verity into things that may be seen, condescends in
part to sanction this infirmity, if so it be, of our human
existence, wherein the world of sense is so much with us,

and welcomed this thought as a kind of keeper and sentinel over his soul therein. [*Miscellaneous Studies*, pp. 186-187]

The dilemma of Florian, Marius, or Gaston de Latour was Pater's very own. A firm believer in the exclusive authority of the senses, he hoped to fasten his religious yearnings on a "sensible vehicle or occasion" adaptable to the motions of the flux. Years earlier, in *The Renaissance*, Pater had optimistically hailed such a "vehicle." Disparaging the abstractions of religion, he welcomed ritual as a visible form of "pagan worship" which had survived despite the Christian belief in the invisible and the immutable. With considerable oversimplification, he suggested that this outward "religious observance," immune to the fluctuations of history, be retained, while dogma, ritual's abstract content, be disregarded as variable, ethereal, and therefore wholly negligible. Borrowing a simile made famous by Marx and Kingsley, Pater continued: "This pagan worship, in spite of local variations, essentially one, is an element in all religions. It is the anodyne which the religious principle, like one administering opiates to the incurable, has added to the law which makes life sombre for the vast majority of mankind" (p. 202).

In the years after *The Renaissance*, Pater became increasingly aware of the necessity for moral "law." Dissatisfied with the inconclusiveness of a creed based on the impression of the moment, he now sought to make amends for his own "infirmity." Yet he was unwilling to abandon his sensationalist standards. Thus, in *Marius the Epicurean* and in his shorter "portraits," Pater addressed himself above all to those concerned with the visible world who were inclined to accept only the "laws" perceived through the senses. But,

by illustrating the clash of motion and rest, his stories only
drew attention again and again to the separation between
"the sensuous and the ideal elements in human knowledge."
Although his essays deal with a few "diaphanous" models
like Raphael, Sir Thomas Browne, or Wordsworth, most of
Pater's subjects find that "the world of sense" is too much
with them. What is more, their example cannot be followed.
In the essays, Browne and Raphael are aided by archaic
Christian beliefs invalidated for their successors; Wordsworth, by a placid pantheism that Pater refuses to accept.
In the stories, only Brother "Apollyon" manages to fuse the
sensuous and the ideal. But as the reincarnation of a deity,
he represents a cyclical continuity denied to ordinary mortals.

Pater's fictional attempts to deal with the collision of
motion and rest gave way once again to an ambitious interpretation of history itself. *Plato and Platonism*, published
in 1893, constitutes Pater's last iteration, still character-
istically hesitant and irresolute, of the question he had treated
so superficially in *The Renaissance*, "this very question of the
reconciliation of the religion of antiquity with the religion of
Christ" (*Renaissance*, p. 33). With the sole exception of
Marius the Epicurean, the work to which it is most closely
related, *Plato and Platonism* is Pater's most "prophetic" piece
of writing. Yet, as such, it also illustrates the characteristics
which differentiate Pater from other Victorian prophets of
culture.

Unlike Matthew Arnold or George Eliot, Pater is not an
actual "reconciler." Although he resorts to methods of qualification and elimination which distinctly resemble Arnold's
own, Pater refuses to merge the empirical and the ideal into
a vague compromise such as his predecessor's "power not
ourselves." Nor can he, for all his yearning for a "diaphanous" character, create a figure who transcends reality

after the manner of George Eliot's Deronda. Instead, Pater pares down religion and philosophy, not only to Victorian "essences" of their content, but also to their "sensible vehicles," ritual and dialectic. In *Plato and Platonism*, as in *Marius*, his avowed use of Hegel's "historic method" is designed to provide his contemporaries with an "atmosphere" designed to conserve morality as well as with a belief in "things that may be seen."

Plato and Platonism furnishes an excellent guide to *Marius the Epicurean*. Pater's fabrication of the "environment" which produced a philosophic tradition of his own devising is intimately connected with his fictional reconstruction of the "atmospheres" affecting the "sensations and ideas" of the young Marius (*Plato and Platonism*, pp. 268-269). Though appearing a full eight years after the publication of his novel, *Plato and Platonism* resorts to an identical system of spatial allusions and cross references. Whereas this system is concealed in the novel, its presentation is all but explicit in the later work, where Pater openly concedes that his sweeping manipulations of history are conditioned by the religious needs of his own time, an era of "decadence," "rich and various in special apprehensions of truth" but "tentative and dubious in its sense of their *ensemble*" (p. 174). Consequently, although both works present a similar "*ensemble*" through an imaginative reshuffling of the past, *Plato and Platonism* dispenses with the disguises adopted in *Marius*. In the novel, Pater removes Marius into a period of "decadence" only obliquely corresponding to the Victorian period; in his lectures on Plato, he addresses himself directly to the doubter of his own generation, "the speculative young man of our own day" (p. 154). He ranges over twenty-five centuries of history in order to extract the remnants of a "religion of sanity" (p. 227), which, unlike the irretrievable "religion of cheerfulness" depicted in *Marius* can still act as a visible bulwark for a dubious age.

Pater's lectures on Plato are above all addressed to the scientific-minded, "speculative" young man who must find solace in the uninspiring observation of matter and its operations, of "organism and environment, or protoplasm perhaps, or evolution, or the *Zeit-geist* and its doings" (p. 154), and also to those who, like Dowson, Wilde, or Moore, regard the visible world as a mere source for pleasurable stimuli, in dangerous emulation of those decadent Athenians who affected what was "least fortunate in the habits, the pleasures, the sordid business, of the class below them" (p. 274). Scientist and aesthete, both students of the palpable, both highly aware of the flux, are thus regarded as prospective converts to Pater's Hellenistic Christianity, a "religion of sanity" to be reconstructed out of the visible remnants of the "tradition, the development," of Plato's thought and method. Pater's purpose is didactic. He hopes to enlist the scientist's interests in a more comprehensive pursuit; he wants to check the aesthete's irresponsible hedonism by leading him to the Platonic "art of discipline."

Although relying far more on the subtleties of inference and suggestion than on open polemics, *Plato and Platonism* follows the cast of Matthew Arnold's theological essays. While Arnold is concerned with the establishment of a humanist tradition outside the realm of Christian doctrine and dogma, Pater attempts to set up a Platonism "independent of, yet true in spirit to, the Platonism of the Platonic Dialogues" (268-269). In either case, a loose application of Hegel's "historic method" is sanctioned by a painful awareness of the "ever-changing 'Time-spirit' or *Zeit-geist*," the perennial flux which renders all things relative (p. 9). Yet the differences between the two men are also noteworthy.

While Arnold upholds the literary permanence of the biblical revelation over the fluidity of the Greek vision, it is precisely this fluidity "with no link on historic time" which attracts Pater to Hellenism (*Greek Studies*, p. 101). To Arnold, the Hellenic "banner of art and science" must yield its place to the Hebraic "banner of righteousness."[23] To Pater, the Greek love of form and knowledge and a Spartan concern with moral "discipline" actually survive in the humanism of Christianity. The Hellenic ideal adapts itself, because of its concreteness, to the laws of change and mutability.

Read correctly then, *Plato and Platonism* may be regarded as a latterday equivalent of *St. Paul and Protestantism* (1870), *Literature and Dogma* (1873), and *God and the Bible* (1875). Searching like Arnold for an "essential" contemporary faith and using Arnold's tools of analogy, antithesis, and imaginative rearrangement, Pater produces a work which is likewise anti-philosophical, anti-abstractionist, and anti-dogmatic in its bias. But whereas Arnold and most other Victorian prophets search for some time-honored and invariable pool of human experience, Pater, forced to rely on an exclusive truth of the senses, "delights in tracing traditions" only to efface them (*Appreciations*, p. 244). The "atmosphere" which he holds out to his prospective "Platonist" is far more tentative than Arnold's forthright, polemical presentation of his "essence" of Christianity. While Arnold boldly tries to recover "the secret of Jesus" through a reinterpretation of the Gospels and the Pauline epistles, Pater cautiously evades any open friction with traditional theology and adheres to a purely secular line of inquiry. Still, despite his insistence on an all-Hellenic heritage, his frame

[23] Cf. *Literature and Dogma* (London, 1873), p. 354: "But conduct, plain matter as it is, is six-eighths of life, while art and science are only two-eighths."

of reference is unmistakably Christian. To Pater, the "environment" of the Platonic dialogues is the fountainhead of all subsequent systems of metaphysics, ethics, and aesthetics; Christianity and its modern "relics" are but the outgrowth (or, at least, the analogous by-product) of the ideas of Plato and his predecessors. Aided by this spatial theory, Pater not only avoids Arnold's frequently clumsy attempts at biblical exegesis, but also manages to side-step any polemical engagements with the established Church.[24]

Pater's historical theories impress on *Plato and Platonism* a scope that is far broader, but also far more facile, than that of Arnold's religious works or of Newman's *Essay on the Development of Christian Doctrine*. In Pater's system, pagan *Gnosis* merely becomes Christian "vision." Pater offers no "secret of Jesus," no "religion new-given"; "Hebraism," "*Aberglaube*," and similar terms integral to the Arnoldian type of inquiry are carefully shunned. Hellenism is a self-sufficient tradition, containing in itself desirable and undesirable elements found also in Judaism or Christianity. Thus, Pater attacks Parmenides as the initiator of an idealism which was to affect Socrates and Plato, although he concedes that in its coldness the Greek's philosophy of "rest" did not "touch the affections" as did its counterpart, "the revelation to Israel" (*Plato and Platonism*, p. 38). Yet he finds this emotionalism in Cleanthes the Stoic, a Parmenidean, whose

[24] Very likely as a result of the controversy over *The Renaissance*, Pater had a marked dislike for open polemics. In his essays, he praises Sir Thomas Browne's suspicion of theological disputations (*Appreciations*, pp. 131-132); he also feels compelled to point out that Pascal's participation in the Jansenist controversies of his time transcended the bounds of partisanship, belonging to disputes not of a single age but of eternal ones (*Miscellaneous Studies*). This same distrust of partisan "solutions" in the realm of religion colors Pater's review of Mrs. Ward's *Robert Elsmere*, discussed below.

"Hymn to the One" becomes the ready equivalent to "Israel's devout response to the announcement: 'The Lord thy God is one Lord'" (p. 49). Similarly, Plato's abstracted and therefore undesirable "Theory of Ideas" is metamorphosed by Pater into the "rude scholasticism of the pedantic Middle Age" or into the "cold-blooded transcendentalism" of philosophers like Marcus Aurelius, Spinoza, or Kant, whose search for an "ideal city" is, like the search for the one "way" in *Marius*, destined to come to nought (pp. 31, 164). Again, the "old Heracliteanism" of Plato's predecessors merely becomes the new Darwinian hypothesis, encouraging, then as now, "the destructiveness of undisciplined youth" (p. 18).

Conversely, the Platonic "environment" examined by Pater has its positive side as well. Plato's skepticism and the dialectical method of Socrates have allowed unbelievers from Marius the Epicurean down to Montaigne and to Pater's contemporary "young man" to find refuge in an "endless dialogue, with one's self," a "habit" of "tentative thinking and suspended judgment" which avoids the dogmata of theism and materialism (pp. 177, 195). What is more, Pater's "independent" Platonic tradition also offers a tangible religious "atmosphere," available even to those who have labored throughout the ages "with no prospect of Israel's reward" (p. 233). A "religion of sanity," based on the ritual and discipline of Sparta and adopted by Plato for his republic, can still be found among the relics of modern Christianity. For, to Pater, the "graceful polytheism" of the Greeks merges easily into "the *dulia* of saints and angels in the catholic church" (p. 33); the "music" of the temperate Lacedaemonians reverberates still in the chants of the Gregorian monks; the "hieratic Dorian architecture" of the Greek temples manages to survive in the "Cistercian Gothic" of the Middle Ages (pp. 278-279).

The aim of *Plato and Platonism*, like that of the writings of Arnold, Hennell, and the German "Higher Critics," is to recover a "positive" creed for the nineteenth century through an imaginative reinterpretation of this creed's historic "origins." Yet, while Pater's predecessors placed this "origin" in the era of Christ and St. Paul, his own use of an all-Hellenic tradition allows him to go back even farther in time to the "environment" created for Plato by three of his forerunners (Heraclitus, Parmenides, and Pythagoras), by his master Socrates, and by the disciplined worship of the Lacedaemonians. Somewhat passively, like the subjects of Pater's "imaginary portraits," his Plato holds all of these strands together for a brief moment in history, before their inevitable fragmentation by the *Zeitgeist*. He fuses the Heraclitean "doctrine of motion"—a doctrine openly identified with "the entire modern theory of 'development'" (p. 19)—with the Parmenidean "doctrine of rest" or "the immutable"—a doctrine likened to the "revelation" of Judaeo-Christian faith (p. 38). To effect his synthesis of these rival doctrines, Pater's Plato avails himself of a third philosophical system, the Pythagorean "doctrine of number," which finds its visible counterpart in the Dorian worship of the Spartans. Plato thus manages to fuse matter and idea into a harmonious whole, into a "true Hellenism" which perceives and embodies in the operations of the visible world a symbol of the unseen. His genius consists in the magnitude of his combination, in the successful merging of his "*visual* power" with his yearning for the absolute: "for him, all gifts of sense and intelligence converge in one supreme faculty of theoretic vision, Θεωρία, the imaginative reason" (pp. 142, 140).[25]

[25] Pater's use of Plato as a fountainhead bears comparison to F. D. Maurice's more factual treatment of the philosopher in his *Moral and Metaphysical Philosophy: Ancient Philosophy* (London

But Plato's fusion cannot be imitated. It is a monument of the past, whose value is primarily antiquarian. Pater's "speculative young man" can at best hope to recover some of the elements that went into the construction of an "environment" long since invalidated by the historical flux. Pater's own meticulous rebuilding of this lost "environment," piece by piece, is conducted with an eye toward the present: the reconstructed ruins contain the material for a new foundation. This foundation is provided by a "positive" Platonic tradition which Pater emphatically distinguishes from that usually associated with Aristotle, the Schoolmen, Spinoza, Hegel, and all "those mystic aspirants to 'vision,' " the "so-called Neo-Platonists of all ages, from Proclus to Schelling" (p. 193). Pater thus must detach his own "independent" Platonism from its undesirable connections with Plato's "Theory of Ideas"; he must provide his "speculative young man" with a humanist creed separable from the abstractionist doctrines of religion and philosophy.

If, in Pater's pre-Christian, all-Hellenic system, Plato is regarded as a sort of pagan St. Paul, the repository of the doctrines of his predecessors, an Ur-visionary who holds out the promise of "the City of the Perfect, *The Republic*, Καλλίπολις, *Uranopolis*, *Utopia*, *Civitas Dei*, *The Kingdom*

---

and Glasgow, 1854). Both writers see Plato as a reconciler who kept "men's judgments in a perpetual equilibrium" (Maurice, p. 244); both regard the Dialogues as the initiation of "a habit of entire interminable scepticism" (Maurice, p. 244), of "scepticism, in a recognisable philosophic tradition" (*Plato and Platonism*, p. 194); both hold that this skepticism eventually splintered the Platonic fusion into Epicurean and Stoic halves. To Maurice, a Hebraist, this fragmentation is irrelevant: his book opens with a section on the "Hebrew Historical Books" and ends with a treatment of St. John, "A Jew the Reconciler of the Old and New." To Pater, a Hellenist, the fragments are all.

of Heaven" conveniently rolled into one (p. 266), it is
Socrates, Plato's teacher, who corresponds to Arnold's conception of Jesus. Pater's Socrates embodies a "peculiar religiousness" and a sense of "mission" which originate in, but
transcend, Parmenides' more sterile search for the "One,"
just as, in the scheme of *Literature and Dogma*, the "sweet
reasonableness" of Jesus arises from, but transcends the
Hebraic belief in a "power not ourselves." But while Arnold
is forced to dismiss the theological import of Christ's crucifixion and resurrection because of the discrepancies within
the Gospels, Pater can fully exploit the "historic" significance
of Socrates' self-immolation for an ideal of truth. Pointing
to the detailed account of Socrates' death given in the *Apology* and the *Phaedo*, Pater can emphasize the "purely human" aspects of the philosopher's last hours and can disclaim
any similarity to the "one sacred scene to which they have
sometimes been compared" (p. 78).[26]

Pater's Socrates has a dual effect on his disciple. On the
negative side, his "philosophy of the unseen" (p. 126) stirs
up Plato's "religious soul" and stimulates the "mystic intel-
lectualism" of the later neo-Platonists (p. 85). On the positive side, however, his relativism, his ironic profession of
ignorance, endow Plato with a means of balance: the dialectic. The philosopher's death, like that of Marius the Epicurean, is therefore not to be regarded as an act of religious
martyrdom. Though accused of fabricating a "new deity"
and though teaching Plato, "the sensuous lover," to become
a "lover of the invisible," Socrates, unlike Jesus, brings no
"religion new-given," no promise of divine redemption
through his sacrifice. Indeed, it is only Plato's acute "impress

---

[26] Pater was undoubtedly thinking of J. S. Mill's famous comparison of the trial of the "man named Socrates" to that of "the
man" executed on Calvary in the second chapter of *On Liberty*.

of visible reality" (p. 129), his Paterian responsiveness to his own senses, which allows him to transcend the "somewhat sad-coloured school of Socrates" by blending "the material and the spiritual" (pp. 127, 135). Like Marius, Socrates dies as a victim of the relativity of knowledge. In Pater's scheme of things, it is he who brings "philosophy down from heaven to earth" (p. 81) by teaching Plato (and modern man) that he was to remain "a mere seeker after wisdom he might never attain" (p. 99). It is his earthly skepticism and not his love of the invisible which initiates the "independent" Platonism sought by Pater.

To Pater, Socrates is the initiator of the "dialogue of the mind with itself" (p. 183), which he, like Arnold, regards as an essential requirement for the formulation of modern thought. The Socratic dialectic of Plato's Dialogues is of particular value to the thinker who can believe in neither the "metaphysical reassertions" of religion or philosophy, nor in that "sort of certainty which is afforded by empirical science" (p. 194). Abstractions, "even under the direction of Plato," are as faulty as "the promise of 'ontological' science": neither can fully satisfy Pater's presumptive reader, "the speculative young man of our own time." It is here, then, that "that other sort of Platonism" comes into play (p. 195). Pater's "young man" must learn to question the assertions of both science and metaphysics. Like Marius the Epicurean, he must somehow convert this doubt into a personal creed fit for "an age which thirsts for intellectual security, but cannot make up its mind. *Que scais-je?* it cries, in the words of Montaigne; but in the spirit also of the Platonic Socrates, with whom such dubitation had been nothing less than a religious duty or service" (p. 195).

Grim as this exhortation is, Pater does not conclude *Plato and Platonism* with a cult of doubt. The Socratic dialectic merely yields the "temper" for a faith, and to Pater any such faith must be predicated on the visible and the tangible. Unlike *Marius*, where Pater directs his protagonist to the "atmosphere" of a lost primitive church, and unlike *Gaston de Latour*, where he conducts his hero to the pantheism of Giordano Bruno, the "speculative young man" of *Plato and Platonism* must look at the surroundings of the nineteenth century. He must feed on sensations approved and tested by the past. Thus, Pater directs his reader to still another component of Plato's "environment," the "poetic religious system" of the Lacedaemonians, and to its surviving counterparts in the Victorian age (p. 226).

According to Pater, "the Lacedaemonians were the hereditary and privileged guardians" of that "catholic or general centre of Greek religion" which concerned itself with the worship of Apollo, but "of Apollo in a peculiar development of his deity":

In the dramatic business of Lacedaemon, centering in these almost liturgical dances, there was little comic acting. The fondness of the slaves for buffoonery and loud laughter, was to their master, who had no taste for the like, a reassuring note of his superiority. He therefore indulged them in it on occasion, and you might fancy that the religion of a people so strenuous, ever so full of their dignity, must have been a religion of gloom. It was otherwise. The Lacedaemonians, like those monastic persons of whom they so often remind one, as a matter of fact however surprising, were a very cheerful people; and the religion of which they had so much, deeply imbued everywhere with an optimism as of hopeful youth, encouraged that disposition, was above all a religion of sanity. The observant Platonic visitor might have taken note that something of that purgation of religious thought and sentiment, of its expression in literature, recommended in Plato's *Republic*, had been already quietly effected here, towards the establishment of a kind of cheerful daylight in men's tempers. [pp. 226-227]

Pater's monastic Spartans are thus able to impose a moral discipline on the worship of natural forces embodied by Apollo. Their very worship of the god is based on a respect for his "mental powers," and not on an exaltation of the "physical forces of production, which he also mystically represents" (p. 227). Pater is careful to contrast the Spartan Apollonians to their Athenian counterparts. While the Spartans practice a "religion of sanity," their cousins indulge in "an orgiastic, an unintellectual, or even an immoral service" (pp. 227, 228).

According to Pater, the religion of sanity of the Lacedae-monians is intimately related to Plato's own desire to impose order on the Heraclitean world of the senses. With a canni-ness that almost seems Darwinian, Pater's Plato understands the extent to which men are dependent on their environment: "Men, children, are susceptible beings, in great measure conditioned by the mere look of their 'medium.' Like those insects, we might fancy, of which naturalists tell us, taking colour from the plants they lodge on, they will come to match with much servility the aspects of the world about them" (p. 272). Fully aware of man's mimetic nature, Plato realized the importance of art as a guide to the perception of the ideal. Yet an art based on nature was necessarily amoral, reproducing the Ionian world of flux and not the Dorian goals of harmony and order. Plato thus rejected an art knowing "no purpose but itself" (p. 275); imposing a "simplification of human nature" on the founders of his

Republic (p. 273), he demanded that the art of the City of the Perfect create "strictly moral effects" (p. 272). To Pater, "the somewhat visionary towers of Plato's *Republic* blend . . . with those of the *Civitas Dei*" of a Christianity he cannot accept (p. 243). But the concrete counterpart of Plato's theoretical fusion of aesthetics and ethics, the Apollonian festival of the "*Hyacinthia*" with its "harmonizing" of natural gaiety and sober mourning, still survives in the Christian celebration of All Souls' Day.

Thus, in the conclusion of *Plato and Platonism*, Pater's "young man," already armed with the skepticism of Socrates, is directed to the same "sacred liturgy" which once allowed the Lacedaemonians and the inhabitants of Plato's imaginary community to avoid a "vicious" tendency inherent in a life based only on the senses (p. 273). Having conducted the prospective convert to his "independent" Platonism on an imaginative excursion through time and space, Pater returns to his original point of departure. Symbolic analogues fade away and the present again comes into focus: Pater's "religion of sanity" is finally given a locality still available to the Victorian skeptic. Examining the disciplined art of the Middle Ages with a sympathy far greater than that shown in *The Renaissance*, twenty years before, Pater places the "saving Dorian soul" of his "true" Hellenism amidst the ritual mass of Christianity itself.

The great cathedrals of the Middle Ages still seem to Pater "a long way from the Parthenon," but he reasons that they are after all the evolutionary end-product of "the Platonic aesthetics" (p. 279). It is Lacedaemon and not Athens, the Doric rather than the Ionic ideal, moral artifice rather than unbridled sensationalism, which must be upheld:

Those Churches of the Middle Ages have, as we all feel, their loveliness, yet of a stern sort, which fascinates while perhaps it repels us. We may try hard to like as well or better architecture of a more or less different kind, but coming back to them again find that the secret of final success is theirs. The rigid logic of their charm controls our taste, as logic proper binds the intelligence: we would have something of that quality, if we might, for ourselves, in what we do or make; feel, under its influence, very diffident of our own loose, or gaudy, or literally insignificant, decorations. "Stay then," says the Platonist, too sanguine perhaps,—"Abide," he says to youth, "in these places, and the like of them, and mechanically, irresistibly, the soul of them will impregnate yours. . . ." [pp. 279-280]

This then is Pater's exhortation to "youth," to the young doubter who wanders throughout his essays and "imaginary portraits": allow yourself to come under the influence of the moral environment expressly created by ecclesiastical art and ritual; if in sympathy with its "soul," you may, like Marius, at least succumb to "its saving salt, even in ages of decadence" (p. 282). The Ruskinian bias of this exhortation is deliberately faint-hearted, coming as it does from a disillusioned sensationalist, yearning for a wider range of experience, but distrustful of the aestheticism of a Whistler or a Wilde.

Pater thus directs his prospective "Platonist" to the surviving rites of the Catholic Church, the only remnant of a lost "Hellenic lineage" (p. 282).[27] Again the tone is mildly apologetic: "The diamond, we are told, if it be a fine one, may gain in value by what is cut away. It was after such fashion that the manly youth of Lacedaemon had been cut and carved. Lenten or monastic colours, brown and black,

[27] The last two works published during Pater's lifetime were his studies of the "atmospheres" of the French cathedrals of Notre-Dame d'Amiens and Vézelay (1894).

white and grey, give their utmost value for the eye (so much is obvious) to the scarlet flower, the lighted candle, the cloth of gold" (p. 282). It is in these residual acts of faith, in a faint worship of religious form, that Pater's young man may hope to find "even in ages of decadence" some of the substance of Plato's fusion and thus to get "something of that irrepressible conscience of art, that spirit of control" prescribed in the *Republic*. But Plato's reconciliation itself remains out of reach. For his "vision," like that of the church, depends on a belief in the Immutable, invalidated for Pater by his own belief in the *Zeitgeist* or "relative" spirit.

In his important review of Mrs. Humphry Ward's *Robert Elsmere*,[28] Pater deplored the clergyman's abrupt decision to abandon institutional Christianity in order to found a church of his own. Supported by a relativism which made him quite willing to recognize Christianity as a perpetual "possibility," Pater professed surprise at the ease with which Elsmere's faith was shattered by his sudden confrontation with the historical Jesus of the "Higher Criticism." Pater's comments have been attacked as being both shallow and insincere in the light of his own pronounced agnosticism.[29] A reading of *Plato and Platonism*, however, will confirm that there is no reason to question his sincerity. In his review, reprinted in *Essays from "The Guardian,"* Pater declared Elsmere's unbelief to be as dogmatic and unbending as orthodox faith: "Had he possessed a perfectly philosophic or scientific temper he would have hesitated" (p. 67). *Plato and Platonism* is the last of Pater's own hesitant endeavors to provide such a "temper" for the "Elsmeres" of his own age. By asking these doubters to stay within the physical confines of a church offering at least an atmosphere based on the "positive image-

[28] *The Guardian*, March 28, 1888.
[29] Cf. Geoffrey Faber, *Jowett* (London, 1957), pp. 382-383.

ries of a faith, so richly beset with persons, things, historical incidents" (*Imaginary Portraits*, p. 98), Pater hoped to preserve a more flexible faith than Robert Elsmere's drab Socialist Christianity: "It is the infinite nature of Christ which had led to such diversities of genius in preaching as St. Francis, and Taylor, and Wesley" (*"The Guardian,"* p. 69).

In the final lines of *Plato and Platonism* Pater casts a longing look at the "Greek clay" safely stored in the British Museum as a still visible "correlative" of Plato's unattainable fusion (p. 283). Wearily, he prescribes "patience, 'infinite patience,' " (p. 284), for all those temperamentally unable to accept the philosopher's invisible world of ideas or the equivalent "promises" of Christianity (p. 264). The same air of fatigue and satiety which prevails in the conclusion of *Marius* permeates the end of Pater's last work, as his "speculative" young pupil, like the meditative Marius, is forced to seek shelter in a compound of ritual and skepticism. As Pater possibly realized, it is on his deliberate avoidance of metaphysics (and of its relation to ethics) that the framework of *Plato and Platonism* rests and ultimately falls. His "religion of sanity" is the product of a reduction. Pater's refusal to consider the validity of Plato's "vision," his adroit circumscription of the basis of Christian belief, and his nontheological line of inquiry give him the flexibility necessary to construct a creed approved and confirmed by the convolutions of the *Zeitgeist*. Yet, despite this imaginative enlistment of the "historic" method, Pater rebuilds only in order to eliminate and to exclude.

Pater's most "public" utterance is ultimately confounded by its very preciosity. *Plato and Platonism* remains above all an exercise in tasteful selection, that "faculty of choosing and rejecting" so vividly described in the essay on "Style" as the act of arriving at a preconceived unity of design (*Ap-*

preciations, p. 26). Forever dependent on the impressions of the individual seeker, Pater's "religion of sanity" is far more frail and exclusive than the humanist cults of his contemporaries. Ironically enough, the imposing historical façade of *Plato and Platonism* is erected, like that of *Marius the Epicurean*, to house the most intimate of all the personal cults of Victorian unbelief.

VI

The "Atmospheres" of
Marius the Epicurean

Three or four years ago I re-read Marius the Epicurean, *expecting to find I cared for it no longer, but it still seemed to me, as I think it seemed to us all, the only great prose in modern English, and yet I began to wonder if it, or the attitude of mind of which it was the noblest expression, had not caused the disaster of my friends. It taught us to walk upon a rope, tightly stretched through serene air, and we were left to keep our feet upon a swaying rope in a storm.*

—WILLIAM BUTLER YEATS

Marius the Epicurean: His Sensations and Ideas is Walter Pater's most extended "imaginary portrait." Its protagonist is the same "speculative young man" addressed in *Plato and Platonism*, the habitual seeker who recurs in Pater's shorter fiction, a character "more given to contemplation than to action,"[1] who, in his "impressibility" and "susceptibility" to influences, must yield to a succession of physical and intellectual "atmospheres" before he is able to renounce his philosophic quest and become sublimated by the refining power of death. But Pater's novel is far more than a drawn-out version of the awkward "Sebastian van Storck." Its integration of separate episodes into an all-encompassing mixture of decadence and renascence, and its incorporation of a much wider range of experience than that depicted in the shorter

[1] *Marius the Epicurean: His Sensations and Ideas*, 2 vols., Library Edition (London, 1910), chap. 2, p. 24. Subsequent references to this edition of Pater's works are given in the text.

stories, make *Marius*, next to *Plato and Platonism*, the most ambitious formulation of Pater's lifelong search for a religious creed.

Marius the Epicurean occupies a central position in the development of Pater's thought. Written as a reconsideration of the "principles" of *The Renaissance*, the novel tests out the assumptions underlying Pater's later stories and prepares the way for the "religion of sanity" of *Plato and Platonism*. Like all of these works, *Marius* displays the basic opposition of permanence to change, of rest to motion and flux. While *Plato and Platonism* goes back to the initial "environment" of Western philosophy, *Marius* turns to the "environment" which shaped the religion of the early Christians. Like *Plato and Platonism* or *The Renaissance*, Pater's novel reinterprets the "origins" of a crucial cycle of history in order to establish a possible link between seemingly incompatible opposites, "the religion of antiquity" and "the religion of Christ" (*Renaissance*, p. 33). The "portrait" of Marius therefore is designed to illuminate this link: it is intended to demonstrate the tangency between the young Roman's curiously "Hebraic" Hellenism and the "Hellenic" Hebraism of the early Christians, to stress the sameness of man's search for a first principle, and to trace the continuity of his formal expressions of worship. As in *Plato and Platonism*, where Pater is concerned with the recovery of an "independent" Platonic tradition opposed to the metaphysical Platonism later absorbed by Christianity, the emphasis in *Marius* is on an earlier, simpler, but "natural" Christian religion, a crystalline faith muddied only by the complexity of its later evolution: "The kingdom of Christ was to grow up in a somewhat false alienation from the light and beauty of the kingdom of nature, of the natural man, with a partly mistaken tradition concerning it, and an incapacity, as it might almost seem at times, for eventual reconciliation thereto" (*Marius*, ch. 17, p. 29).

Although Pater's novel is by no means free from the defects inherent in his mode of philosophico-historical fiction, it possesses a greater unity and coherence than the stories examined in the previous chapter. The very length of the work allows Pater to unfold the character of Marius with a greater regard for detail. Although the young Pagan still remains a blueprint of a character, a lifeless recipient of "sensations and ideas," his very lifelessness is justified by the given circumstances of his peculiar early upbringing. An understanding of the childhood "atmosphere" which molds the temperament of Marius is essential for an understanding of his weary end.[2] Equally important for the book's unity, however, is Pater's control of his story through the use of several cumulative metaphors: those of the way and the wayfarer, of the house and the city, of the fading flower, and of the face of death.[3] The image of the road is symbolic of Marius' quest for truth, for the security and "rest" he hopes to find in the shelter of the various "houses" he encounters on his pilgrimage, as well as in that "unseen Celestial City, Uranopolis, Callipolis, *Urbs Beata*" sought by his fellow-pilgrim, the Neo-Platonist Marcus Aurelius (ch. 17, p. 39). The images of the flower and of death, on the other hand, are employed as symbols of decay and mutability, of the perpetual "motion" of the Heraclitean flux that Marius, like Pater, believes in, but despairs of; they only accentuate

[2] See Billie Andrew Inman, "The Organic Structure of *Marius the Epicurean*," *Philological Quarterly*, XLI (April 1962), 475-491.

[3] See Jean Sudrann, "Victorian Compromise and Modern Revolution," *English Literary History*, XXVI (September 1959), 425-444. Although Miss Sudrann's evaluation of three of these metaphors and her interpretation differ considerably from my own emphasis and arrangement, her excellent analysis has greatly facilitated my own.

Marius' increasing need for a creed or temper which will prepare him for the finality of death and reconcile him to the existence of evil and suffering.

Marius the Epicurean is divided into four parts, roughly equivalent to four stages of the young man's spiritual evolution. Each part contains a set of "perspectives" deeply affecting his sensations and ideas. In each of these parts, death, the death of another being and ultimately the death of Marius himself, effects a break by bringing with it a rejection. Each of the four parts thus sets the tone for a distinctive "mental atmosphere," integrated into the total atmosphere of decay and rebirth which prevails in the novel. In each case this "atmosphere" is of a physical as well as of a numinous nature. In each case the impressions of an actual house (the villa of "White-Nights," the temple of Aesculapius, the Pisan academy of Marius' tutor, the palace of Aurelius, the "two curious houses" of Apuleius and Cecilia,[4] and the hut of the Christian peasants who minister to Marius) provide a form of religious or philosophic experience affecting also the "house" of Marius' "thoughts" (ch. 19, p. 63).

Viewed in a somewhat different manner, the novel is patterned by two sets of oppositions. It portrays the clash of the two philosophical systems whose development Pater was to trace in *Plato and Platonism*: a materialist view of life based on the Heraclitean flux (Epicureanism or the "New Cyrenaicism") and an idealist view based on incorporality (Cynicism or Roman Stoicism). Facing these two philosophical traditions are the two "natural" religions placed at the opening and the conclusion of the book: the old Greco-Roman cult of Numa which surrounds Marius' childhood, a religious stage not unlike the *"Aberglaube"* defined in

---

[4] "Two Curious Houses" is the joint title of chapters 20 and 21 of the novel.

Arnold's *Literature and Dogma,* and the new eclectic religion of the early Christians, itself a "generous" mixture of Gnostic, Jewish, and Pagan sources, which surrounds Marius' death. The materialistic systems encountered by Marius, as well as the idealistic systems of Cornelius Fronto, Aurelius, and Apuleius, have all a common denominator: Plato; while the worship of the early Christians turns out to be merely a higher development of the Greek religion Marius disdained as a child. The young Roman's life thus bridges two cycles of history. He belongs to a sophisticated paganism which would eventually have brought about a perfect fusion of Hellenism and Hebraism by assimilating the spirit of the Christians, were not its own culture inherently flawed and externally threatened by a barbarism ready to impress on Christianity an altogether different growth. For, according to Pater, "the gracious spirit of the primitive church" was not destined to reappear until the Renaissance, an era he had already examined in his previous book: "As if in anticipation of the sixteenth century, the church was becoming 'humanistic,' in an earlier, and unimpeachable *Renaissance*" (ch. 22, pp. 118, 125).[5]

In *Marius,* as in all of his "imaginary portraits," Pater's choice of environment carries with it a wealth of spatial inferences for his own age: "That age and our own have much in common—many difficulties and hopes. Let the reader pardon me if here and there I seem to be passing from Marius to his modern representatives—from Rome, to Paris or London" (ch. 16, p. 14). The dilemma of Marius, his split of allegiances "between that old, ancestral Roman religion, now becomes so incredible to him and the

[5] Cf., in this connection, Pater's explanatory footnote to his "Conclusion" in the third edition of *The Renaissance,* quoted in Chapter V, section 1.

honest action of his own untroubled, unassisted intelligence"
(ch. 8, p. 125), becomes, by extension, the dilemma faced
by the "honest" Victorian doubter forced to reject not only
the verities of orthodox religion but also the pantheism of the
Romantics. For, despite his allegiance to a materialistic
philosophy, Marius is subject to visionary spells in which the
"purely material world, that close, impassable prison-wall"
seems to be "the unreal thing, to be actually dissolving away
all around him" (ch. 19, p. 70.)

Just as the aesthete-philosopher of *Plato and Platonism*
must realize that the idealism of a Coleridge or Spinoza has
been invalidated by the *Zeitgeist*, so must Marius renounce
the transcendence offered to him by Aurelius, "the imperial
wayfarer, he had been able to go along with so far on his
intellectual pilgrimage" (ch. 19, p. 64). Even though
Marius' brief moments of vision are less abstracted than the
Emperor's grandiose reveries, they do accentuate his failure
to endow his own idealism with a distinctly human object and
shape. Thus, Marius' dreamy absorption of the "mysterious
and visionary" landscape on his way to Rome is given an
entirely new meaning by the "personal presence" of the
Christian Cornelius; his sudden awareness of an incorporeal
"person beside him," later in the novel, merely prepares him
for his experience in the church in the house of Cecilia,
where the serene faces of the worshippers confirm his earlier
intuition through "an actual picture." The faces of human
beings again animate Marius' last vision: they blend with the
carved image of Christ, and provide the feverish Pagan with
the final, hazy, but gratifying, sense of "a living person at
his side" on his journey to death (ch. 28, p. 218).

Marius can no more recover the Platonic fusion of Heraclitean flux and Parmenidean rest than can his successors in
the *Imaginary Portraits* or the modern speculative young

man of *Plato and Platonism.* The "theoretic vision" of Plato is irretrievable. Only death and ritual can escape the flux: death by providing relief; ritual by satisfying the Paterian hunger for "a spiritual verity in things that may be seen." To Marius, as to Daniel Deronda, "vision" merely amounts to "the *being* something" (ch. 28, p. 218); but while Deronda at least recovers his father's heritage by an act of providence and will, the fatherless Marius passively partakes of the "mystic bread" of the Christians in "the moments of his extreme helplessness" (ch. 28, p. 224). Unlike Deronda, he cannot translate his fragmented perception of an Ideal into a program of action: "Revelation, vision, the discovery of a vision, the *seeing* of a perfect humanity, in a perfect world— through all his alternations of mind, by some dominant instinct, determined by the original necessities of his own nature and character, he had always set that above the *having*, or even the *doing*, of anything" (ch. 28, p. 218).

1. THE PILGRIMAGE OF MARIUS

a. *Four Materialist Systems*

If the course and conclusion of Marius' pilgrimage are "determined by the original necessities of his own nature," these "necessities" are in turn determined by the imprint left on his psyche by the northern country house of "White-Nights." Living with his widowed mother in a world of dead usages and "antique traditions," Marius is the last survivor of an "ancient family." Marius' morbidity, his acute awareness of disease, suffering, and death, impressed upon him by "the material abode" of "White-Nights," as well as his deep "sense of conscious powers external to ourselves," cannot find an expression in the old religion of Numa. Neither the domestic observances maintained by his father as "a matter of family pride" nor the gay and simple faith of the rustics who worship Ceres and Bacchus appeal to his "great seriousness" and "instinct of devotion" (ch. 1, pp. 5, 6, 5). Marius' seriousness and devotion thus take the form of a "speculative activity" which does not satisfy the emotional needs of his heart. Although his intellect demands the clarity of "definite history and dogmatic interpretation" which the anthropomorphic religion derived from the Greeks cannot provide, his feelings are molded by the atmosphere of awe and repression which surrounds him: he is awed by the thought of his dead father, "awed by his mother's sorrow," awed by the severity of a home which has become converted into a mausoleum dedicated to memory and regrets.

This initial "atmosphere," rural, yet somehow depressingly funereal, endows Marius' character with the fixity it is to maintain throughout the novel. Despite his assimilation of subsequent atmospheres, despite the succession of "houses" he is to haunt in his search for "cities" heavenly and earthly, "White-Nights" has stamped his character indelibly. From the villa Marius derives a dreamy sense of isolation, the "cloistral or monastic" temperament which later attracts him to the lonely Aurelius and to the single-minded Christian "Knight" Cornelius. His unworldliness ultimately causes him to shrink away from an attachment to Cecilia, the Christian widow he idealizes into a symbol of maternity; yet it also prevents him from succumbing to a reduction or perversion of his dedication to truth: "It kept him serious and dignified amid the Epicurean speculations which in after years much engrossed him, and when he had learned to think of all religions as indifferent, serious amid many fopperies and through many languid days, and made him anticipate all his life long as a thing towards which he must carefully train himself, some great occasion of self-devotion, such as really came . . ." (ch. 2, p. 18). "White-Nights" thus endows Marius with more than a sense of detachment. The villa and its rural surroundings also impress on him the sympathy which will culminate in that "great occasion of self-devotion" which, in the book's central irony, makes a Christian saint out of a pagan skeptic.

Marius the Epicurean: His Sensations and Ideas depicts, among other things, how the feelings implanted by childhood "sensations" can oppose the reasonable "ideas" of maturity. Hence, it is "White-Nights" which provides Marius with the "heart" that, in Pater's scheme, as in that of George Eliot's *Middlemarch*, asserts itself above the systems of the mind: "One important principle, of fruit afterwards in his Roman life, that relish for the country fixed deeply in him; in the winters especially, when the sufferings of the animal world became so palpable even to the least observant. It fixed in him a sympathy for all creatures, for the almost human troubles and sicknesses of the flocks, for instance. It was a feeling which had in it something of religious veneration for life as such—for that mysterious essence which man is powerless to create in even the feeblest degree" (ch. 2, pp. 21-22). It is this feeling of commiseration and helplessness which, allied to his recognition of evil, eventually causes Marius to turn away from the philosophies which permit or ignore the "manly amusement" of the Roman arena and attracts him instead to the mixture of sympathy and joy contained in the faith of the early Christians.[6] Indeed, even the sight of a writhing serpent arouses in the boy a "moral feeling" that is to be reawakened in his later life as a compound of pity and loathing for a being "far gone in corruption" (ch. 2, p. 24).[7]

---

[6] "Manly Amusement" is the title of chapter 14 of the novel.

[7] The symbol of the snake recurs throughout the novel as an

Fresh from "White-Nights," Marius encounters four systems based on the Heraclitean flux or "doctrine of motion." All four of these systems (the Aesculapian religion of bodily health, the hedonistic "Euphuism" of his friend Flavian, the philosophies of Heraclitus, Epicurus, and Lucretius, and, finally, the "New Cyrenaicism" adopted by Marius) are of a materialist nature. Pater's careful discrimination between these forms of epicureanism is designed as an obvious elaboration of the views he had maintained in the suppressed "Conclusion" of *The Renaissance.* Pater wants to emphasize to the young men he might have led astray by his "Conclusion" that a belief in the exclusive validity of the senses need not degenerate into an "orgiastic" sensationalism. Just as in *Plato and Platonism* he was to distinguish between the irresponsible hedonism of the Athenians and the graver "religion of sanity" of the Lacedaemonians, so does he, in *Marius,* emphasize the distinction between the capricious absorption of momentary pleasures and the controlled, contemplative search for gratification as the true end of life.

Marius' contact with the brotherhood of the *Asclepiadae,* a monastic society worshipping the healer-son of Apollo as the "son of God," is brief. Although from the vantage point

---

emblem of worldly depravity: Marius shrinks from the "agreeable sense" of the religion of Aesculapius at the thought that the god with the caduceus might appear as a "sallow-hued" snake (ch. 3, pp. 30-31); his Pisan hedonism is marred by "an African showman exhibiting a great serpent" (chap. 2, p. 23); in Rome, a second "showman with his serpents" reminds the young philosopher that beauty must coexist with "what was repugnant to the eye" (chap. 2, p. 24). Marius' own unworldliness becomes evident when he unconsciously converts Apuleius' racy story of Cupid and Psyche into a parable in which the lustful god becomes not the "evil serpent-thing" or "deadly serpent" he has been rumored to be, but a symbol of ideal love (chap. 5, pp. 64, 73).

of his later learning Marius eventually will come to recognize in the brotherhood's teachings the "old Greek temperance" of Plato's *Charmides* and the "love of visible beauty" of the *Phaedrus*, he is too naïve to understand the Neo-Platonic vision announced by its priests, "some vision, as of a new city coming down 'like a bride out of heaven'" (ch. 3, p. 32). Like some of the young readers of Pater's "Conclusion," Marius lacks the philosophical training necessary to understand the implications of a creed which merely appeals to his sense of physical beauty and his desire for bodily sanity. His mistaken cult of the body is soon undermined as he returns home, "brown with health," only to discover the "health of his mother failing" (ch. 3, p. 41). Her death, which instills new fears and regrets in Marius, terminates his first, short change of air, and, correspondingly, marks an important change in his character.[8] It alienates the adolescent from the "sensations" of "White-Nights" and leads him to pour his emotionalism into the pursuit of a wider range of speculative "ideas": "It would hardly have been possible to feel more seriously than did Marius in those grave years of his early life. But the death of his mother turned seriousness of feeling into a matter of the intelligence: it made him a questioner. . . . There were days when he could suspect, though it was a suspicion he was careful at first to put from him, that that early, much cherished religion of the villa might come to count with him as but one form of poetic beauty, or of the ideal, in things; as but one voice, in a world where there were many voices it would be a moral weakness not to listen to" (ch. 4, pp. 43-44). Accordingly, for the rest of the novel, Marius listens to the "voices" of past and present. His first formal instruction comes in the environment

[8] "Change of Air" is the title of chapter 3 of the novel.

provided by his tutor's Pisan lyceum, "one of many imitations of Plato's Academy" (ch. 4, p. 46).

Pisa, possessed of "the urbanities, the graceful follies, of a bathing-place," is in direct contrast to "that gray monastic tranquillity" of Marius' earlier days at the villa (ch. 4, p. 47). There, the boy had spent his days in "an imaginative exaltation of the past"; now, the modernity of "the present" promises an "entire liberty of heart and brain," a freedom which Pater describes ominously as appealing to Marius' "appetite for experience, for adventure, whether physical or of the spirit" (ch. 4, p. 48). The spokesman for this new atmosphere is Marius' older colleague, Flavian, "the brilliant youth who loved dress, and dainty food, and flowers" (ch. 4, p. 51). Flavian introduces Marius to two writers whom the young patrician is to meet much later in the novel under wholly different circumstances and in a wholly different light: "one Lucian" and Apuleius, the celebrated author of "the 'golden' book of that day," the *Metamorphoses*, or *The Golden Ass*.

Flavian reads the book as a manifesto for his own aestheticism, the Roman "Euphuism" which leads him to demand a more intense and poetic way of life, not unlike that which Pater had himself demanded in his "Conclusion." Marius, however, approaches Apuleius in an altogether different spirit. He singles out the satirist's tale of "Cupid and Psyche," strips it of its mockery, and converts it into an "allegory" of a "gentle idealism" by reading into it "far more than was really there for any other reader" (ch. 6, p. 94): "So the famous story composed itself in the memory of Marius, with an expression changed in some ways from the original and on the whole graver. The petulant, boyish Cupid of Apuleius was become more like that 'Lord, of terrible aspect,' who

stood at Dante's bedside and wept, or had at least grown
to the manly earnestness of the *Erôs* of Praxiteles. Set in relief
amid the coarser matter of the book, this episode of Cupid
and Psyche served to combine many lines of meditation,
already familiar to Marius, into the ideal of a perfect imaginative love, centered upon a type of beauty entirely flawless
and clean—an ideal which never wholly faded from his
thoughts, though he valued it at various times in different
degrees" (ch. 6, p. 92). Marius' apparent misreading of the
tale (rendered in chapter 5 of the novel) is significant. For
not only does it set the stage for his encounter with Apuleius,
near the very end of his intellectual pilgrimage, but it also
marks his impending rejection of Flavian's "Euphuism."⁹

Flavian has no difficulty in reading the "Golden Book"
as a satire on the gods. Perennially excited by the experiences
he cultivates, he regards the old mythology as a mere vehicle
for sensations which are still "untried" and "unexpressed."
But his hedonism proves to be even more vulnerable to
mutability and death than the more temperate cult of the
Asclepiadae. Infected with a pestilence brought by the Emperor's returning armies, the young man lies "amid the rich-
scented flowers" he loves, "rare Paestum roses, and the like"
(ch. 7, p. 112). Flavian tries to ignore his imminent death
by dictating a vernal hymn to Marius, in an ironic touch
which further stresses his inability to reconcile matter to
form. But Pater implies that a unity, unavailable to the
fatally diseased aesthete, will one day supervene. For Flavian's

---

⁹ Two articles on Pater's adaptation of the tale of "Cupid and
Psyche," Paul Turner's "Pater and Apuleius," *Victorian Studies*, III
(March 1960), 290-296, and Eugene J. Brzenk's "Pater and
Apuleius," *Comparative Literature*, X (Winter 1958), 55-60, skirt
the thematic function of Pater's alterations of his Latin original.
This function is discussed by the present writer in *VS*, IV (June
1961), 411-412.

verse carries "something of the rhyming cadence, the sono-
rous organ-music of the medieval Latin" (ch. 7, p. 114).
And Marius himself, soothed by this rhythm, foresees "a
wholly undreamed-of and renewed condition of human body
and soul: as if he saw the heavy yet decrepit old Roman
architecture about him, rebuilding on an intrinsically better
pattern" (ch. 7, p. 114). But Marius' prescience cannot
mitigate the actual suffering of his friend, who dies in pain
amidst an opulent pagan environment. Flavian's cremation
on a funeral pyre only confirms Marius' gloomy unbelief:
"The little marble chest" among "the faded flowers" signifies
for him "nothing less than the soul's extinction" (ch. 8, p.
123).

As a direct consequence of Flavian's death, Marius moves
to a higher form of materialist philosophy. Discovering that
both his artistic and intellectual faculties are satisfied by "the
severer reasoning" of Epicureanism, he turns to a system
providing "the actually aesthetic charm of a cold austerity
of mind" (ch. 8, p. 124). His choice is not without its
penalty. For the "heart" of Marius, we are told, remains
encased "there in the urn with the material ashes of Flavian":
"It was to the sentiment of the body, and the affections it
defined—the flesh, of whose force and colour that wandering
Platonic soul was but so frail a residue or abstract—he must
cling. The various pathetic traits of the beloved, suffering,
perished body of Flavian, so deeply pondered, had made him
a materialist, but with something of the temper of a devotee"
(ch. 8, pp. 125). Thus, at the age of eighteen, Marius lays
aside his poetry and examines the works of Lucretius, Epicurus, and "the teacher of both, Heraclitus of Ionia." From
Heraclitus, Marius learns the " 'doctrine of motion' " (ch.
8, p. 131), as well as the relativism of Socrates and the

Sophists, "a philosophy of the despair of knowledge" (ch. 8, p. 132).

Marius cannot fully accept the "bold mental flight" of his new master. He cannot pass "from the fleeting, competing objects of experience to that one universal life" and detect unity in multiplicity (ch. 8, p. 132). He consequently regards the doctrines of Heraclitus after the fashion in which Pater regards the evolutionist systems of his own times: "as hypothesis only—the hypothesis he actually preferred, as in itself most credible, however scantily realisable even by the imagination—yet still as but one unverified hypothesis, among many others, concerning the first principle of things" (ch. 8, p. 132). Heraclitus offers Marius a vision of the perpetual flux, "of that constant motion of things—the drift of flowers, of little or great souls, of ambitious systems, in the stream around him" (ch. 8, p. 132). It is this panorama that confirms the young seeker in his decision to rely on the certainty of his own impressions and that draws him to still "another wayfarer on the "journey" to truth, Aristippus of Cyrene, "a genuine disciple of Socrates" (ch. 8, pp. 134, 136).

The teachings of Aristippus go beyond the "hypothesis" of Heraclitus, although they are based on the Ionian's vision of a world dominated by flux. Just as, in Pater's own time, the "higher" utilitarianism of J. S. Mill involved an amplification of the Benthamite ethics, so does the "New Cyrenaicism," which Marius now embraces, retain, but amplify, the hedonic emphasis of earlier materialist philosophers. Almost anti-philosophical in its preference for "practical ethics" over "theoretic interests," the "healthfully sensuous wisdom" of the Cyrenaics is an outright repudiation of any undisciplined sensationalism such as Flavian's: "Not pleasure, but a general completeness of life, was the practical ideal to which this anti-metaphysical metaphysic really pointed" (ch. 8, p. 142).

Somewhat too stridently, Pater assures his readers that this "complete" life is based on "various yet select sensations" and proceeds to defend his protagonist from the "charge of 'hedonism' " by asserting that "the blood, the heart, of Marius were still pure" (ch. 9, p. 150).

Marius' "New Cyrenaicism" represents the fuller "thoughts" Pater spoke of in the restored "Conclusion" to the third edition of *The Renaissance*. By endowing the aestheticism he had advanced in his earlier book with a respectable philosophic tradition and by distinguishing this philosophy from its lesser counterparts, he no longer could be accused of wantonly "misleading" his younger contemporaries. But *Marius the Epicurean* is more than a self-vindication. The "New Cyrenaicism" adopted by Marius is but one roadmark along his pilgrimage. Ironically enough, the attributes which Pater ascribes to Marius' materialist philosophy—"energy, variety, and choice of experience including noble pain and sorrow even"—will be shared by the idealist philosophy of Marcus Aurelius. And, even more ironically, Marius will find solace neither in his own Epicureanism nor in the Stoicism of his Emperor, but in the soothing ritual of a Christianity he cannot believe in.

2. The Pilgrimage of Marius

b. Four Idealistic Systems

Traveling along the Cassian Way through the "heart of the old, mysterious and visionary country of Etruria," Marius undertakes a new lap in his pilgrimage. In Rome, through a counterpoint of visible "atmospheres" and overheard speeches, the young thinker will come in contact with four idealistic systems: the Stoicism of Marcus Aurelius, the humanism of Cornelius Fronto, the pantheism of Apuleius, and the Christian services he observes in the house of Cecilia. But an incident which occurs on the road to Rome sharply affects Marius' "sensations" and prefigures his evaluation of the "ideas" of the systems he will later encounter. Startled by a near-accident which revives "his old vague fear of evil," Marius suddenly feels reassured when a new traveler, the "knight" Cornelius, joins him for the remainder of their journey. Having surrendered himself earlier as "a willing subject . . . to the impressions of the road" (ch. 10, p. 160), the "sentimental Marius" now feels that the fleeting landscape seems "to have been waiting for the passage of this figure to interpret or inform it" (ch. 10, p. 169). The "heart" of Marius revives: "as in his early days with Flavian, a vivid personal presence broke through the dreamy idealism, which had almost come to doubt of other men's reality" (ch. 10, p. 169). Unaware that his new friend is a Christian, Marius attributes his animating powers (which almost recall those of the dead Hallam in Tennyson's "In Memoriam") to the mixture of "severity" and "blitheness" he irradiates. But Marius is still incapable of penetrating and, far less, of sharing the hopefulness of the Christian warrior for whose sake he will eventually die.

On arriving at the capital, the two travelers discover "that Rome was become the romantic home of the wildest superstition" and "religious mania" (ch. 11, p. 180). A multitude of contradictory creeds, deities, and worships, all condescendingly tolerated by the philosophic Emperor, have created a religious eclecticism similar to that reigning in Pater's own time ("that age and ours have much in common—many difficulties and hopes"). To Marius' surprise, his new acquaintance, a veritable embodiment of the "diaphaneitè" that Pater had celebrated in his first essay, quietly sings to himself without paying homage to any "image or sanctuary." Cornelius takes his leave from the puzzled Pagan and rides away, secure in his gleaming armor and with "the staff of a silken standard firm in his hand." Yet Pater points out, with the hindsight of history, that the young Christian's confident monotheism is not at all unrelated to the profusion of Roman gods: "If the comparison may be reverently made, there was something here of the method by which the catholic church has added the *cultus* of the saints to its worship of the one Divine Being" (ch. 11, p. 182).

Before his first true contact with Christianity can take place, however, Marius must examine the philosophy of the Emperor whose preferment he seeks. Aurelius' first speech, a melancholy sermon addressed to a "city of tombs," is in direct opposition to Marius' creed that the end of life is life itself. Like a medieval "hermit," Marcus Aurelius upholds "rest" above the "motion" of life by mocking "the corpse which had made so much of itself in life." As he speaks, oblivious of his audience, eagles drive smaller birds across the sky and "the winter roses from Carthage" are more "lustrously yellow and red" than ever (ch. 12, p. 211). But the Emperor ignores these omens of mutability. Reversing the creed of Marius, he opposes "the seen to the unseen, as falsehood to truth": "Marius could but contrast all that with his own Cyrenaic eagerness, just then, to taste and see and touch; reflecting on the opposite issues deducible from the same text. 'The world, within me and without, flows away like a river,' he had said; 'therefore let me make the most of what is here and now.'—'The world and the thinker .upon it, are consumed like a flame,' said Aurelius, 'therefore will I turn away my eyes from vanity: renounce: withdraw myself alike from all affections' " (ch. 12, p. 201).

Marcus Aurelius, " 'a master in Israel' " whose personal letters have something in common "with the old Judaic unction of friendship" (ch. 13, p. 226), represents the Parmenidean Hebraism of *Plato and Platonism*. Pater's portrayal of Aurelius as a Roman equivalent of the Savonarola that George Eliot had depicted rather unsympathetically in *Romola* must have startled those humanists who, after the manner of Matthew Arnold, regarded the Emperor's Stoic philosophy as a model for their own blends of "righteousness," "sweetness," and reason.[10] In a celebrated passage in the second chapter of *On Liberty*, J. S. Mill had called Aurelius a better Christian in all but the dogmatic sense of the word, who had, nonetheless, sinned against the relativism of truth by assuming his opinions to be infallible. By exaggerating the "Hebraistic" qualities of Aurelius' beliefs, Pater went a step beyond Mill. To him, not only Aurelius but also those Victorian agnostics who regarded the Emperor as a model for their own creeds are guilty of an assumption of infallibility. Pater implies that any attempt to mold human nature after a purely abstracted pattern is bound to end in failure. Stoicism can at best yield a temper suited to a few; it cannot be codified into a coherent system applicable to all men, unmindful of their heredity and environment. Thus, even the dreamy Marius, whose "habitual reserve of manner" resembles that of his Emperor and who is as deeply moved by the "profound religiousness" of the ruler's palace as by the atmosphere of "White-Nights," will be unable to adopt the Emperor's idealistic philosophy.

[10] Matthew Arnold, "Marcus Aurelius," *Essays in Criticism* (New York, 1883), pp. 364, 373; to Arnold, Aurelius rivals the historical Jesus as "perhaps the most beautiful figure in history" (p. 354). In "The Genesis of *Marius the Epicurean*," *CL*, XIV (Summer 1962), 242-260, Prof. Louise M. Rosenblatt not only disproves the notion that Pater's novel was primarily stimulated by Arnold's essay, but also demonstrates very convincingly that the book's chief source was Arnold's French mentor, Ernest Renan.

Pater probes skillfully into the weaknesses inherent in Aurelius' doctrines, and, by extension, also undermines those Victorian creeds which preached "renunciation" and the annulment of all passion. The same dispassionateness which allows Aurelius to regulate his own life also removes him from the life around him. In one of the rare instances of physical characterization in his fiction, Pater juxtaposes the ascetic physiognomy of the philosopher-king to the animalistic features of Lucius Verus, his imperial associate; he likewise contrasts the Emperor's glacial asceticism to the licentiousness of Faustina, his adulterous Empress, who is observed by Marius as she warms her hands over a fire, while her son, rumored by some to have been fathered by a murdered gladiator, plucks "a rose to pieces over the hearth" (ch. 13, p. 218). Unaffected by these discordant ties, Aurelius persists in his arbitrary "determination that the world should be to him simply what the higher reason preferred to conceive it" (ch. 13, p. 219). The impotence of his "sanguine and optimist philosophy" becomes apparent later on. The death of Lucius Verus prompts Aurelius to assert his arrogant belief in "the sanctity of kings" and reveals his aspirations toward godliness and personal salvation. The death of an infant son breaks down the Emperor's philosophic detachment and eventually leads to Marius' final rejection of his Stoic faith.

For the time being, however, Marius is moved to reconsider his initial antagonism to the "ascetic pride which lurks under all Platonism" (ch. 12, p. 200). The influence of "White-Nights," which had at one time made Marius "a kind of 'idealist,'" again comes to the fore. For Marius' Cyrenaicism is only skin-deep. Observing that the ruler's "intellectual loneliness" is mitigated by his "affectionate and helpful contact with other wayfarers, very unlike himself,"

Marius gradually comes to appreciate Aurelius' concept of charity: "From the great Stoic idea, that we are all fellow-citizens of one city, he had derived a tenderer, a more equitable estimate than was common among Stoics, of the eternal shortcomings of men and women" (ch. 13, p. 219). Marius, whose sympathy for others harks back to the days at "White-Nights," is attracted to this creed of toleration. Soon, however, he realizes that something is wanted to convert intellectual tolerance into active charity.

At the "manly amusement" of the Roman amphitheatre, Marius watches Marcus Aurelius sitting impassive and indifferent through a spectacle of unnecessary suffering and cruelty. Frankly horrified, Marius is indignant at the pagan religion which relishes "the dexterously contrived escape of the young from their mother's torn bosoms" as a homage to Diana, the "special protectress of new-born creatures" (ch. 14, p. 238). The carnage is designed to celebrate the nuptials of Lucius Verus and "troops of white-shirted boys," who cover the "great red patches" with sand, are showered with "a rain of flowers and perfume" by the "good-natured audience." Earlier in the day, Marius had been fortified by the sight of Cornelius, whose array he regards as an enigmatic armor or vesture, a "sign or symbol" emblematic of "some other thing far beyond it" (ch. 14, p. 233). The charm of Cornelius reminds Marius of his earlier attachment to Flavian, but he is painfully aware that the young hedonist would have observed the sports of the arena with a "light heart."

Now "feeling isolated in the great slaughter-house," Marius once again watches the Emperor (ch. 14, p. 240). Though he will make one more effort to accommodate his views to those of Aurelius, he cannot repress his present contempt for the Emperor's indifference to evil and suffering:

"There was something in a tolerance such as this, in the bare fact that he could sit patiently through a scene like this, which seemed to Marius to mark Aurelius as his inferior now and for ever on the question of *righteousness*; to set them on opposite sides, in some great conflict, of which that difference was but a single presentment. . . . Yes! what was needed was the *heart* that would make it impossible to witness all this; and the future would be with the forces that could beget a heart like that" (ch. 14, pp. 241-242; italics added).

The second part of *Marius* ends with this recognition of the necessity for a faith of the heart.[11] Fronto's "Religion of Humanity" at first seems to fulfill the expectations of Marius, whose "conscience" is still "vibrating painfully under the shock of that scene in the amphitheatre, and full of the ethical charm of Cornelius," as he listens eagerly to the words of the Stoic professor (ch. 15, p. 6). Fronto tries to reconcile the "old morality" with Aurelius' system. He emphasizes above all the ethical duties to be adopted by the inhabitants of the latter's ideal commonwealth. Fired by the rhetorician's eloquence, Marius looks around him to find a visible correlative for Fronto's words. He sees nothing: "Humanity, a universal order, the great polity, its aristocracy of elect spirits, the mastery of their example over their successors—these were the ideas, stimulating enough in their way, by association with which the Stoic professor had attempted to elevate, to unite under a single principle, men's moral efforts, himself lifted up with so genuine an enthusiasm. But where might Marius search for all this, as more than an

[11] Placed at the end of part two, Marius' recognition carries a greater stress in the original two-volume edition of *Marius the Epicurean* than is apparent in a single-volume text such as that issued by The Modern Library.

intellectual abstraction? Where were those elect souls in whom the claim of Humanity became so amiable, winning, persuasive . . ." (ch. 15, pp. 11-12)? The answer is as damning to Fronto's "Religion of Humanity" as it is to its Victorian counterparts. For, turning away from the rhetorician, Marius looks at the motion outside the walls and detects the Christian Cornelius riding by in a military procession. The cheerful "knight" is adorned with wreaths of olive, symbols no more of mutability, but of an indestructible and visible hopefulness which Fronto's address to the "very finest flower" of Roman society cannot purvey.

Marius now re-examines his Cyrenaicism, "anxious to try the lastingness of his own Epicurean rose-garden" (ch. 17, p. 14). The result is a revival of the more instinctive need for a poetic worship such as that he had rejected in the religion of Numa. Once again spurred on by the face of death—this time by that of Lucius Verus, whom Aurelius wants to canonize in deference to his purely personal feelings—Marius decides to test the Emperor's vision one more time. But he is again repelled by Aurelius' intellectuality, his "coldness of heart" (ch. 18, p. 41). A growing sense of dissidence only confirms the impressions of the arena. Finally, as he sees "weakness and defeat" cloud the philosopher's acceptance of the death of an infant son, Marius pronounces Stoicism to be as flawed as the Cyrenaicism he has rejected. Aurelius' "heart," it would seem, is after all at odds with his system. And so, only the "diaphanous" Cornelius remains as a symbol, more spirit than man, as a sanction for that "reverent delight" produced for Marius by "the visible body of man" (ch. 18, p. 53).

It is at this point that Marius has a vision of his own. In the country outside Rome, a setting not unlike that of "White-Nights," Marius tries to organize "the house of his thoughts." After a good rest and a dream of a fair city, he awakes refreshed as in "one of those old joyful wakings of childhood, now becoming rarer and rarer with him" (ch. 19, p. 62). Reflecting on the "imperial wayfarer" with whose company he has parted, he reviews his own life-pilgrimage. Sitting down in an olive garden, Marius thinks of mutability and afterlife, and weighs the possibility that the will might itself be "an organ of knowledge, of vision." Suddenly, he becomes convinced that "some other companion, an unfailing companion" must have stood beside Flavian, Cornelius, and himself. For once, the physical atmosphere surrounding Marius seems to confirm his intuition: "It was as if there were not one only, but two wayfarers, side by side, visible there across the plain, as he indulged his fancy. A bird came and sang among the wattled hedge-roses: an animal feeding crept nearer: the child who kept it was gazing quietly: and the scene and the hours still conspiring, he passed from that mere fantasy of a self not himself, beside him in his coming and going, to those divinations of a living and companionable spirit at work in all things" (ch. 19, pp. 67-68).

It is thus that Marius perceives, not with the absolute certainty of the mystic nor through the abstract logic of the philosopher, a divinity "of which he had become aware from time to time in his old philosophic readings—in Plato and others, last but not least in Aurelius" (ch. 19, p. 68). Although Marius' sensations and ideas never again fall "precisely into focus as on that day," he has been able to identify his tentative "divinations" with that "reasonable Ideal to which the Old Testament gives the name of *Creator*" (ch. 19, pp. 71, 68). He now realizes that the remainder of his life must be devoted to a search for a human correlative of this Ideal, an "equivalent" among "so-called actual things." The fourth part of *Marius the Epicurean* places this "equivalent" amidst the ritual of early Christianity.[12]

3. THE CHRISTIAN DEATH OF A PAGAN

Before Marius can come in contact with the youthful religion of the church in the house of Cecilia, he finds a strange reverberation of "his own early boyish hero-worship" when he attends a banquet for Apuleius (ch. 20, p. 76). This scene is deemed by Pater to be important enough to be linked with the meeting in the Cecilian villa by the dual chapter heading of "Two Curious Houses." The chapter in which Marius meets Apuleius is headed by the inscription, "Your old men shall dream dreams." The chapter depicting his contact with the Christians completes the epigraph: "Your old men shall dream dreams, and your young men shall see visions." To Marius' great surprise, his former idealization of the satirist's fable, long since deplored by him as a mistake, turns out to be correct after all: "For a moment his [Apuleius'] fantastic foppishness and his pretensions to ideal vision seemed to fall into some intelligible congruity with each other. . . . Apuleius was a Platonist: only, for him, the *Ideas* of Plato were no creatures of logical abstraction, but in very truth informing souls, in every type and variety of sensible things" (ch. 20, pp. 86-87). Apuleius' pantheism, correctly "misread" by the adolescent Marius before his initiation into philosophy, stresses the circularity of any pil-

[12] The "self not himself" now accepted by Marius resembles the "not ourselves" defined in *Literature and Dogma*; however, there is a key difference in the manner in which this "power" is perceived. To Pater, any faith must be intellectually visible—a faith of form. To Arnold, religion may be attained through a critical perusal of the "best that has been thought and said." *Marius the Epicurean* refutes such a contention. Absorbing the very best of pagan and Christian culture, Marius still dies a skeptic.

grimage of the mind. What is more it establishes an actual link between the spent "dreams" of pagan philosophy and the unsophisticated, but fresh and vital, "vision" of the young Christian religion, which, as Marius now perceives, is a genuine religion of the "heart."

Pater emphasizes the youthfulness of the Christian spirit. In the hopeful singing of children Marius perceives the rhythm of the best of pagan culture, the "poetic sound" of Flavian's doomed verses. The joyousness of the young religion, its "expression not altogether of mirth, yet of some wonderful sort of happiness," attracts the melancholic Pagan and allows him to recall again the old Greco-Roman religion of nature which surrounded his own childhood at "White-Nights" (ch. 21, p. 96). This joyousness stamps both—the receding worship of the rural deities of old and the rising reverence for a "Good Shepherd" who cares for his flock—as anthropomorphic "religions of sanity," such as that which Pater was to celebrate in *Plato and Platonism*. To Marius, Christianity provides the visible symbols he had missed in the systems of Fronto or Aurelius. The congregated choir-boys, who are so utterly unlike the "white-shirted boys" of the blood-stained arena, embody for him "the virginal beauty of the mother and her children" (ch. 21, p. 106). The adoration of the Holy Family is prompted by an "instinct of family life" that is highly meaningful to the orphan of "White-Nights" (ch. 21, p. 98).

The early Roman church thus satisfies that "which all hearts had desired," including Marius' own (ch. 22, p. 115). It is a "religion of cheerfulness" in which the divinity of Christ merely represents "the final consummation of that bold and brilliant hopefulness in man's nature, which had sustained him so far through his immense labours, his immense sorrows, and of which pagan gaiety in the handling of life, is but a minor achievement" (ch. 22, pp. 114, 115). But, like the paganism before it, Christianity is to be distorted by the *Zeitgeist*, the shadow of events to come. The gracious spirit of the primitive church is but a "beautiful, brief, chapter of ecclesiastical history" (p. 120), which will give way to "the exclusiveness, the puritanism, the ascetic gloom" of a church driven by misunderstanding and oppression "inwards upon herself" in a "world of tasteless controversy" (ch. 22, p. 118).

How then is the spirit of this church, the spirit of Hellenism even, to survive through the convolutions of history? Pater's answer is given in the chapter entitled "Divine Service." There, the house that Marius has sought for so long is finally located in the "environment" of a ritualistic church.[13] Just as in *Plato and Platonism* Pater's young doubter is left only with the moral atmosphere of the cathedrals of the past to perpetuate an adaptable faith, so in the novel, ritual, the visible form of faith, is depicted as the only principle capable of self-renovation. Significantly enough, the service attended by Marius celebrates the Nativity: the "anniversary of his birth as a little child." To Marius the Eucharistic celebration brings with it a vision as sharp as that perceived by him in the olive garden: "It was the image of a young man giving up voluntarily, one by one, for the greatest of ends, the greatest gifts; actually parting with himself, above all, with the serenity, the divine serenity, of his own soul; yet from the midst of his desolation crying out upon the greatness of his success, as if foreseeing this very worship" (ch. 23, pp. 138-139).

The image of the suffering Christ is impressed upon the

[13] The chapter bears the epigraph: "Wisdom hath builded herself a house: she hath mingled her wine: she hath also prepared for herself a table."

sensationalist Marius only through the reality of the ritual before him, "the suggestions of that mysterious old Jewish psalmody, so new to him" (ch. 23, p. 138). Like Daniel Deronda at the synagogue in Frankfort, Marius can connect this psalmody with an experience which is ageless. The sacrifice of the young man it speaks of is as visible to him as it will be to Saint Lewis of France in a later age, "across the dimness of many centuries," for it reminds him also of "the most natural and enduringly significant of old pagan sacrifices" (ch. 23, p. 136). Ritual, by virtue of its evolutionary nature, is the only permanent worship of the "heart": "As if in anticipation of the sixteenth century, the church was becoming 'humanistic,' in an earlier, and unimpeachable *Renaissance*. Singing there had been in abundance from the first; though often it dared only be 'of the heart.' And it burst forth, when it might, into the beginnings of a true ecclesiastical music; the Jewish psalter, inherited from the synagogue, turning now, gradually, from Greek into Latin—broken Latin, into Italian, as the ritual use of the rich, fresh, expressive vernacular superseded the earlier authorised language of the Church" (ch. 22, p. 125). Religious ritual, then, embodies the "music" or "harmony" praised in *Plato and Platonism* and defies the brittleness of the philosophic doctrines and religious dogmas tested by Marius. Unlike these, it accommodates itself to the laws of change: "Ritual, in fact, like all other elements of religion, must grow and cannot be made—grow by the same law of development which prevails everywhere else, in the moral as in the physical world" (ch. 22, p. 126).

It is through his observation of the Christian rites that Marius can now emulate the symbolic sacrifice they have made meaningful to him. For the young Pagan has reached the end of his pilgrimage. Along the "Queen of Ways," an

Appian Road studded with sepulchres, Marius and "the famous writer Lucian" stop a young Epicurean, Hermotimus, "still at the beginning of . . . [his] journey." It is "the time of *roses*" and many a funeral procession passes by with its floral offerings (ch. 24, p. 142). In the ensuing "conversation not imaginary,"[14] Lucian employs his wry Socratic irony to demolish young Hermotimus' belief that his predetermined path will conduct him to absolute truth. Resorting to the metaphors of the "way" and of the "city," Lucian points out caustically that Stoics, Epicureans, or Platonists are all the same weary "wayfarers from afar": "*There is but one road that leads to Corinth*" (ch. 24, p. 154). It is impossible for the true philosopher, he argues, to finish the journey with the preconceived ideas held at the beginning of it. No one philosophy holds the exclusive road—the presumptive disciple of any one system may as well choose his affiliation by asking a little child to draw the name of the philosopher to be followed throughout life. Lucian departs, the disillusioned disciple goes "on his way," and Marius, having met a personification of the "relative" spirit defined in *Plato and Platonism*, is left alone, reading the "sepulchral inscriptions" along the road, painfully aware of a misspent life. But as he travels back to the city, the "atmosphere" of the Appian Way impresses upon him the full import of a "certain Christian legend he had heard," built around "an image, almost ghastly in the traces of its great sorrows— bearing along for ever, on bleeding feet, the instrument of its punishment" (ch. 24, p. 171). For the first time, Marius discovers "some new meaning in that terror of isolation" brought about by mutability and death.

Now fully aware that his philosophical speculations have

[14] "A Conversation Not Imaginary" is the title of chapter 24 of the novel.

been in vain, Marius is left only with the feelings engendered by "White-Nights." He has fashioned a sentimental creed of his own by worshipping the "permanent and general power of compassion—humanity's standing force of self-pity" (ch. 25, p. 182). It is this creed of sympathy which leads to Marius' end. Returning to "White-Nights," Marius is appalled by the decaying funerary urns of his ancestors. He decides to bury them all, no longer afraid of the finality of death. At this precise point, the mysterious Cornelius, "then, as it happened, on a journey and travelling near the place," reappears (ch. 28, p. 209). Traveling together back to Rome, Marius and Cornelius join a group of Christians praying at the tomb of their martyr, Hyacinthus, "hardly less terrified and overwrought by the haunting sickness about them than their pagan neighbours" (ch. 28, p. 211). For, an ominous "menace in the dark masses of hill," like that sensed by Marius on his first trip to Rome, oppresses the superstitious people of the town. Suddenly, an earthquake rolls the hills "like a sea in motion." The pagan majority seizes the Christians, and with them, Marius and Cornelius. Pretending that he, and not Cornelius, is the Christian among the two, Marius secures his friend's release and takes his place. But when he dies, it is not as "hero" or "heroic martyr," but as the victim of a sudden disease. Cared for by a solicitous group of Christian peasants, Marius is given "in the moments of his extreme helplessness their mystic bread" and dies in their hut, a presumed martyr to their cause (ch. 28, p. 224).

The irony of Marius' passive absorption of this final "atmosphere" informs the novel's entire meaning. Despite its sympathetic treatment of an apostolic Christianity, *Marius the Epicurean* cannot be read as a reasoned plea for an all-encompassing faith.[15] Dying "amid the memory of certain touching actual words and images," Marius can at best experience a hopeful satisfaction. The philosophies he has examined have produced a state of "candid discontent," a "receptivity of soul" which has left "the house ready for the possible guest" and "the tablet of the mind white and smooth, for whatsoever divine fingers might choose to write there" (ch. 28, p. 220). But Christianity is but another of the "many voices it would be a moral weakness not to listen to" (ch. 4, p. 44); it is "a plea, a perpetual after-thought, which humanity henceforth would ever possess in reserve, against any wholly mechanical and disheartening theory of itself" (ch. 28, p. 221). Therefore it is Pater's insistence on the relativity of all such "theories," and not the momentary glimpse of the crucified Jesus perceived by the dying Marius, which prevails most strongly in the novel. The book's intricate system of juxtaposition and analogy is designed to obviate the exclusiveness of any one religion. Its final effect is derived, not from its structured ascent to Christianity, but from the blunting oppositions and realignments which make Christianity a strong possibility, but a possibility only.

In Pater's relativist scheme of things, there can be no ultimate stage for apprehending truth, a platitude brought home by Lucian's "conversation not imaginary." Every system examined by Marius is "interpreted" with such a burst of enthusiasm that Marius or the reader believes each time that the ultimate level of "vision" has been reached. But each vision is superseded by the next, and the totality of Pater's reconstructed "atmospheres" merely demonstrates

[15] For an entirely different reading of the novel, see Bernard Duffey, "The Religion of Pater's *Marius*," *Texas Studies of Literature and Language*, II (Spring 1960), 103-114.

that no one is exclusive. The Socratic dialectic of Lucian proves, if anything, that no single way leads to the "Heavenly City" so fervently desired by Marius. But if Christianity does not afford the "way," it can at least endow Marius with the "spirit" with which he approaches the death he has feared for so long. This spirit is nondoctrinal. For Marius is impressed by the "visible" only: the serene beauty of Cornelius' faith, the faces of the boys who sing a mysterious Jewish psalmody, the symbol of the Eucharist. The value of a "humanistic" Christianity capable of reassuring the unbeliever lies in its powers of perpetuation, its adaptability to the flux which makes all things relative. Above all, the religion of form of the early Christians provides continuity. For continuity, the adaptation to change and death, is the novel's main theme. *Marius the Epicurean* illustrates primarily the similarities between presumably antagonistic ways of life: between the materialism of Epicurus and the idealism of Aurelius, between the satirical Apuleius of Flavian's "Euphuism" and the idealistic Apuleius concocted by Marius, between the anthropomorphic religion of Numa and the ritualistic religion of Christ, all illustrations of the dictum that "opposite issues" are "deducible from the same text" (ch. 12, p. 201). The central illustration of this text is the Christian death of a pagan by an almost accidental act of will.

The pilgrimage of the "constitutionally impressible" Marius is in many ways defective. As a fictional creation, the passive young Epicurean who exposes himself to every "sensation" and "idea" available to him, belies his avowed desire to attain a "constantly renewed mobility of character" (ch. 8, p. 139). Barely able to recover the "heart" he already possessed as an adolescent, Marius is utterly paralyzed by the systems he examines. Even his "New Cyrenaicism," presumably attuned with the "soul of motion" of Heraclitus, is as immobile as the abstractionism it opposes: " 'Not what I do, but what I am . . . is what were indeed pleasing to the gods!' " (ch. 9, p. 154) Although this passivity is meant to characterize a deliberate defect in Marius' mental make-up, it robs the conclusion of the novel of its mildly "positive" effect. Marius' sacrifice is far less convincing as an active exercise of the "heart" than either Dorothea Brooke's vindication of Tertius Lydgate or Daniel Deronda's adoption of his people's cause. Marius' act of sympathy relies excessively on the credibility of the Christian knight, so "visibly" real to the young philosopher, but not to the reader. Nor does Pater's belated attempt to provide Marius with a plausible motivation at all strengthen the book's conclusion. Marius' death remains a convenient escape; it parodies, rather than re-enacts, the myth of the self-sacrificing God common to the religions of Christ and Apollo.

Consequently, *Marius the Epicurean* is far more impressive in its negations than in its celebration of the "heart." Pater's description of Christianity's hold on Marius is almost in the nature of an apology: "To understand the influence upon him of what follows the reader must remember that it was an experience which came amid a deep sense of vacuity in life" (ch. 23, p. 128). Though pleading against "any wholly mechanical and disheartening theory" of life, Pater is at his best when he depicts the "disheartening" convolutions of the historical flux. The "religion" he proposes in *Plato and Platonism* is built from the ruins of the Christianity whose birth is depicted in *Marius*; this Christianity is in turn dependent on the residues of a pagan and Hebrew past.[16] To this world of mutability, the melancholy Marius

[16] The most notable difference between the "religions" of *Marius* and *Plato and Platonism* is the greater importance which Pater

can only oppose his "own solitary self-pity" (ch. 25, p. 184). He must convert the symbols he perceives through his senses into a sentimental faith based on "the mere clinging of human creatures to each other" (ch. 25, p. 184), a faith far more subjective than the stoical "religions of humanity" that he has rejected. In Pater's passive religion of the senses, man is forced to reconstruct God in his own image. Marius can at best "dare" to hope that "a heart, even as ours" exists behind the disheartening world he faces (ch. 25, p. 185).

Marius' intellectual pilgrimage is a thinly veiled autobiography which reveals, sometimes too painfully, the most intimate obsessions of its author. Primarily, however, it reflects the plight of an artistic temperament unable to reconcile the physical world of the senses with the ideal world of morality and religion.[17] A Hellenist by temperament, Walter Pater rejected the Heracliteanism of *The Renaissance* by yielding halfway to the morality of his time. For George Eliot, a Hebraist, there had been less of a conflict; for her, the visions of Dorothea Brooke and Daniel Deronda correspond to

---

gives to *askesis* in the later work. In *Marius*, the Hebraic "ideal of asceticism" is regarded as the inferior counterpart of the "ideal of culture" presumably pursued by the early church (chap. 22, p. 121). In *Plato and Platonism*, this same asceticism is credited for creating temperate and "disciplined" atmospheres of worship.

[17] Contemporary reviewers of *Marius* were dissatisfied with the book's resolution. Mrs. Humphry Ward deplored Pater's identification of Christianity with a vague "atmosphere of feeling and sensation" and contrasted Pater's evasive conclusion to the "nobler" counsel of Arthur Clough ("Marius the Epicurean," *Macmillan's Magazine*, LII, June 1885, 132ff.). The anonymous reviewer in *The Atheneum*, though sympathetic, pointed out that a reconciliation between pagan philosophy and Christian faith would have been clearly impossible "even if death had not intervened" (*The Atheneum*, No. 2992, February 28, 1885, pp. 271-273).

the "will" of a traditional past. Pater would also like to regard the "Will as Vision." But he exhausts himself and his creation by questioning, at the very threshold of vision, whether the way of vision is after all the one to be followed: "Our pilgrimage is meant indeed to end in nothing less than the *vision* of what we seek. But can we ever be quite sure that we are really come to that? By what sign or test?" (*Plato and Platonism*, p. 192) Thus Marius' pilgrimage ends with an exaltation of the same feelings with which he began his journey. Marius is confounded by the variety of "signs" and "tests" with which he is confronted. He is defeated by the multiplicity of ways open to him, by the discordance between the many wayfarers to whose guidance he yields. His one act of "will" allows him to die as a pagan, but a pagan drained of his lifeblood, glorying in his passive superiority to his Emperor on "the question of righteousness." Even more than Daniel Deronda, Marius hovers insecurely between two antagonistic worlds which he can span only through his death.

It was another novelist and Pater's contemporary, Samuel Butler, who was to provide the span that Pater had hoped for, by declaring that in the world of matter, "will" and "vision" were one and the same. Like Pater, Butler resorted to a fictionalized autobiography. Like Pater, he played the systems of philosophy and religion against each other with destructive irony. But unlike Pater, Butler filled the vacuum created by his relativism with the inverted Utopia of his imagination. He dismissed creatures such as Marius for being hybrids and not the "sane" and normal animals they ought to be; he laughed away the whole question of "righteousness"; and, through satire and paradox, declared that the way of the flesh was the only way to salvation.

VII

Samuel Butler:
The Search for a Religious Crossing

*It is common to hear men wonder what new faith will
be adopted by mankind if disbelief in the Christian
religion should become general. They seem to expect
that some new theological or quasi-theological system
will arise, which, mutatis mutandis, shall be Christianity
over again. . . . . But how can people set up a new superstition, knowing it to be a superstition?*

—Samuel Butler

*Creative Evolution is already a religion, and is indeed
now unmistakably the religion of the twentieth century,
newly arisen from the ashes of pseudo-Christianity, of
mere scepticism, and of the soulless affirmations and
blind negations of the Mechanists and Neo-Darwinists.*

—George Bernard Shaw

In 1873 Miss Eliza Mary Ann Savage prodded Samuel
Butler into reading *Middlemarch*. In a letter to her friend,
she made sure to ridicule George Eliot in order to suggest
that she held his powers to be far superior to those of the
famous novelist. Miss Savage's purpose was quite explicit:
"The moral is this:—That I want a novel—ever so many
novels—and that I have come to look upon you as an
admirable novel-making machine and that you ought to be
set going."[1] As always, Miss Savage's tone was carefully
chosen; as always, her intentions were both shrewd and
benevolent. She had just read a portion of the manuscript

---

[1] Henry Festing Jones, *Samuel Butler, Author of Erewhon: A
Memoir in Two Volumes* (London, 1919), I, 174.

of *The Fair Haven*. Already responsible to a large extent for the moderate success of *Erewhon* (1872), Miss Savage was now trying to steer Butler away from the practice of disguising his self-questioning with a barrage of perversely argued, highly complex, but utterly ambivalent disputations ascribed to Erewhonian professors or imaginary Bible critics. Instead, it was the ingenuity that had gone into the creation of these figures that she wanted to stimulate. For Miss Savage recognized Butler's genius; she saw that only as a novelist could he hope to channel his brilliant but unruly dialectic into consistency and control. What is more, she realized that an "ideological" type of fiction, such as George Eliot's, would allow Butler to deal with the same issues he had treated in *Erewhon* or *The Fair Haven*, that it would provide him with a safer and more open mode of criticism, and that, if successful, it would endow him with what he wanted the most, recognition and money.

Still, Miss Savage had to proceed cautiously if she was to be successful in "setting" her friend to go in the direction she wanted. She would have to convince him that she was by no means suggesting the heresy that he write like "George Eliot and make a lot of money by it."[2] She would have to pretend that her sole aim was to expose to Butler how laughably easy it was to write a mediocre novel of the kind acclaimed by the Victorian reading public. Her scheme was partially successful. Butler read *Middlemarch*, predictably pronounced it to be "bad and not interesting," and was moved to write a "better" novel of his own, *The Way of All Flesh*.[3] But his interest soon began to flag. Even Miss

[2] *The Note-Books of Samuel Butler*, Shrewsbury Edition of the Works of Samuel Butler (London and New York, 1923-1926), p. 159. All subsequent references to this edition of Butler's works are given in the text.

[3] Jones, p. 184.

Savage's loyal assurance, years later, that George Eliot's *Theophrastus Such* contained a "most barefaced crib" from *Erewhon* failed to evoke the desired response.[4] For, by then, Butler had found a new adversary, Darwin, and had proceeded to transform his Erewhonian equivocations into the construction of an actual creed.

From 1873 to 1887, Butler worked only intermittently on his novel. His main attention was riveted on the fabrication and consolidation of the creed he had first propounded in *Life and Habit* (1877). Through a succession of "scientific" treatises, he began to joust against the Darwinians with increasing self-assurance. Far from becoming the first of the many public novels Miss Savage had hoped for, *The Way of All Flesh* became a private exercise, written and rewritten to test out Butler's theories about heredity, theories which were themselves an attempt to free himself from his personal doubts. By 1887, *The Way of All Flesh* lay stowed away in a drawer, never to be reworked. Butler's father had died the previous winter, Miss Savage two years before. *Luck or Cunning?* (1886-1887), the feeblest of Butler's anti-Darwinian tracts, had exhausted his desire for polemical engagements over the subject of evolution, and his mind was now full of *Narcissus*, the Handelian cantata he was composing with Henry Festing Jones.

When, in the same year, the wife of his former art instructor asked Butler to enter a new arena of controversy by making a pronouncement on the "sexual question," he replied evasively: "At present I have the religious world bitterly hostile; the scientific and literary world are even more hostile than the religious; if to this hostility I am to add that of the respectable world, I may as well shut up shop at once for all the use I shall be to myself or anyone

[4] Jones, p. 310.

else. Let me get a real strong position like that of Ruskin, Carlyle, or even Matthew Arnold, and I may be relied upon to give the public to the full as much as they will endure without rebellion; but I will not jeopardise what I believe to be a fair chance of future usefulness by trying to do more than I can."[5] Suddenly unwilling to offend the "respectable" world, Butler was readying himself for a life of "future usefulness." But ahead were only his Odyssey theories, his Italian travelogues, his dogged justification of Shakespeare's sonnets, and a sentimentalized biography of the same grandfather who had been so acidly satirized in *The Way of All Flesh*.

From 1887 on, Butler's watchword resembled the aging Swift's "vive la bagatelle." The man who had tilted against the orthodox dogmas of Christianity and then against the scientific theory of an evolutionary world without design, now singled out for combat the windmills provided by classicists, Shakespeare scholars, and the imaginary detractors of Dr. Butler's memory. Presumably also for "future usefulness," Butler spent his later years in editing his literary "remains" by rearranging the samples of his earlier wit and by writing out lengthy afterthoughts as postscripts to the letters he had accumulated over the years. Only one work of this later period, *Erewhon Revisited* (1901), displays the talent Miss Savage had hoped to enlist. But, mellowed and subdued in tone, itself in the nature of an afterthought, Butler's last burlesque almost pleads for the illusion which its author, "a true lover of consistency," had attacked all his life long.[6]

[5] Jones, II, 49-50.
[6] "A true lover of consistency, it was intolerable to him to say one thing with his lips and another with his actions" ("Memoir of the late John Pickard Owen," *The Fair Haven*, p. 47).

In the rush of attention which followed the posthumous publication of the *Note-Books* and his neglected novel, Butler was hailed as a "modern" iconoclast who dared to clear his era of "English Victorian rubbish."[7] Later critics, recovering from the hero worship of the Edwardians, soon reversed this judgment. Butler now became "not so much the Anti-Victorian, as the Ultimate Victorian,"[8] a *fin-de-siècle* coward who, lacking the arrogance of a Wilde, found refuge in the neurosis of his Erewhonian daydreams. Neither of these evaluations is wholly correct. But they crystallize the difficulties involved in an objective appraisal of Butler's career. Butler does not belong to Mr. Holloway's elite of Victorian "sages"; he is not one of Professor Willey's "honest doubters."[9] Yet the man who aggrandized himself, as Shaw did after him, into "the *enfant terrible* of literature and science" (*Note-Books*, p. 182), also yearned for "a real strong position like that of Ruskin, Carlyle, or even Matthew Arnold." Butler told himself that established society had forced him into "the Ishmaelitish line which I have been led and driven to take in literature," and reasoned that a visit to the annual dinner held at Shrewsbury, the institution he had satirized as "Roughborough" in his novel, was therefore to be avoided as a dangerous clash with "the enemy's camp"; yet he proudly claimed never to have "missed a single one of these functions since writing the above" and eventually donated

[7] Abel Chevalley, *The Modern English Novel*, trans. Ben Ray Redman (New York, 1925), p. 104; traces of this approach are still evident in Clara Gruening Stillman's *Samuel Butler: A Mid-Victorian Modern* (New York, 1932).

[8] Malcolm Muggeridge, *The Earnest Atheist: A Study of Samuel Butler* (New York, 1937), p. xi.

[9] Professor Willey has more than repaired this omission by supervising P. N. Furbank's excellent *Samuel Butler (1835-1902)* (Cambridge, 1948) and by his own *Darwin and Butler: Two Versions of Evolution* (London, 1960).

the manuscript of *The Life and Letters of Dr. Samuel Butler, Head-Master of Shrewsbury School* to his alma mater.[10] Butler's life, as Kingsley Amis puts it so well, came "to be built on saying one thing, meaning another, and doing a third."[11]

Butler failed to see that *Middlemarch* embodied, through symbol and indirection, many of the ideas later arrived at in his closely argued books. But this in itself was not the cause of his denunciation of the novel as a "long-winded piece of studied brag, clever enough I daresay, but to me at any rate singularly unattractive."[12] What made George Eliot, Matthew Arnold, John Morley, and all the other Victorian reconcilers so objectionable to Butler was their "middle way," their settlement for a "double truth" he deemed impossible. As a "lover of consistency," he could not hold contradictions in equilibrium by saying with George Eliot and Dr. Johnson that two opposing beliefs could at the same time both be true. Compromise was unthinkable. Thus, he seized on paradox itself and gave it his unqualified assent. To the multiple discrepancies offered by actuality, he added his own. He inverted, transposed, and transmuted, until obsessed by paradox, he made it the very basis of his ontology.

The Victorians believed in public solutions and public airings of their private dilemmas. Butler, too, ascribed a collective significance to his personal doubts. What is more, he needed controversy and paradox in order to produce, and to him the greatest paradox remained that of the Christian society which he accused of having stunted his development and which he identified with his parents and with his grand-father. In *The Fair Haven*, a work published in the same

[10] Jones, II, 39.
[11] "Afterword," *Erewhon* (New York, 1961), p. 239.
[12] Jones, I, 184.

year as Arnold's *Literature and Dogma*, Butler groped, like
Arnold, for a solution of the discrepancies between the
Gospels. Like the son of Rugby's master, the grandson of
the master of Shrewsbury brought wit and irony to the
"Higher Criticism" his forebears had so gravely ignored.
But his ironies remained tentative and private. Butler hid
behind the mask of John Pickard Owen, the book's fictitious
author. He portrayed Owen's father as an exact reverse of
Canon Butler, and then proceeded to sing a hosanna to
parental love and to the love of God the Father. He disguised
his scriptural criticism so elaborately that the book was
generally misread as a defense of orthodoxy.

Although more popular than *The Fair Haven*, *Erewhon*
suffers from a similar obscurantism. Like *Middlemarch* itself
(the first part of which was published only four months
before *Erewhon*), Butler's satire relies primarily on a negative criticism of church and society. But, whereas George
Eliot presents her ideals clearly through her adroit handling
of "the irony of events," Butler fails to sustain his point of
view. Through her ironic equipoise, George Eliot can mock
the self-righteousness of a Bulstrode and still be sympathetic
to the strict "Hebraism" of his wife; she can expose the flaws
inherent in Lydgate's separation of morality and biology,
and yet manage to convince the reader of his high-minded-
ness. Butler is incapable of such a balance, for his ideals are
not yet clear to himself. By depicting a nation in which
good health and ethics are equal and in which disease and
disability are regarded as crimes, he creates an extreme by
which he can satirize Victorian self-righteousness. Yet, at
the same time, he wants the reader to regard the physical
perfection of the Erewhonians as an actual ideal. Thus, the
verdict of the judge who condemns a prisoner for "the great
crime of labouring under pulmonary consumption" (*Ere-*

whon, ch. 11, p. 84) is enlisted, on the one hand, as a mock
parallel of the rigid moralism of Victorian justice, while,
on the other, it is entirely consonant with the "Hellenic"
ideal represented by Higgs's handsome captors, who perpetuate their racial purity through a Spartan process of natural
selection. The magistrate's role, already made ambivalent, is
further complicated by Butler's reproduction of his "axiom of
morality" that "luck is the only fit object of human veneration" (ch. 11, p. 81). For this belief in "luck," like the
judge's heartless decision to eliminate the sick, the weak,
and the malformed among the Erewhonians, is based on the
Darwinian concept of fortuitous selection, a concept which
Butler regards with great misgivings as the only serious
obstacle for his own hopeful belief in a power which can
bequeath strength, beauty, and wealth to those who are conscious of their weakness, ugliness, and financial dependence.

The remainder of this chapter retraces the steps by which
Samuel Butler eventually found this wishful belief, the vitalist
"religion" of the flesh he scrupulously tested out by converting an Ernest Pontifex enfeebled by the past into a bridge-
builder confident of the future. After testing his new-found
faith in his novel, Butler was able to lead a life of inconsistencies without further qualms. Buoyed by Miss Savage's
devotion and by the adoration of Jones, comforted by the
stolid loyalty of Alfred, his valet, he could tell himself that
he was a rarity among Victorians, a unique thinker unfettered
by a mediocre coterie, a prophet "who believes himself to
have practised what he preaches" (*Note-Books*, p. 156).
Butler thrived on this self-deception. It was the archparadox
by which he could transform insipid friends like Pauli, Jones,
Faesch, or Alfred into a circle of cognoscenti. It was the
difference which made it possible for him to condone his
own inconsistencies, allowing him to practice a "graceful"

alienation which mimicked the values of his Philistine family, and to preach bachelorhood and the separation of the child from the parent in the very face of his own theories about inherited identity and the unity of ancestor and offspring.

Butler needed this fictitiously secured independence. He nursed it even more than his perennial sense of neglect. Without these two elements, Canon Butler would never have become Theobald Pontifex, the public dethronement of Darwin would never have been dared, and the rejected miracle of the Resurrection would never have become metamorphosed into the credible phenomenon of inherited memory. Also without these two elements, Butler would have muffled himself into protective silence; his attempt to substitute evolutionism for Christianity would not have taken place; and his one great novel, so fervently encouraged by Miss Savage, would never have been written.

1. THE CREATION OF A FAITH (1859-1872)

Butler's alienation from his parents, his rejection of Christianity, and his gradual emergence as an evolutionary thinker are so intimately related to the composition of *The Way of All Flesh* that they must be considered in conjunction with each other.[13] Unlike other Victorian "Elsmeres," whose unbelief was prompted by the development theory, Butler had hardly come under the influence of the standard generators of doubt when he refused to become ordained upon his graduation from Cambridge in 1858. It was not until his journey to New Zealand in the fall of 1859 that he even

[13] Most studies of Butler do not fully deal with this interdependence. Writers who are interested in Butler's role of the renegade usually minimize the import of his evolutionary doctrines; those who examine Butler as a vitalist thinker are too quick in dismissing the role played by his loss of faith in the shaping of these doctrines.

read Gibbon's *The Decline and Fall of the Roman Empire,*
and not until well after his arrival that he secured a copy
of the recently published *Origin of Species,* written by his
father's schoolfellow. To the practical young sheep-farmer
at work in a new environment, Darwin's theories came as a
deliverance. They confirmed his break with the past, extri-
cated him from his sense of guilt, and sanctioned the literal-
istic bent which had led him to dismiss a supernaturalism he
could accept neither as truth nor as symbol. Butler found
that the *Origin* supported his own failure to follow the
ecclesiastical footsteps of his father and grandfather, and that
it provided him with a clear-cut and logical system which
would do away once and for all with inconsistencies of his
upbringing. It was only much later, and upon discovering
that it too was erratic, that Butler was faced with the task
of revising this substitute system as well.

Darwin's immediate assistance is exemplified by the curious
article, "Darwin on the Origin of Species: A Dialogue,"
which Butler published in December 1862 in the Christ-
church (New Zealand) *Press.*[14] Though professing to ex-
pound Darwin's ideas, Butler emphasized two points of extreme relevance to himself: first, the fact that though an
offspring resembles its parent, any slight variation which
could make the offspring better adapted would tend to im-
prove its line; second, the Lamarckian corollary (only briefly
noted by Darwin) that such a variation could be induced by
a change in climate or other environmental conditions. Although Butler was still willing to subordinate this corollary
to Darwin's emphasis on a random process of selection, it
eventually became the basis of his own "teleological evolutionism." In Ernest Pontifex, Butler was to illustrate the

[14] The dialogue is reprinted with *A First Year in Canterbury
Settlement* in the Shrewsbury edition of Butler's works.

variation of an offspring who improves on his heredity by deliberately altering the climate of his Christian upbringing.

If the *Origin* clearly supported Butler's contravention of family tradition, it also endowed him with the "scientific" frame of mind he now proclaimed to have gained through the "entire uprooting of all past habits."[15] In Butler's essay, the disputation between the evolutionist "F" and the orthodox Christian "C" is clearly enlisted to define the characteristics of a new "habit of mind."

> F. . . . whether the lawyer-like faculty of swearing both sides of a question and attaching the full value to both is acquired or natural in Darwin's case, you will admit that such a habit of mind is essential for any really valuable and scientific investigation.
>
> C. I admit it. Science is all head—she has no heart at all.
>
> F. You are right. But a man of science may be a man of other things besides science, and though he may have, and ought to have no heart during a scientific investigation, yet when he has come to a conclusion he may be hearty enough in support of it, and in his other capacities may be of as warm a temperament as even you can desire.
> [*Canterbury Settlement*, p. 189]

Butler's 1862 essay confirmed him in the role of "man of science" who must also be a "man of other things besides science." It impressed upon him the value (and the potential fun) of "swearing both sides of a question," and thus led him to employ the dramatic self-division that was to become a hallmark of his writings. Butler is represented by "C," the Christian conservative, almost as much as he is by "F,"

---

[15] Jones, I, 96.

the radical evolutionist. Pronouncing Darwin's hypothesis to be "very horrid," "C" points out that it denies the fall of man and consequently invalidates any hope for redemption (p. 193). But "F" minimizes "C"'s (and Butler's) fear of future inconsistencies: "I believe in Christianity, and I believe in Darwin. The two appear irreconcilable. My answer to those who accuse me of inconsistency is, that both being undoubtedly true, the one must be reconcilable with the other, and that the impossibility of reconciling them must be only apparent and temporary, not real" (pp. 193-194). "F"'s statement seems to have been intended as a device to throw the unwary reader into the "true" camp of evolution. But its dualism was to plague Butler for the rest of his life. "C"'s voice could never be fully silenced. Willy-nilly, almost mechanically, Butler was thrown into the role of reconciler of faith and science.

With the exception of a series of letters defending his dialogue from the comments of a mysterious opponent,[16] the next results of Butler's conversion to the Darwinian habit of mind are to be found in three ironic examinations of the mechanistic system so unreservedly hailed by "F." The first article, "Darwin Among the Machines," published in the *Press* in 1863, whimsically holds that man's identity may be annulled by his superior offspring, the machine. Since a new "mechanical life" may well supplant human existence, man must act immediately. He must practice the "survival of the fittest" and kill the machine. Butler's next article in order

[16] Butler's dialogue was answered in the *Press* by a writer who signed himself as "Savoyard." In view of his later practice of answering his own letters under different pseudonyms in order to vent problems in a "scientific" spirit, it would seem not unlikely that "Savoyard" was none other than Butler himself. On the other hand, stylistic traits, the erudition, and Butler's own identification of his opponent with the Bishop of Wellington could point to the contrary.

of composition, if not in chronology, was "Lucubratio Ebria" (1865), sent to the New Zealand *Press* from England as a mock answer to the earlier piece. In it, Butler rebukes "the view adopted by a previous correspondent" and sings an equally exaggerated paean to the machine as the most logical extension of the human animal. His third article, "The Mechanical Creation" (1865), attempts to reconcile the other two by arguing that, although machines might actually assume an identity of their own, man's own identity would develop through them.

Although "The Mechanical Creation" still draws an analogy between man's purposive development of the machine and the seemingly erratic evolution of organic matter, it is obvious that the crux of all three articles lies in Butler's reluctance to accept this correspondence. Butler's closer view of Darwin had yielded a series of unanswered questions. Under the guise of burlesque and exaggeration, Butler cautiously explored his increasing dissatisfaction with a system which had never purported to present the logical teleology he now demanded. Was man's individual identity determined by a mechanistic process of selection? Was his short existence purposeless because fortuitous? Having delved into "F" 's evolutionism, Butler looked again at "C" 's objections. In an important letter to the *Reasoner*, published in August of 1865, he re-evaluated his loss of faith.

Butler in his letter still holds that "an atheist may be a very good Christian—such a Christian as Christ would have rejoiced to know" ("Precaution in Free Thought," *Canterbury Settlement*, p. 240). Even if the Christian miracles are false—and Butler implies that they are—"a radical change of opinion" is dangerous because it subverts a faith in the "clear-headedness of one's age," which is "a much more

serious thing than loss of faith in a personal Deity" (p. 240).
Yet it is the loss of this deity which plagues Butler:

> I say personal Deity—I should have said Deity alone—
> for I see not how to believe in an impersonal Deity. It is
> as easy to believe the trinity in unity and unity in trinity,
> as it is for me to conceive the notion of Deity without
> personifying it. If I do not personify the idea, the idea
> itself eludes my grasp—give us half a grain of oxygen and
> our imagination can diffuse it through all space, and invest
> it with intelligence and the other attributes of matter, but
> without it we are powerless. For myself I must have a
> personal Deity or none at all. An impersonal Deity is to
> me an intelligent vacuum. [p. 240]

Earlier in the same year, Butler had published his anonymous pamphlet, "The Evidence of the Resurrection of Jesus
Christ as Contained in the Four Evangelists."[17] In it, he had
attempted to document the basic reasons which had forced
him to reject orthodox Christianity. But, although Darwin
and science had provided him with the "essential" spirit that
validated his loss of faith, they had failed to provide him with
a deity he could substitute for the rejected Christian explanations. Instead of a divine design, Darwinism had given
Butler a "vacuum" which, though admittedly "intelligent,"
was, as he now realized, based on chance and accident. Thus
Butler was forced to accept what George Eliot had detected
almost immediately after the appearance of *The Origin of
Species*, namely that it contained only a description of a

---

[17] Only the year of publication of the pamphlet is known, but it
is reasonable to suppose that it was published before the appearance
of Butler's letter on August 1. The contents of Butler's pamphlet
were transferred to *The Fair Haven*; the Shrewsbury Edition lacks
a transcription of the work.

natural process and not an alternate explanation of the final causes offered by theology or philosophy.

For the next five years Butler abandoned his search for a new "personal Deity" and devoted most of his time to his paintings. Gradually, he became convinced that art was not his true vocation. By 1870, he planned a new book, a work that would be a "mere peg on which to hang anything I had in mind to say." The result was *Erewhon*, published in March 1872 and slightly revised in June 1872. *Erewhon* was a true "peg." It fused Butler's past writings about Darwin and religion with the actual travel experiences he had already recounted in *A Canterbury Settlement* (1863). Specifically, it was the outgrowth of his four essays on evolution, just as *The Fair Haven*, which was published the next year, represented an expansion of his pamphlet on the Resurrection. But *Erewhon* was the first work in which Butler consciously blended religion with evolutionism. Although this process took the shape of a satire against established religion, it helped Butler to clarify some of his own reservations about Darwinism and advanced his ideas with regard to the purposive evolutionism toward which he was moving.

Erewhon has been frequently compared to *Gulliver's Travels*. The analogy is a tenuous one, for the intentions of the two books are radically different. Swift mocks any deviation from the standards of a well-defined, orthodox position usually implicit in his satire; Butler resorts to satire in order to grope for the norms necessary for such a position. Thus, despite its incisiveness, *Erewhon* fails to sustain its satire. Its shifting of points of view, a method traceable to the two "voices" of "F" and "C," obliterates the position of the author and converts his confident laughter into an unsure search. For the book is not only a satire, but also an effort to endow a still wishful Utopia with the evolutionary creed that Butler did not find and establish until the codification of his later theories. Almost thirty years later, on returning to this Utopia with *Erewhon Revisited*, Butler rewrote *Erewhon* as well. In an attempt to make it more consistent with his matured ideas, he introduced two new chapters, "The Rights of Vegetables" and "The Rights of Animals."

However diffuse, the 1872 edition of *Erewhon* possesses a rough unity by its steady reversal of Christian values into their evolutionary counterparts. The country of "Erewhon" or "Nowhere" thus acquires a double function. It is a satiric replica of a nineteenth-century England nominally ruled by the Anglican Church (the Musical Banks), but actually dominated by a worship of conventionality (Ydgrunism) and by a blind acceptance of a false system of education (the Colleges of Unreason), the same elements which conspire against the development of the young Ernest in *The Way of All Flesh*. But at the same time the land of "Nowhere" is depicted as an idealized Utopia whose positive values are even perceived by the impossibly "earnest" narrator Higgs, desirous of converting the Erewhonians to the Church of England. Higgs extols the pagan beauty of his captors, whose mixture of Egyptian, Greek, and Italian characteristics makes them "Ishmaelites" in the fullest sense. He approves of their eugenic practices and admits that only their respect for his own health and good looks prevented him from being massacred.

But Butler was not yet quite ready to exalt health and well-being into a this-worldly state of grace. The morality-disease inversion allowed him to parody the values of the Church of England with destructive wit. He ridiculed its claims of absolute truth and satirized its ministry (the cashiers and the straighteners), as well as the conformism and pietism it imposed on its worshippers (the Nosnibor family). What is more, by creating the myth of the "World of the Unborn," Butler managed to return to the two thorns of his own Cambridge doubts, the efficacy of infant baptism and the miracle of the Resurrection. Through his emphasis on Erewhonian "birth-formulae" which made children responsible for their own blemishes, he satirized the orthodox belief in baptism as a guarantee for redemption in afterlife. Through his creation of a myth about a bodiless, prenatal existence, he was able to poke fun at the Judaeo-Christian concept of a bodiless, posthumous existence.

Yet, as usual, Butler attempts to make up for what he takes away. His burlesque of the "Unborn" hides a deadly serious concern with the question raised by "C" in the New Zealand essay: the question of immortality. Casually and jokingly, Butler introduced in the fantasy about the "Unborn" the teleology with which he intended to replace the Christian afterlife in God and to which he was to give his "earnest" assent in the years to come. Butler's precorporeal "Unborn," like Schopenhauer's "Ideas," strive for a materialization in the phenomenal world; they possess a memory which is destroyed upon their assumption of corporeal forms and which becomes "a bare vital principle, not to be perceived by human senses" (ch. 19, p. 148). Consequently, though earthly existence appears to be ruled by a "free will," it is in reality only an instinctive perpetuation of the knowledge of the "Unborn." Earthly identity, marred by an ignorance of this knowledge, as well as by suffering and pain, is only the illusory counterpart of a truly imperishable Identity, immortalized through the unending evolution of the species. The description of Erewhonian funeral practices (the Erewhonians use artificial tears and scatter the ashes of their dead) is intended to demonstrate that the dissolution of organic life is in itself an argument for life's unity. Butler's ideas about the "Unborn" thus foreshadow his later conclusion that "dying is only a mode of forgetting" and forgetting, "a mode of dying" (*Note-Books*, p. 365).

Glimpses of Butler's forthcoming evolutionary creed are also to be found in his descriptions of "The Colleges of Unreason" and of "Ydgrunism," the worship of conformity. Butler laughs at the physically imperfect professors as enmeshed in their study of "hypothetics" like George Eliot's Mr. Casaubon, and just as deliberately obstructing the dynamics of progress. But he presents a younger professor who vows to be only against arbitrary change and who preaches the subordination of progress to common sense. This positive representation of "Unreason" as an instinctive wisdom, neither lacking in reason nor opposing it, anticipates Butler's later exaltation of "memory," although, in its immediate context, the shift vitiates his satire on the professors and robs his irony of its point.

A similar ambivalence is found in Butler's description of "Ydgrunism," which is to religion what Unreason is to education, and which, like Unreason, is endowed with negative as well as positive qualities. Butler makes sure to distinguish between two forms of conformity, "High Ydgrunism" and "Low Ydgrunism." While Low Ydgrunism implies a slavish, often hypocritical, submission to skin-deep conventions, High Ydgrunism is reserved for the best of the Erewhonians. The High Ydgrunites are an elite: they are "manly," young, generous, and courageous. Unaffected by error or paradox, they are Butler's heroes: "gentlemen in the full sense of the word" (ch. 17, p. 130). Their lack of questioning and self-doubt is "an Ideal which all may look upon for a shilling" (ch. 17, p. 132). Butler exalted this type of figure in his characterizations of Towneley in *The Way of All Flesh* and of George in *Erewhon Revisited*.

To him the innate "gentleman" became the incarnation of the graceful adaptation to environment he was to call "Habit," an instinctive conformity denied both to Ernest Pontifex and to Butler himself.[18]

Butler's aristocratic "High Ydgrunites" have no need of a religion at all. Higgs, the would-be missionary, deplores that their happiness and "clearness," so similar to the "*diaphaneitè*" of Marius' friend Cornelius, cannot be adopted by others. But he finds a "step in advance" from unexpected quarters: a small sect, holding out "a future state of some sort," preaches an evolutionary religion by which "those who had been born strong and healthy and handsome would be rewarded for ever and ever" (ch. 17, p. 134). Though only a small minority, scoffed at by most Erewhonians, these enthusiasts are hopefully eyed by Higgs as the pioneers of a new religion able to combine the immortality demanded by "C" with the eugenics postulated by "F."

Erewhon comes close to this rapprochement. Butler's distrust of an "impersonal" process of evolution is not only illustrated by his nascent vitalism, but also by the three chapters entitled "The Book of Machines," an outgrowth of his earlier three articles. Machines are banned in Erewhon ever since, five hundred years before the arrival of Higgs, a controversy erupted between machinists and anti-machinists. Although some appliances were saved because the Professors of Inconsistency and Evasion failed to carry the new principles to their legitimate conclusion, the arguments against the machine ended in the destruction of most mechanical artifacts. These arguments, catalogued in "The Book of Machines" and dutifully reproduced by Higgs, constitute an expansion of those advanced in "Darwin Among the

[18] Mr. Muggeridge calls this type "Nice Person" and makes much of Butler's sense of inferiority.

Machines." Butler believed that their satirical intention was sufficiently clear; his readers, however, misread his irony by identifying "The Book of Machines" with *The Origin of Species*. In the Preface to the second edition of *Erewhon*, Butler felt compelled to deny that the three chapters were anti-Darwinian. Himself adopting the tone of a Professor of Inconsistency and Evasion, he professed surprise that "the book at which such an example of specious misuse of analogy would seem most naturally levelled should have occurred to no reviewer" (p. xx).[19]

Butler's protestation is significant. He had actually swerved farther away from Darwin than he himself realized. *Erewhon* had anticipated his later theories. He had expressed his belief in the importance of acquired habit; he had related habit to the concomitant idea of unconscious memory; and he had intimated his faith in a vital principle. It remained for him to shift from fantasy to reality, from burlesque to earnestness, to fuse the two voices of his early New Zealand "Dialogue" into a personal creed. This process began after the publication of *The Fair Haven* in 1873 and culminated with *Life and Habit* in 1877. With the latter, Butler's theories were complete. Only minor alterations followed, together with the adjustments necessary to enlist the corroboration of Buffon, Lamarck, Erasmus Darwin, and Professor Ewald Hering in his subsequent three works, *Evolution Old and New* (1879), *Unconscious Memory* (1880), and *Luck or Cunning?* (1886). Butler therefore consolidated his evolutionary doctrines in the period running from 1873 to 1886, a period which exactly overlaps that of his sporadic work

[19] In addition to the *Analogy of Religion* by his namesake, Joseph Butler, Butler probably was also thinking of Paley's *Natural Theology*, ridiculed as a fallible proof for cosmic design in chapter 7 of the book.

on *The Way of All Flesh*.[20] Butler's novel was a repository
for his theories. By a fictionalized analysis of his youth and
maturation, he was able to test the efficacy of his new
"religion" in the experimental spirit he had hailed in Darwin.
The next section examines the tenets of Butler's evolutionary
faith.

2. THE CONSOLIDATION OF A FAITH (1873-1886)

Flushed by the success of *Erewhon*, Butler next proceeded
to clear the way for the "eugenic" religion it had adum-
brated. He expanded his earlier pamphlet on the Resurrection
into *The Fair Haven* and intensified his destructive treatment of the central dogma of Christianity through a double
assault. Echoing earlier "Higher Critics," Butler hinted
that the conflicting versions of the Crucifixion invalidated a
belief in Christ's resurrection as well as in His divinity. In
addition, he set out to confound the Judaeo-Christian notion
of a Heavenly Father by intimating that any such personification was wholly dependent on individual bias and aberration. To bring home these two points Butler again devised a
clever satiric scheme which would allow him to mask his
own position. By examining the Gospels in the guise of an
agnostic turned believer, John Pickard Owen, he would
meet the arguments against orthodox belief with such feeble-
ness and lack of logic that the reader would have to be converted to agnosticism. Furthermore, by creating an elaborate
"Memoir" of Owen's life, written by still another *persona*,

---

[20] *The Way of All Flesh* was written in three main spurts of composition: 1873-1874, 1878, and 1883-1884. Butler rewrote the novel
once and revised some segments twice so as to adjust them to his theories. According to Daniel F. Howard, Butler's creativity was stimulated
by altercations with his father (see "The Critical Significance of
Autobiography in *The Way of All Flesh*," *Victorian Newsletter*, 17,
Spring 1960, pp. 1-3).

William Bickersteth Owen, the author's brother and the editor of the entire work, he could illustrate his contention that a man's conception of God was the product of his peculiar environment and heredity.

Butler's ingenious plan misfired because of his veiled authorship and hidden point of view, further obscured by his introduction of quotations from "an anonymous pamphlet" (his own 1865 essay) and from the opinions of "a gentleman who is well known to the public, but who does not authorize me to give his name" (*The Fair Haven*, p. 140). It was the "Memoir," however, which prompted Miss Savage to persuade Butler that he had the makings of a novelist and to stir him into writing the initial draft of what was to become *The Way of All Flesh*. One of the main parallels between the "Memoir" and the novel lies in their association of religion with family life. The early death of Owen's father, "a singularly gentle and humorous playmate," makes his children dependent on the religious zeal of their mother, "trained in the lowest school of Evangelical literalism—a school which in after life both my brother and myself came to regard as the main obstacle to the complete overthrow of unbelief" (p. 3). Owen's recollection of his father, an exact antithesis of Canon Butler, leads him to draw a revealing analogy:

> I may perhaps be allowed to say here, in reference to a remark in the preceding paragraph, that both my brother and myself used to notice it as an almost invariable rule that children's earliest ideas of God are modelled upon the character of their father—if they have one. Should the father be kind, considerate, full of the warmest love, fond of showing it, and reserved only about his displeasure, the child, having learned to look upon God as his Heavenly

Father through the Lord's Prayer and our Church Services, will feel towards God as he does towards his own
father; this conception will stick to a man for years and
years after he has attained manhood—probably it will
never leave him. For all children love their fathers and
mothers, if these last will only let them; it is not a little
unkindness that will kill so hardy a plant as the love of a
child for its parents. Nature has allowed ample margin for
many blunders, provided there be a genuine desire on the
parent's part to make the child feel that he is loved, and
that his natural feelings are respected. This is all the religious education which a child should have. [p. 8]

Yet this ideal education, so similar to that which produced
the "High Ydgrunites" in Erewhon, is followed by the
description of an education more like Butler's very own.

On the other hand, if a man has found his earthly father
harsh and uncongenial, his conception of his Heavenly
Parent will be painful. He will begin by seeing God as an
exaggerated likeness of his father. He will therefore shrink
from Him. The rottenness of still-born love in the heart
of a child poisons the blood of the soul, and hence, later,
crime. [p. 9]

Ostensibly both passages mock man's urge to personify
God, a procedure which Butler was to satirize far more
effectively in *Erewhon Revisited*. Yet they also reveal his
own very palpable need to "personify the idea," to refashion
the vacuum left by his childhood experiences. Had Butler
been a Dickens he would merely have translated these experiences into a grim vision of "earthly" horrors. Instead, he
sought to systematize his vision. He expanded "love" into
the "natural feelings" of all organic beings, he made this

"love" coequal with the will of a "hardy plant," and wound up by substituting the benevolent and provident Evolutionary Personality of his own creation for a "painful" Heavenly Parent. For Butler could not give his assent to a mere "essence" of Christianity. In the climactic chapter entitled "The Christ-Ideal" Butler rejected the attempts of those who, like Arnold, George Eliot, or Pater, were at least trying to conserve a kernel of traditional faith.

Although *Literature and Dogma* had preceded the publication of *The Fair Haven* by little more than a month, Butler may well have had Arnold's work in mind in "The Christ-Ideal." In this chapter, Butler has Owen praise "the spiritual value of the Christ-Ideal," after the manner of Arnold's exaltation of the "secret of Jesus." With feigned gravity, Butler has Owen contend that the very contradictions between the Gospels only attest to the "many-sidedness of Christ," allowing the modern believer to appreciate a "spiritual essence" unnoticed during the actual life of Jesus. In what is the most fiercely ironical passage of *The Fair Haven*, Butler contrasts the disembodied "Christ-Ideal" with its worldly Hellenic counterpart:

How infinitely nobler and more soul-satisfying is the ideal of the Christian saint with wasted limbs, and clothed in the garb of poverty—his upturned eyes piercing the very heavens in the ecstasy of a divine despair—than any of the fleshly ideals of gross human conception such as have already been alluded to. If a man does not feel this instinctively for himself, let him test it thus—whom does his heart of hearts tell him that his son will be most like God in resembling? The Theseus? The Discobolus? or the St. Peters and St. Pauls of Guido and Domenichino? Who can hesitate for a moment as to which ideal presents the higher development of human nature? And this I take it should suffice; the natural instinct which draws us to the Christ-ideal in preference to all others as soon as it has been once presented to us, is a sufficient guarantee of its being the one most tending to the general well-being of the world. [pp. 230-231]

Although presumably it was this passage which led reviewers of the book to praise its "almost pathetic earnestness" (p. xxi), Butler's irony is evident. He has no sympathy for an asceticism which demands a rejection of "fleshly ideals." To him, man's "natural instinct" for perfection should draw him, not to the Christ-Ideal, but to the Discobolus which was for him, as for Walter Pater, a symbol of Hellenic "grace."[21] Butler therefore differs from Arnold and George Eliot in his far greater mutilation of Christian ethics. Nor does he see his way to combine these ethics with the Hellenic ideal of grace, after the timid fashion of Walter Pater. For Butler accepts the hedonism Pater tries to evade. In a significant criticism of *Literature and Dogma* made some time later, Butler argued that Arnold's insistence on a power of "righteousness" was only a diluted replica of Christianity's insistence on a righteous God. Happiness, he asserted with Benthamite candor, could come only "the more we confine our attention to the things immediately round about us which seem, so to speak, entrusted to us as the natural and legitimate sphere of our activity" (*Note-Books*, p. 202).

For Butler *The Fair Haven* was a purge. He was now

[21] Pater built his essay on "The Age of Athletic Prizeman: A Chapter in Greek Art" around the figure of the Discobolus, which he regarded as a symbol of arrested motion; Butler's painting "Mr. Heatherley's Holiday" and his poem "A Psalm of Montreal" rely on the contrast between an old man, a stuffed owl, and the ever-youthful figure of the Discobolus.

ready for his utopian reconstruction. He laid aside his novel and devoted his full time to the systematization of the ideas that had been fermenting in his mind since his New Zealand days. The system presented itself in *Life and Habit* in 1877, a book which begins in Butler's semiserious, casual manner and ends with a startled plea for the creed that suggested itself to him as he was writing. In a remarkably candid confession at the end of the book, Butler betrays his own surprise: "I admit that when I began to write upon my subject I did not seriously believe in it. I saw, as it were, a pebble upon the ground, with a sheen that pleased me; taking it up, I turned it over and over for my amusement, and found it always grow brighter and brighter the more I examined it. At length I became fascinated, and gave loose rein to self-illusion. The aspect of the world seemed changed; the trifle which I had picked up idly had proved to be a talisman of inestimable value . . ." (*Life and Habit*, pp. 249-250).

The final exhortation of *Life and Habit* contains a fusion of the faith of "C" with the skepticism of "F," the two voices of Butler's initial dialogue: "Will the reader bid me wake with him to a world of chance and blindness? Or can I persuade him to dream with me of a more living faith than either he or I had as yet conceived as possible? As I have said, reason points remorselessly to an awakening, but faith and hope still beckon to the dream" (p. 250). If *The Fair Haven* had succeeded in tearing "C" away from the impossible dream of a vestigial orthodoxy, *Life and Habit* now removed "F" from the remorseless reason of the Darwinians.[22] A compromise had been reached: reason could be

[22] Butler gave notice to Francis Darwin that *Life and Habit* had "resolved itself into a downright attack upon your father's view of evolution" (Jones, I, 257). The friendship and later estrange-

propitiated by a dream that did not depend on the night-mares of childhood. After *Life and Habit* Butler set out to protect himself from the "awakening" he feared by vindica-ting his logic to himself. To do this, he turned to his novel once again and refashioned it in the light of his new theories.

In order to give substance to Ernest's Cambridge doubts and his rejection of holy orders, Butler took up the paradox of the Victorian "Elsmere," the agnostic clergyman, in a fictitious series of letters which appeared in *The Examiner* from February to June of 1879. More ambitiously, he sought to convert his "dream" into an all-embracing meta-physical system in "God the Known and God the Unknown," a series of articles published by *The Examiner* at around the same time. His antagonism began to shift. The "living faith" of *Life and Habit* had made him regard himself as a religious thinker; now it was Darwin, and not orthodox Christianity, who threatened to disturb his vision of a har-monious universe. In *Evolution Old and New* (1879), *Unconscious Memory* (1880), and *Luck or Cunning?* (1886), Butler poured on Darwin's cohorts the same cor-rosive irony he had employed against his father's religion. Christianity seemed less repellent. In his correspondence with the Bishop of Carlisle and in an article on "Rome and Pantheism" (1880), Butler even toyed with the prospects of an "unholy" alliance between his creed and established religion; he flirted with the Rosminian fathers in 1882 and became reconciled to his family after his father's death in 1886. He identified himself with his namesake, Bishop Samuel Butler, in his grandfather's biography (1896), and defended religion from skepticism in *Erewhon Revisited*

---

ment of Butler and the Darwins are analyzed by Professor Willey in his book.

(1901). *The Way of All Flesh,* however, remained un-altered as a document of his permutation of the old religion into a new faith.

The main tenets of this faith and their relevance to Butler's ethical thought are essential for an understanding of his novel. Chief among his ideas is his belief in the unity of organic life, the oneness of personality Butler had already embodied in the Erewhonian myth of the "Unborn." This oneness, according to Butler, not only holds between parent and offspring, but also between all species of a common ancestry. Just as cells make up the body of a single man, so are men themselves "only component atoms of a single compound creature, LIFE, which has probably a distinct con-ception of its own personality though none whatever of ours" (*Life and Habit,* p. 105). Individual identity is there-fore subordinated to the identity of the entire evolutionary organism, the Continued Personality which becomes Butler's equivalent of the rejected "personal Deity" of religion. This Personality can offer "immortality" to man, but no "resur-rection from the dead" ("God the Known and God the Unknown," *Collected Essays,* I, p. 43).

In defining the dynamics of this Evolutionary Personality, Butler distinguishes between three stages of operation which underlie all change. Animating all three of the stages is the vital principle which provides the emotional core of his creed and which is described as "faith, or as the desire to know, or do, or live at all" (*Life and Habit,* p. 105). "Plants and animals are living forms of faith, or faiths of form" (*Evolution Old and New,* p. 299), and suicide or the death-wish is a lack of faith nonexistent among plants and animals, and rare even among those humans who "rail at life most bitterly" (*God the Known,* p. 43). Although faith or the will to live is not a first cause in itself, it is the initial stage of any organic change.

The concept of the vital principle is tied to that of unconscious memory. Both are a requisite for life. "Matter which can remember is living; matter which cannot remember is dead" (*Life and Habit*, p. 244). To induce an organic change, matter, like the Erewhonian "Unborn," must pass from an instinctive, unconscious stage to consciousness; it must transform the vital principle into an awareness of effort and power. Challenged by a new environment or a new climate, the awakened organism calls forth a conscious modification, solidifies it into a *law*, and passes it on to subsequent generations as a *habit*. If unable to perform this change, the organism becomes extinct; if successful, its habitual reiteration of the law allows its descendants to relapse again into unconscious memory. This memory remains latent, powerful, and "charged" so that, when rekindled by associated ideas, an organism can again recall its "past existences" and, if necessary, reiterate the processes undergone before.

"Life, then," in Butler's materialistic system, "is faith founded upon experience, which experience is in its turn founded upon faith—or more simply, it is memory" (*Life and Habit*, p. 243). It follows therefore that the best life is that of a "creature well supported by a mass of healthy ancestral memory," an Erewhonian "High Ydgrunite" turned into reality (*ibid.*). Perennially "young and growing," such beings are attuned to the mechanics of evolution by virtue of their *good breeding*; they are in a state of *grace* (as opposed to a state of *law*). As we shall see in the next chapter, it is this state, embodied by the gentlemanly Towneley, which Ernest Pontifex manages to regain for his children, although it remains denied to himself.

Butler's theory of heredity is unlike Darwin's in its insistence on an absolute faith in instinct, memory, and habit. In "How I Came To Write *Life and Habit*," the second chapter of *Unconscious Memory*, Butler professed to have been "horrified" at Darwin's contention that "the most wonderful instincts with which we are acquainted . . . could not possibly have been acquired by habit" (p. 25). Defiantly, he responded: "Until continued personality and memory are connected with the idea of heredity, heredity of any kind is little more than a term for something which one does not understand" (*Life and Habit*, p. 207). Butler cherished his "dream." It was something he could understand, the personification of an "idea." It is not surprising that he protected it from imaginary intruders. For his faith was all-encompassing, applicable to men as well as plants and animals. It was rooted in the physical nature of man, demanded no abstract dogmas or visible rituals, and yet offered an immortality of sorts by incorporating individual life into that of the Continuous Personality. It exalted a life of "instinct," but recognized the "lawful" preservation of habits until these had become mnemonic and instinctive in themselves.

Butler's system was utopian. But he could now balance all the extremes which had warred within him. Pagan "grace" and Hebraic "law," reason and faith, change and conservatism, rebellion and conformity could finally be held in equipoise. In a sense, Butler had achieved exactly what George Eliot had set out to do in *Middlemarch*. Even his conclusions resembled those of the novelist whose book Miss Savage had recommended to him. He had come to share her relativism, even her belief in a "double truth." Just as George Eliot had implied in *Daniel Deronda* that a "power not ourselves" might exist outside the causal "will" operating in *Middlemarch*, so Butler now conceded that a "God the Unknown" might well exist beyond the volition of the Continuous Personality he openly called "God the Known." *Daniel Deronda* is artistically unsuccessful; *God the Known and God the Unknown* is philosophically unsound. Butler admitted his faulty metaphysics and resigned himself by regarding his "religion" as a practicable ethic, just as George Eliot and Arnold had done with their humanist cults.

Butler had achieved a precarious balance, but he was content with it. Truth remained double-sided, yet this very duality allowed him to retreat toward the minor paradoxes and literary "bagatelles" which kept him sufficiently puzzled for the last sixteen years of his life. To be sure, the "two voices" were not drowned out. They were heard once more in *Erewhon Revisited*, but their former dissonance now blended into a joint laughter at the two-facedness of reality. Butler was fully aware that this final harmony was not that of Handel or Shakespeare. He was too shrewd to believe in his philosophy, but he was too faithful to question the "dream." Thus, in the last of his scientific treatises, he settled for an apotheosis of paradox:

> I know that contradiction in terms lurks within much that I have said, but the texture of the world is a warp and woof of contradiction in terms; of continuity in discontinuity, and discontinuity in continuity; of unity in diversity, and of diversity in unity. As in the development of a fugue, where, when the subject and counter subject have been enounced, there must henceforth be nothing new, and yet all must be new, so throughout organic life —which is as a fugue developed to great length from a very simple subject—everything is linked on to and grows out of that which comes next to it in order—errors and

omissions excepted. It crosses and thwarts what comes next to it with difference that involves resemblance, and resemblance that involves difference, and there is no juxtaposition of things that differ too widely by omission of necessary links, or too sudden departure from recognized methods of procedure. [*Luck or Cunning?*, pp. 234-235]

Ultimately, Butler's system yielded a relativism quite similar to that underlying the humanist creeds of other Victorian thinkers. Yet his ethic remained at odds with that of George Eliot, Arnold, and Pater. Whereas Arnold and George Eliot advocate self-renunciation as a stoic discipline by which to check the egoism inherent in human nature, whereas even Pater prescribes the creation of strictly moral "atmospheres" for the edification of the sensations, Butler regards man's instinct as the only power which can ensure his adaptation to the evolving order of life. Thus, while Arnold, Pater, and George Eliot appeal to conscience as a guide for morality, Butler stresses the power of the unconscious. While they exalt the "divine gift of memory" as a cultural heritage that enables man to raise himself out of the flux of life, Butler converts memory into a biological force perpetuated by breeding and heredity. Butler refuses to see any great merit in "a notoriously Hebrew contribution to our moral and intellectual well-being" (*Note-Books*, p. 200) or to ascribe any significance to the example of Christ. By paring down Arnold's "power not ourselves" into a "power within ourselves," the instinctive wisdom or "cunning" he venerated as a life-force, he provided a transition to the vitalism of George Bernard Shaw or D. H. Lawrence.

In their efforts to retain an old faith stripped of all its

"unscientific" elements, the Victorian humanists were driven
into some highly unnatural extremes of their own. Their
cults made man too much a God, and God too much a man.
George Eliot glorified a "Choir Invisible" made up of dis-
carnate Saints of Humanity; Butler sang joyful hymns to
an Evolutionary Personality moving in clear-cut ways its
wonders to perform. In both cases a distortion was inevitable.
By subordinating physical vitality to an abstracted Hebraic
"righteousness," George Eliot's creed ultimately became
as unnatural as the puritanical bibliolatry she had set out to
replace. Samuel Butler's "Ishmaelitish" cult of vitality erred
equally, although in exactly the opposite direction. He demanded an unquestioning faith in the natural instincts of
the species. Overoptimistically, he assumed that morality
could rely on this faith alone. With tenuous logic, he attributed to instinct a rational wisdom wholly denied by those
among his successors who converted his cautious and prim
admiration for physical "grace" into a strident mass-worship
of irrationality, the superphallus, and the superman. Through
a highly ironic twist in the history of ideas that Butler
would have been the first to appreciate, his conservative
Victorian "religion" was adopted by those radicals most eager
to break the moral "shackles" of the nineteenth century.

VIII

Reality and Utopia in
The Way of All Flesh

*We then offer immortality, but we do not offer resur-
rection from the dead.* —SAMUEL BUTLER

*"If I don't feel I'm immortal now what's the good of
fussing about it later on?"* —D. H. LAWRENCE

The Way of All Flesh can be read in a variety of ways. In
one of its most limited and pettiest forms, the book is an
indignant self-catharsis and self-excoriation reflecting Butler's
misgivings about his own parentage and personality. Seen
in a much wider perspective, the novel illustrates the dilemma
of all Ernest Pontifexes who find their identity to be predetermined by antecedent generations, which either have or
have not infused them with "grace," vitality, and an instinctual wisdom. Through Ernest's return to the ways of
the flesh, Butler dramatized the power of the "talisman"
he had found in *Life and Habit*. Ernest is allowed to recover
the "habits" of his great-grandfather by following the stric-
tures of that continuous Evolutionary Personality which
Butler named "God the Known." In this sense, *The Way
of All Flesh* is a religious novel. It investigates the workings
of a faith which allows for change as well as permanence,
death as well as immortality. It tests the efficacy of this
faith's "grace" by contrasting it to the "grace" offered by
the more traditional forms of worship and education.[1]

---

[1] Although A. R. Streatfeild noted in his Preface to the first
edition of the novel that it contained a practical illustration of the
theories embodied in *Life and Habit*, a surprisingly small number

Despite the magnitude of such an undertaking, the scope of the novel entitled *Ernest Pontifex, or, The Way of All Flesh: A Story of English Domestic Life* is far more compact than that of *Middlemarch: A Study of Provincial Life.* Though Butler's examination of organic change is as ingenious as George Eliot's more massive investigation of the dynamics of human progress, he does not require a framework as complex as hers. His analysis of a Continuous Personality is confined to a study of five generations of the Pontifex family and centered on the development of its main component "cell," Ernest. Even the satirical treatment of George, Theobald, and Christina Pontifex in the first quarter of the novel is consistent with the author's desire to concentrate on Ernest's story. This opening section *is* Ernest's story: George, Theobald, and Christina are merely the young man's prenatal "selves," the "past existences" described in *Life and Habit.* The detailed scrutiny of Ernest's parentage is no Shandean mockery of his antemundane existence. If Ernest's adoption of new "habits" is to involve a conversion or reconversion to the vitality of John Pontifex, then there must be a documentation made of the totality of his "identity": "Accidents which happen to a man before he is born, in the persons of his ancestors, will, if he remembers them at all, leave an indelible impression on him; they will have moulded his character so that, do what he

---

of critics have followed his lead. Two studies of *The Way of All Flesh* as a "novel of evolution" are Claude T. Bissell's article in *Nineteenth Century Studies* (Ithaca, 1940), and Ellis Shorb's chapter on the novel in "Samuel Butler's Concept of a Vital Principle" (unpubl. diss., University of North Carolina, 1956). Interpretations of the novel as a *Bildungsroman*, as a satire or novel of revolt, and as an autobiographical work are more abundant. Obviously, the novel belongs to no one of these genres, but to all.

will, it is hardly possible for him to escape their consequences."[2] Ernest Pontifex has to pay for the "consequences" of
his heredity. He is the victim of John Pontifex's injudicious
marriage, of George Pontifex's transplantation, of Theobald
Pontifex's timidity and weakness. He is the accumulation of
their mistakes.

Butler was fully aware that it would never do to make
Ernest a direct replica of himself if he was to maintain the
"scientific" spirit of detachment he had once praised in
Darwin. He therefore introduced a few significant changes
in Ernest's characterization. Unlike Butler, Ernest becomes
ordained upon his graduation; although he considers mi-
grating to Australia or New Zealand in order to undergo
an "uprooting" similar to Butler's own, he remains in London for his "three and a half years' apprenticeship to a rough
life" (ch. 78, p. 345). Butler's sheep-farming was entirely
financed by his father; Ernest must manage with a paltry
hundred pounds given to him by Theobald. While Butler
remained a bachelor, Ernest passes on the "grace" he has
regained to his and Ellen's children.

Still, in order to assure himself of the full impersonality
he required as a novelist and "man of science," Butler relied
on a further means of detachment. Resorting to his habitual
method of self-division, he created the persona of Edward
Overton as the narrator of Ernest's story. Through the eyes
of this elderly "Ishmaelitish" observer, Butler could bear to
look at Ernest's predicament without himself becoming
plagued by the fogging overearnestness which marred the
fictionalized "autobiographies" of Victorian doubters such as
Froude, William Arnold, or "Mark Rutherford." What is

[2] *The Way of All Flesh*, Shrewsbury Edition of the Works of
Samuel Butler (London and New York, 1923-1926), chap. 63, p.
276. Future references to the novel are given in the text.

more, he could view Ernest, his younger self, from the vantage point of an independent thinker abreast of the new evolutionary doctrines "being put forward nowadays" and quite capable of giving a puff to Butler's own theories through casual quotations from *Life and Habit*.[3]

Unlike Ernest and unlike Theobald, whose exact contemporary he is, Overton has been educated by a sage parent. His father, who resembles the genial Owen Senior in *The Fair Haven*, inculcates in his son a respect for the intuitive wisdom of the species. In a speech which anticipates the credo of an Ernest Hemingway, Overton Senior defends the primitive creativity of John Pontifex, the carpenter, as an example of the highest vitality: "If a man has done enough either in painting, music, or the affairs of life to make me feel that I might trust him in an emergency, he has done enough. It is not by what a man has actually put upon his canvas, nor yet by the acts which he has set down, so to speak, upon the canvas of his life that I will judge him, but by what he made me feel that he felt and aimed at. If he has made me feel that he felt those things to be lovable which I hold lovable myself I ask no more; his grammar may have been imperfect, but still I have understood him . . ." (ch. 1, p. 5). Nonetheless, we know little about Overton's own life. He is a detached commentator, a mask, an ironist who has demonstrated his dissociation from false moral standards by writing burlesque stage plays mimicking the "righteous" Puritan ethos hated by Butler. He is a repository of scientific facts, full of organic similes and metaphors. In short, Overton is the figure described in "Darwin on the Origin of the Species" as the man of science who must also be "a man of other things besides science."

---

[3] The next-to-last paragraph in chapter 33 of the novel is taken verbatim from chapter 15 of *Life and Habit*.

The creation of Overton gave Butler's novel a consistency it would otherwise have lacked.[4] The satiric indignation showered on George, Theobald, and Christina Pontifex is balanced by Overton's adoption of a more tolerant, but still highly ironical, view of Ernest's own priggishness. Overton's semiserious attitude prevents Butler from falling into an excessive commiseration over Ernest's plight or into an excessive exultation over his deliverance and conversion. Overton's tone also provides a perfect vehicle for the aphorisms, inverted quotations, and bon mots which had been so conspicuously out of place in Butler's "serious" works. Butler realized the value of this tone and promptly added "love of fun" to the desirable eugenic qualities he had enumerated in *Life and Habit*. In the novel, Overton's sense of humor is shared by John Pontifex, Alethea, and, eventually, by Ernest himself; it is conspicuously absent in the characters of Mrs. John Pontifex, George, Theobald, and Christina.

Yet when all is said, *The Way of All Flesh* remains uneven as a work of art. In the novel's stagy resolution, Ernest is liberated from marriage by the opportune revelation of Ellen's previous attachment and is freed from the ungentlemanly sin of poverty by Overton's long-withheld disclosure of Aunt Alethea's legacy. The theatricality of this ending befits Overton, the creator of stage plays. The author of a farce based on *Pilgrim's Progress* has had too complete a control over Ernest's pilgrimage. Overton manipulates Ernest with the skill of a puppet-master. He regards his godson's tribulations as amusing gyrations which he alone can regulate and bring to their spectacular ending. Overton's decision to give Ernest his Aunt Alethea's money is rendered

[4] See William H. Marshall, "*The Way of All Flesh*: The Dual Function of Edward Overton," University of Texas *Studies in Literature and Language*, IV, 1963, 583-590.

in the bemused manner of a busy playwright who, on rummaging through his old manuscripts, is a trifle surprised at his own ingenuity in saving the draft of an unfinished play he had at one time decided to discard: "After all I suppose I was right; I suppose things did turn out all the better in the end for having been left to settle themselves—at any rate whether they did or did not, the whole thing was in too great a muddle for me to venture to tackle it so long as Ellen was upon the scene; now, however, that she was removed, all my interest in my godson revived, and I turned over many times in my mind what I had better do with him" (ch. 78, p. 345).

Overton's smugness resembles that of Butler in the conclusion of *Life and Habit*. He has picked up a bauble, a theory, and it has worked: "I saw, as it were, a pebble upon the ground, with a sheen that pleased me; taking it up, I turned it over and over for my amusement, and found it always grow brighter and brighter the more I examined it" (*Life and Habit*, pp. 249-250). In *Life and Habit* Butler's self-amusement changes its pitch and turns into a plea to the reader to worship his newly found "pebble" as a talisman promising "a more living faith than either he or I had as yet conceived as possible" (p. 250). In *The Way of All Flesh* Overton switches from his delight in the success of Ernest the puppet to a violent praise of the success of Ernest the vitalist convert. In either case the change is too abrupt. Its effect is not unlike that produced by Chaucer's Pardoner when he caps his witty self-confession by asking the Host to "kisse the relikes." The modern reader who sees in Ernest Pontifex a forerunner of Lawrence's heroines or Joyce's Stephen Daedalus is neither converted nor amused. His reaction necessarily becomes that of the Host.

In bridging "reason" and "dream" Samuel Butler tried

to lapse from wit to earnestness. There is a deliberate self-blinding in Overton's apologia for the inverted faith on which the entire novel is structured: "What culture is comparable to this? What a lie, what a sickly debilitating debauch did not Ernest's school and university career now seem to him, in comparison with his life in prison and as a tailor in Blackfriars." Yet, in the next sentence, Overton undermines his own plea by adding with playful candor: "I have heard him say he would have gone through all he had suffered if it were only for the deeper insight it gave him into the spirit of the Grecian and the Surrey pantomimes" (ch. 78, p. 346). It is this arbitrary compression of levity and seriousness which causes *The Way of All Flesh* to fall short of becoming the masterpiece it might have been. Butler was unable to maintain the Shakespearean balance that George Eliot herself had lost in *Daniel Deronda.* Nor does his comic juxtaposition of Ernest Pontifex and Edward Overton even resemble Joyce's opposition of Stephen Daedalus to Leopold Bloom. For at the end of *The Way of All Flesh* a curious metamorphosis has taken place.

Overton, the aging writer of extravaganzas, and Ernest, the budding author of religious essays, have become indistinguishable one from another. Both are bachelors, both are wealthy and independent, both have adopted an "Ishmaelitish line" by laughing at society and by congratulating each other for their cleverness. Ernest has become Overton and Overton has dropped his mask. He has refashioned Ernest after his own image; he has revealed himself as a successful theorist and experimenter. His training of Ernest's unconscious has produced the desired results; but this training has also proved to be more devastating than Theobald and Christina's overprotective strangulation of the conscious Ernest. As Ernest's substitute parent, Overton has achieved what Theobald was unable to attain. He has appropriated for himself the young man's identity, or, in nonevolutionary terms, his soul.

In the novel's conclusion Ernest and Overton undertake a channel-crossing prescribed by a doctor well versed in evolutionary lore. "Crossing," says this wise physician, "is the great medical discovery of the age . . . and this is crossing—shaking yourself into something else and something else into you" (ch. 79, p. 352). Ostensibly, the doctor's remark is an irreverent pun contrasting the worldly grace of a biological crossing to the spiritual grace offered by the sign of the Cross.[5] But, although like Overton he speaks "laughingly," it is "plain he was serious." Butler's rejection of the miracle of the Crucifixion led him to pour his faith in a substitute myth of his own construction, a myth in which Ernest could be "shaken into something else." Thrown into "deep waters," Ernest regains "his own power to swim" (ch. 78, p. 346). Ernest's children, apprenticed to a bargeman, can cross over to a better race and to a more natural faith. Ernest the bridge-builder has provided for their crossing by trying to close the gap between "F" and "C," between Overton and Theobald, between "reason" and the "dream." But his bridge is unstable. We are unconvinced by Ernest's conversion because, inherent in Butler's method, lies his own latent distrust of the "dream."

The Way of All Flesh is a parody of its own grave search for the way to cross. It illustrates, in any case, that the comic conventions of nineteenth-century English fiction had

[5] Cf. *The Note-Books*, p. 277: "How rudimentary is the action of an old priest! I saw one once at Venice in the dining-room of the Hotel la Luna who crossed himself by a rapid motion of his fork just before he began to eat, and Miss Bertha Thomas told me she saw an Italian lady at Varallo at the table-d'hôte cross herself with her fan."

become inadequate to deal with the artist's despair over his identity in a world of flux. The novel demanded new directions. Butler's vitalist "dream" was to be carried on in full earnestness in D. H. Lawrence's sexual ethic; Butler's "reason" was to find a new expression in the experimental comedy of James Joyce.

1. The "Past Selves" of Ernest Pontifex

In a vivid passage in *Life and Habit*, Butler describes the internal battle fought by those who, like Ernest Pontifex, defy the identity forced upon them by their ancestors:

> It is one against legion when a creature tries to differ from his own past selves. He must yield or die if he wants to differ widely, so as to lack natural instincts, such as hunger or thirst, or not to gratify them. . . . His past selves are living in unruly hordes within him at this moment and overmastering him. "Do this, this, this which we too have done, and found our profit in it," cry the souls of his forefathers within him. Faint are the far ones, coming and going as the sound of bells wafted on to a high mountain; loud and clear are the near ones, urgent as an alarm of fire. "Withhold," cry some. "Go on boldly," cry others. "Me, me, me, revert hitherward, my descendant," shouts one as it were from some high vantage-ground over the heads of the clamorous multitude. "Nay, but me, me, me," echoes another; and our former selves fight within us and wrangle for our possession. Have we not here what is commonly called an *internal tumult*, when dead pleasures and pains tug within us hither and thither? Then may the battle be decided by what people are pleased to call our own experience. [p. 43]

In *The Way of All Flesh*, Ernest's "internal tumult" is depicted through an external struggle with his "past selves." With scientific economy, Butler chooses only those voices which are nearest to Ernest and therefore most loud, clear, and urgent. Butler devotes two chapters to Ernest's great-grandfather, the carpenter John Pontifex; five chapters to his grandfather, George Pontifex; and approximately half of the novel to Theobald and Christina's wrangling for the possession of their son.

John Pontifex is seen in a haze quite similar to that which prevails in George Eliot's novels. An idealized craftsman like Adam Bede or Caleb Garth, he is industrious, conservative, shrewd, and inarticulate. Creative and self-reliant, he is the author of drawings "which were always of local subjects" and the builder of two organs, one for the Paleham church, the other for his private use. A true patriarch, the "pontifex" to whom Ernest must revert, he lives to be a healthy eighty-five. John's wife, equally hearty and long-lived, is a humorless shrew who bears her husband a single child under circumstances which parody the birth of Isaac in Genesis: "Hers had long ago been considered a hopeless case, and when on consulting the doctor concerning the meaning of certain symptoms she was informed of their significance, she became very angry and abused the doctor roundly for talking nonsense" (ch. 2, pp. 5-6).[6]

It is Mrs. Pontifex who introduces the unnatural strain which is to affect the identity of John's successors. Her son George derives "the greater part of his nature from this obstinate old lady, his mother—a mother who though she loved no one else in the world except her husband (and him only after a fashion), was most tenderly attached to the

---

[6] Cf. Genesis 18:11-15.

unexpected child of her old age; nevertheless she showed it little" (ch. 2, p. 6). She is also indirectly responsible for George's transplantation, and, with it, for a corresponding alteration in the family's religious outlook: "George Ponti-fex might have been brought up as a carpenter and succeeded in no other way than as succeeding his father as one of the minor magnates of Paleham, and yet have been a more truly successful man than he actually was—for I take it there is not much more solid success in this world than what fell to the lot of old Mr. and Mrs. Pontifex; it happened, however, that about the year 1780, when George was a boy of fifteen, a sister of Mrs. Pontifex's, who had married a Mr. Fairlie, came to pay a few days' visit at Paleham. Mr. Fairlie was a publisher, chiefly of religious works, and had an establishment in Paternoster Row; he had risen in life, and his wife had risen with him" (ch. 2, p. 7).

George's removal to London and his succession to his uncle's business begin a new phase in the Pontifex line. The primitive faith of old Pontifex is replaced by his son's religious cant. Butler skillfully juxtaposes John Pontifex's dignified death amidst a natural surrounding to his son's inflated description of an Alpine scenery. The carpenter's attunement to nature is instinctive and inarticulate:

The old man had a theory about sunsets, and had had two steps built up against a wall in the kitchen garden on which he used to stand and watch the sun go down whenever it was clear. My father came on him in the afternoon, just as the sun was setting, and saw him with his arms resting on top of the wall looking towards the sun over a field through which there was a path on which my father was. My father heard him say "Goodbye, sun;

good-bye, sun," as the sun sank, and saw by his tone and manner that he was feeling very feeble. Before the next sunset he was gone. [ch. 3, p. 12]

In Butler's scheme of things, John Pontifex dies in a state of "grace." Like Abraham, he has had a revelation "when the sun was going down"; he has seen the face of Butler's "God the Known," confident that his seed will be fruitful once again "in the fourth generation," after a period of servitude.[7] Intuitively, he knows that his "theory about sunsets" is true: that he is to live on in the unending continuation of the species.

The shift from the placid death of old Pontifex to the "conventional ecstasy" recorded in his son's travel diary brings about a complete change of tone. George's prose is studded with stale allusions to the "genius" and "sublimity" of the place. Dutifully, he feels compelled to pen a poem which could well have been written by the poet Young, whose "other-worldliness" had already evoked the satire of another Victorian agnostic:

> Lord, while these wonders of thy hand I see,
> My soul in holy reverence bends to thee.
> These awful solitudes, this dread repose,
> Yon pyramid sublime of spotless snows,
> These spiry pinnacles, those smiling plains,
> This sea where one eternal winter reigns,
> These are thy works, and while on them I gaze
> I hear a silent tongue that speaks thy praise.
>
> [ch. 4, p. 14]

The irony is obvious. George's glibness belies the "silent tongue" of his father. Conscious hypocrisy has replaced the

[7] Genesis 16:12-16.

wisdom of the unconscious. For George makes sure to record his poem in the visitor's book of a Swiss resort mostly frequented by English tourists who are likely to buy the pious works printed by his publishing house. While John Pontifex's religion is as personal as the organ he builds for his private use, that of his son is meant only for public display. The poem in the visitor's book is transcribed with a clear and immaculate hand; but the original version in George's notebook has been smudged by the many erasures.

George Pontifex is a radical who jumps out of the "old groove" of genetic descent by rejecting his father's healthy "habits." Through his calculating adoption of a religionism inimical to his father's faith, George becomes a "hybrid" who impresses a dangerous change on the Pontifex line. According to Overton, "he is a new animal, arising from the coming together of many unfamiliar elements, and it is well known that the reproduction of abnormal growths, whether animal or vegetable, is irregular and not to be depended upon, even when they are not absolutely sterile" (ch. 5, pp. 19-20). His exploitation of a religion he does not believe in, though beneficial to his pockets, stunts the development of both his son and his grandson, who are brought up in the pietistic atmosphere he has introduced. But if this atmosphere is to blunt the growth of Theobald and Ernest, George's "pecuniary characteristics," inherited by his daughter Alethea, ultimately liberate the young man. For Butler makes it clear that George Pontifex is not to be condemned for his ability to make more money than old John. To him, there is no distinction between God and Mammon. Yet, it is George's misuse of religion and wealth that he resents. Though rich and healthy himself, the publisher is unconcerned about the well-being of his descendants. He overeats, overdrinks, and overvalues the worth of his money: "when a man is very fond of his money," Overton assures us with mock-gravity, "it is not easy for him at all times to be very fond of his children also" (ch. 5, p. 20).

George Pontifex is the villain of *The Way of All Flesh*; he is Butler's version of the banker Bulstrode. As a clear-sighted egotist concerned with his temporal self rather than with the perpetuation of the species, George Pontifex sins against the primary law of Butler's evolutionary canon. For Theobald, his weakly son, is the result of George's false transplantation. Timid, "dull and deficient in animal spirits," Theobald hardly resembles his brother John and his sisters Eliza and Mary, all replicas of their father and therefore of old Mrs. Pontifex. What is more, he is totally unlike his lively sister Alethea, who has inherited the genuine vitality of John Pontifex. Theobald also carries the identity of his grandfather. But Alethea's attempts to "join forces with him as much as she could (for they two were the hares of the family, the rest being all hounds)" is of "no use" (ch. 32, p. 134). For, despite his warlike name, Theobald is quickly cowed into submission by his father: "Before he was well out of frocks it was settled that he was to be a clergyman. It was seemly that Mr. Pontifex, the well-known publisher of religious books, should devote at least one of his sons to the Church; this might tend to bring business, or at any rate to keep it in the firm" (ch. 7, p. 29).

Theobald is unable to see through his father's hypocrisy and believes in "the righteousness of the whole transaction." For a moment, a small flicker of revolt betrays the ancestral voice of John Pontifex stirring within him. But his rebelliousness, which is to be echoed by Ernest in the next generation, is soon quelled by George Pontifex, who bullies his son into ordination. Thereafter, Theobald's vitality is extinguished. It will blossom again in Georgie, Ernest's re-educated son, who reminds Overton of "what Theobald would have been if he had been a sailor." But for the remainder of his own life, Theobald accepts the other-worldliness implanted by his father and makes it his duty "to see the honour and glory of God through the eyes of a Church which had lived three hundred years without finding reason to change a single one of its opinions" (ch. 26, p. 109).

If George Pontifex resembles George Eliot's Bulstrode, Theobald is Butler's version of Mr. Casaubon, the clergyman who is dead to life. Performing uneasily those ecclesiastical duties which call for human contact, Theobald finds relief in pasting snippets of the Old Testament against their counterparts in the New. His "Harmony of the Old and New Testaments" is a labor as futile as Mr. Casaubon's "Key to All Mythologies." For Theobald illustrates Overton's dictum that "Every change is a shock; every shock is a *pro tanto* death" (ch. 53, p. 237). If George Pontifex has induced a change, it is his offspring, and not he, who has been deadened by the shock. After Theobald bolts away from his ineffectual ministration to a dying woman, Mrs. Thompson, Overton remarks drily: "Poor fellow! He has done his best, but what does a fish's best come to when the fish is out of water?" (ch. 15, p. 66).

In *Middlemarch*, Mr. Casaubon's courtship and marriage of Dorothea Brooke constitutes one of the ironic highlights of the novel; in *The Way of All Flesh*, Theobald's wooing and wedding of Christina Allaby is a satirical masterpiece. In both cases, the ridicule of the unnaturalness of the union contains a condemnation of the unnatural religious views which make it possible. Christina is almost a parody of George Eliot's heroine. Like Dorothea, she blindly pours her emotionality into a religious zeal which falsifies the natural drives with which she is endowed. But Dorothea is young

and ingenuous. It is her naïve "sweetness" which causes
her to worship the "light" of Mr. Casaubon and leads her
to ignore his decrepitude. Christina, on the other hand, is
four years older than her suitor. After six years of engagement, she is "thirty-three years old, and looked it." Two of
her four unmarried sisters are her elders. Christina knows
very well that her father's assistant "was not the ideal she
had dreamed of when reading Byron upstairs with her sisters,
but he was an actual within the bounds of possibility, and
after all not a bad actual as actuals went" (ch. 11, p. 44).
Accordingly, the drowning Christina clings to a "straw,"
Theobald. In what is a superb parody of the fortuitous process of Darwinian selection, she plays cards "with Theobald
for the stakes" and wins herself a husband (ch. 11, p. 43).

Religion is the only meeting-ground for Christina and
Theobald. It allows Theobald to mask his utter "lack of
fervour" about the approaching hymeneal joys and enables
Christina to disguise the "actual," the ways of the flesh.
Their respective delusions are skillfully rendered in their
conversations "about the glory of God, and the completeness
with which they would devote themselves to it":

> "We, dearest Theobald," she exclaimed, "will be ever
> faithful. We will stand firm and support one another even
> in the hour of death itself. God in his mercy may spare
> us from being burnt alive. He may or may not do so. O
> Lord" (and she turned her eyes prayerfully to Heaven),
> "spare my Theobald, or grant that he may be beheaded."

> "My dearest," said Theobald gravely, "do not let us
> agitate ourselves unduly. If the hour of trial comes we
> shall be best prepared to meet it by having led a quiet
> unobtrusive life of self-denial and devotion to God's
> glory. Such a life let us pray God that it may please Him
> to enable us to pray that we may lead."

"Dearest Theobald," exclaimed Christina, drying the tears that had gathered in her eyes, "you are always, always right. Let us be self-denying, pure, upright, truthful in word and deed." She clasped her hands and looked up to Heaven as she spoke.

"Dearest," rejoined her lover, "we have ever hitherto endeavoured to be all of these things; we have not been worldly people; let us watch and pray that we may so continue to the end."

The moon had risen and the arbour was getting damp, so they adjourned further aspirations for a more convenient season. [ch. 12, p. 53]

To Christina, this other-worldliness is an outlet for her feelings; to Theobald, it is a convenient disguise for his dearth of feeling. Both "keep their ignorance of the world from themselves by calling it the pursuit of heavenly things" (ch. 63, p. 274). But Christina is forced to shut her eyes far more violently than her husband. She must obliterate the instinctual strength which resulted in her one act of "cunning" and prevented her from remaining a spinster. She therefore mortifies the flesh through the observance of unnatural dietary laws that Butler was to satirize again in "The Rights of Animals," the chapter he added to the 1901 edition of *Erewhon*. Above all, Christina tells herself that she is supremely happy with her destiny, that she and Theobald have "nearly everything in this world that they could wish for." But her worldliness even slips into her most pious dreams: "She could imagine no position more honourable than that of a clergyman's wife unless indeed it were a bishop's. Considering his father's influence it was not at all impossible that Theobald might be a bishop some day—and then— then would occur to her that one little flaw in the practice of the Church of England—a flaw not indeed in its doctrine, but in its policy, which she believed on the whole to be a mistaken one in this respect. I mean the fact that a bishop's wife does not take the rank of her husband" (ch. 16, p. 71).

Christina is a tribute to Butler's power of characterization. Though exaggerated, she remains utterly convincing; though satirized, she manages to arouse a measure of good will. Her spiritual reveries always disclose, as if by accident, the worldliness of her ambitions. But Christina is not a hypocrite. Pathetically, she idolizes Theobald as "the bravest man in the whole world" and meekly surrenders her son to his blundering education. Possessing even "a smaller share of personal bravery than hens generally have" (ch. 13, p. 60), she disregards the strongest of all instincts: the mother's preservation of its young. "Christina did not remonstrate with Theobald concerning the severity of the tasks imposed upon their boy, nor yet as to the continual whippings that were found necessary at lesson times. . . . nevertheless she was fond of her boy, which Theobald never was, and it was long before she could destroy all affection for herself in the mind of her first-born. But she persevered" (ch. 20, p. 89).

Overton repeatedly describes Ernest as "his mother's son." Although Christina is as fully responsible as Theobald for Ernest's inability to deal with the way of the world, she also has a beneficent effect on her offspring. For, as even she realizes, "blood is blood as much through the female line as the male" (ch. 29, p. 123). Overton assures the reader that "if Theobald had been kinder Ernest would have modelled himself upon him entirely"; as it is, however, the boy inherits the temper of his mother, "who, when not frightened, and when there was nothing on the horizon which might cross the slightest whim of her husband, was an amiable, good-natured woman" (ch. 35, pp. 147-148). Christina endows Ernest with the power of feeling so manifestly absent in her husband. Ridiculous as she is, she represents after all the "heart" in Butler's novel. In the scheme of *Middlemarch*, Dorothea alters her religion while rebelling against the unnaturalness of her first marriage. Her change, which leads to her remarriage, attunes her to the dynamics of progress. A similar process takes place in *The Way of All Flesh* where, in view of Butler's temporal structure, this change is delayed for another generation. It is Ernest, his mother's son, and not Christina herself, who must rebel against the marriage and the religion of which he is a product. And yet, the young man's conversion, like that of Dorothea Brooke or Marius the Epicurean, is brought about by a capability to feel, which for Ernest is none other than that of his mother, stripped of its other-worldliness and false zeal.

In a highly ironical scene in the latter part of the book, the "converted" Ernest faces his dying mother. Christina is ill and feverish, frightened by her impending death. Though genuinely cheered by her son's return, she is above all concerned about a remission of her "worldly" sins. Theobald, as ineffectual in soothing his wife as he was in ministering to Mrs. Thompson, and Ernest's brother Joey, a clergyman like his father, cannot allay Christina's fears. Thus, it is Ernest, the renegade clergyman and vitalist convert, who listens to his mother's confession. Guiltily, Christina admits "that she had not been so spiritually minded as she ought to have been" (ch. 83, p. 379). She alludes to a mysterious angelic visitation vouchsafed to one of her children but denied to her or Theobald. Ernest is puzzled. He wants to know whether "the angel had appeared to Joey or to Charlotte," but Christina brushes the question aside: "Ernest could not of course press the subject, so he never found out which of his near relations it was who had had direct communication with an immortal" (ch. 83, pp. 379-380). Butler's irony is obvious. Unknown to Christina and only unconsciously apparent to Ernest himself, it is Ernest who has responded to the voice of John Pontifex and who has thereby recovered the "grace" promised to the old carpenter. And, paradoxically enough, it is Christina's irrepressible worldliness, and not her false spirituality, which has helped Ernest to regain the way of all flesh commanded by Butler's "God the Known." As the beneficiary of the vitality that his mother has stifled throughout her life, it is Ernest who can allay her fears. What is more, in his regained optimism, he can be far more merciful than his clergyman-father:

> Ernest interrupted: "My dear mother," he said, "you are ill and your mind is unstrung; others can now judge better about you than you can; I assure you that to me you seem to have been the most devotedly unselfish wife and mother that ever lived. Even if you have not literally given up all for Christ's sake, you have done so practically as far as it was in your power, and more than this is not required of anyone. I believe you will not only be a saint, but a very distinguished one."
>
> At these words Christina brightened. "You give me hope, you give me hope," she cried, and dried her eyes. She made him assure her over and over again that this was his solemn conviction; she did not care about being a distinguished saint now; she would be quite content to be among the meanest who actually got into heaven, provided she could make sure of escaping that awful Hell. The fear of this evidently was omnipresent with her, and in spite of all Ernest could say he did not quite dispel it.

She was rather ungrateful, I must confess, for after more than an hour's consolation from Ernest she prayed for him that he might have every blessing in this world, inasmuch as she always feared that he was the only one of her children whom she should never meet in heaven; but she was then wandering, and was hardly aware of his presence; her mind in fact was reverting to states in which it had been before her illness. [ch. 83, pp. 380-381]

Christina does not know that the immortality promised to her by her son is not the Christian resurrection from the dead but the very same blessing "in *this* world" that she now invokes with such superiority. Thus, for a brief moment, Butler suggests that the vitalist creed of Ernest and the "Christ-Ideal" of his mother can merge one into another; that they are, in effect, one and the same. For Ernest has ensured his mother's redemption. In the shape of Ernest's future "selves," a generation of better Pontifexes, Christina can live on. Though not a saint, she is among the mean who are allowed to enter Butler's evolutionary heaven. Ironically enough, her fleshly "immortality" has been brought about by an Ernest who has had to suffer for her grievous mistakes.

2. THE CONVERSION OF ERNEST PONTIFEX

To shed his past selves, recover the "grace" of his great-grandfather, and return his children to their rightful evolutionary groove, Ernest Pontifex must effect a "crossing." But according to Butler's vitalist theories, such a crossing can be willed only by a memory awakened from the unconscious through the stimulus of a sharp change. Ernest's first changes in environment are insufficient to arouse in him the "dumb" voice of "that other Ernest that dwelt within him, and was so much stronger and more real than the Ernest of which he was conscious" (ch. 31, p. 130). Aware that this ancestral voice cannot be "translated into such debatable things as words," Butler nonetheless has Overton reproduce its unheeded message:

> "You are surrounded on every side by lies which would deceive even the elect, if the elect were not generally so uncommonly wide awake; the self of which you are conscious, your reasoning and reflecting self, will believe these lies and bid you act in accordance with them. This conscious self of yours, Ernest, is a prig begotten of prigs and trained in priggishness; I will not allow it to shape your actions, though it will doubtless shape your words for many a year to come. Your papa is not here to beat you now; this is a change in the conditions of your existence, and should be followed by changed actions. Obey *me*, your true self and things will go tolerably well with you, but only listen to that outward and visible old husk of yours which is called your father, and I will rend you in pieces even into the third and fourth generation as one who has hated God; for I, Ernest, am the God who made you."
> [ch. 31, p. 131]

Ernest, still a "prig," cannot hear this inner voice. But he will eventually recognize its truth and obey the mandate of Butler's Evolutionary Personality, "the God who made [him]." Nonetheless, Ernest will never become an "elect," one of those fortunate beings who, like the High Ydgrunites of Erewhon or old John, Towneley, and his Aunt Alethea, are protected by their ever-wakeful instincts. Instead, Ernest must act through his "reasoning and reflecting self." He must rely on consciousness in order to recall his ancestral experience, to induce a modification, and to pass it on to his descendants as a "law." Ernest's children, or rather his children's children's children, will again be able to revert to "habit" and join the elect.

Ernest's reconversion to his "true self" is depicted in three separate stages. The first stage portrays Ernest at Battersby and at Roughborough as the victim of the heritage introduced by George Pontifex. The second stage depicts the adolescent at Cambridge and in London, where he is imposed upon by a succession of false prophets. Still misusing the changed "conditions of his existence," Ernest finally succumbs to a crisis which illustrates the insufficiency of his training. In the third stage of his career, to be examined in the last section of this chapter, Ernest finally tries to unlearn the false habits of the past two generations. This final schooling produces Ernest's misguided marriage, but ends "tolerably well" with a "pontifex" who can build a bridge from the past into the future.

Although Butler stresses the negative aspects of Ernest's education, he also provides, through Ernest's Aunt Alethea, his friend Towneley, and the ever-present Overton, a series of ideal characters who prevent the "dumb" Ernest from succumbing to the priggish self that his schooling has produced.[8] As godmother and second godfather to Ernest, Alethea and Overton take an active interest in his development. Their intervention on his behalf begins at the boy's christening, even though they can do little to counteract the

---

[8] In addition to these three characters and to Old John Pontifex, Butler also idealizes the vitality of Theobald's rustic parishioners, of John the coachman, Mr. Shaw the atheist tinker, and Mr. and Mrs. Rollings, the foster parents of Ernest's children. His admiration for the instinctual powers of Mrs. Jupp, the promiscuous landlady who understands the "language of flowers," is, as Malcolm Muggeridge has pointed out, not far removed from D. H. Lawrence's exaltation of potent gamekeepers and coal miners.

influence of George Pontifex, his first godfather, who suggests his grandson's Christian name and provides the adulterated baptismal water with which he is christened. In the first stage of Ernest's evolution, Alethea's practical training partially offsets the instruction offered by Dr. Skinner, "a God-fearing earnest Christian." In the second stage, it is Towneley who acts as a foil to the Cambridge Simeonites, Badcock and Hawke, and to Ernest's fellow curate, Pryer. In the third stage of Ernest's growth, Overton restores Alethea's fortune to her godson and thus frees him from further entanglements.

Still, despite the support of these three benefactors, Ernest must largely shift for himself. Towneley only makes a brief appearance. As "Ernest's idol," his role is essentially passive. Like Cornelius in *Marius the Epicurean*, he exemplifies what the protagonist "should most like to be," but cannot become (ch. 80, p. 361). Alethea's premature death prevents her from fulfilling her intention "to be to [Ernest] in the place of parents, and to find in him a son rather than a nephew" (ch. 34, p. 147). Although she is a more rounded character than Towneley, she too remains a device designed to return Ernest to the "true self" of John Pontifex. As her Greek name indicates, Alethea embodies a truth opposed to that preached by the professional truth-tellers she detests. Overton's function is equally artificial. His desire to view Ernest from the standpoint of a theoretician conflicts with his presumed sympathy for his godson. Yet his detachment, like that of Towneley and Alethea, is deliberate. Ernest must face experience without the interference of friend or foe. His predicament is likened to that of a fly observed by Overton as it "crosses" a cup of hot coffee. Overton does not help the insect in its "supermuscan efforts"; instead, he decides that it must will its own salvation: "As I watched him I fancied that so supreme a moment of difficulty and danger might leave him with an increase of moral and physical power which might even descend in some measure to his offspring. But surely he would not have got the increased moral power if he could have helped it, and he will not knowingly alight upon another cup of hot coffee" (ch. 80, pp. 358-359).

Ernest's own "moral and physical power" can hardly increase during his residence at Battersby, with its horrors and privations. But his removal to the school of the "famous Dr. Skinner of Roughborough" is more beneficial. Although the eminent theologian proves to be a magnified Theobald and his schooling a mere extension of the Battersby education, Ernest's growth is given a definite impetus by the intervention of his aunt. Alethea Pontifex does not belittle the intuitive powers of the young. She tests Ernest and detects in him a trace of the vitality lost by her brother. Fooled neither by his unprepossessing appearance nor by his "priggishness," she regards his trustfulness and his deep dislike of Dr. Skinner as definite eugenic qualities. Most encouraging to her is Ernest's "purely instinctive" appreciation of the organ music of a nearby church. This mnemonic association with the past "self" of John Pontifex leads to Alethea's decision "that the boy was worth taking pains with." She leaves London, moves to Roughborough, and trains the "dumb" Ernest by having the boy build an organ in the fashion of her grandfather.[9]

Alethea's intentions are obvious. Noting her nephew's

[9] Like Pater (or Proust), Butler holds that "a smell may remind an old man of eighty of some incident of his childhood"; but, unlike Pater, he asserts that such recollections can transcend the span of a man's life: "Our memory is mainly called into action by force of association and similarity in the surroundings. We want to go on doing what we did when we were last as we are now" (*Life and Habit*, pp. 133, 135-136).

lack of physical strength and moral stamina, she resolves to have him re-enact the "habit" lost by George and Theobald. Ernest responds to his aunt's trick: "he rose as eagerly to the bait as she could have desired, and wanted to begin learning to saw and plane so that he might make the wooden pipes at once" (ch. 34, p. 142). His "true self" begins to function. Oblivious to his father's pedantic appeals to his "reasoning and reflecting self," Ernest begins to "do a little plain carpentering, so as to get to know how to use his tools." He is flushed with excitement: "His inner self never told him that this was humbug, as it did about Latin and Greek" (ch. 34, p. 146).

But Alethea Pontifex knows that she cannot do the impossible. She cannot alter her nephew's heredity or "undo the effect of such surroundings as the boy had had at Battersby." Like the fly observed by Overton, Ernest must generate his own "moral and physical power." Though pleased to see that Ernest partakes of Christina's good nature, Alethea is anxious about the vanity, impulsiveness, and impressionability he has also inherited from his mother: "It was her perception of this which led her to take the action which she was so soon called upon to take" (ch. 35, p. 148). Alethea's "action" consists of the conditions set down in her testament, "an unusually foolish will" for "an unusually foolish boy." Ostensibly leaving her fortune to Overton, she actually delegates to him her guardianship of Ernest. Her abrupt death ends the training of the "dumb" Ernest and forces his "conscious" self into the multiple mistakes she has foreseen.

With the exception of his quixotic gesture in behalf of the servant-girl Ellen, Ernest rounds out the first phase of his career still wholly under the influence of Battersby and Roughborough. But Aunt Alethea has sown her seed. As

Ernest leaves Dr. Skinner's establishment and meditates over his past and present calamities, he unwittingly assumes the eternal youthfulness of John Pontifex. He stares into the mists covering the sun and suddenly breaks out into a laugh:

> Exactly at this moment the light veil of cloud parted from the sun, and he was brought to *terra firma* by the breaking forth of the sunshine. On this he became aware that he was being watched attentively by a fellow-traveller opposite to him, an elderly gentleman with a large head and iron-grey hair.
>
> "My young friend," said he, good-naturedly, "you really must not carry on conversations with people in the sun, while you are in a public railway carriage." [ch. 44, pp. 194-195]

Ernest's unconscious conversation recalls that of his grandfather, who also addressed the sun as a symbol for his confidence in the benignity of nature. But it is a long time before Ernest can cross back to his ancestor's faith.

The second stage of Ernest's evolution finds him in Cambridge and in London. Ernest's readiness to become a clergyman is even more unquestioning than Theobald's compliance with his own father's wishes. What is more, his inherited weakness and lack of experience also make him an easy victim for the "spiritual thieves or coiners" who now prey on him. Cambridge has helped little to liberate Ernest. Like the Erewhonian "Colleges of Unreason," the university's concern is with "hypothetics," not with the new intellectual trends rising all around it:

> It must be remembered that the year 1858 was the last of a term during which the peace of the Church of England was singularly unbroken. Between 1844, when

Vestiges of Creation appeared, and 1859, when *Essays and Reviews* marked the commencement of that storm which raged until many years afterwards,[10] there was not a single book published in England that caused serious commotion within the bosom of the Church. . . .

I need hardly say that the calm was only on the surface. Older men, who knew more than undergraduates were likely to do, must have seen that the wave of scepticism which had already broken over Germany was setting towards our own shores, nor was it long, indeed, before it reached them. Ernest had hardly been ordained before three works in quick succession arrested the attention even of those who paid least heed to theological controversy. I mean *Essays and Reviews*, Charles Darwin's *Origin of Species*, and Bishop Colenso's *Criticisms on the Pentateuch*.[11] [ch. 47, pp. 205-206]

At Cambridge the "conscious" Ernest is courted by the evangelical set of the Simeonites, "a gloomy, seedy-looking *confrérie*, who had as little to glory in clothes and manners as in the flesh itself" (ch. 47, p. 206). The "dumb" Ernest,

[10] Butler's memory, whether conscious or unconscious, is faulty here: *Essays and Reviews* was published in 1860.

[11] This whole passage is reproduced from the first of a series of letters Butler published in the *Examiner* from February to May 1879, reprinted under the title of "A Clergyman's Doubts" in the first volume of the *Collected Essays* in the Shrewsbury Edition. The careful planning and spacing of the letters by the three principal correspondents ("Earnest Clergyman," a minister ordained around the same time as Ernest Pontifex; "Cantab," an Arnoldian advocating a "cultured scepticism" within the Church; and "Oxoniensis," a radical demanding a complete break) would indicate that Butler was using his characteristic method of arguing with himself in order to arrive at some solution. This solution, advanced in the last letter by "Earnest Clergyman," is a creed quite similar to that adopted by the matured Ernest Pontifex.

however, is instinctively attracted to the worldly Towneley, "the handsomest man whom he ever had seen or ever could see." Ernest worships "his especial hero," who has had the fortune to lose his parents when he was only two years old, and is grateful for a "nod and a few good-natured words" from him. But Ernest is Christina's son. He soon turns to the spiritual blandishments of the Simeonites whose leader not only is "ugly, dirty, ill-dressed, bumptious," and physically deformed, but also responds to the pointedly "unnatural" name of Badcock. Aware of the antipathy he arouses, Badcock shrewdly borrows the oratory of another preacher, the Reverend Gideon Hawke, who understands how to "hawk Christ about in the streets" in order to attract reluctant undergraduates.

Mr. Hawke's sermon provides a direct antithesis to Ernest's later absolution of his mother. For the minister threatens those who take up "the pleasures of this brief life" with the "torments of eternity" (ch. 49, p. 221). His "earnest manner, striking countenance and excellent delivery" are even more effective than his words. Ernest, still "his mother's son," is particularly stirred by Mr. Hawke's mysterious allusion to a voice which had informed that a "chosen vessel" was to be among his listeners. Naïvely, Ernest assumes that he is the one for whose benefit Mr. Hawke has been sent, and, with extreme suddenness, he becomes an enthusiast. He writes to his parents that, while his fellow students are doomed to perdition, he alone is "going towards Christ." But the reception to his letter is hardly a warm one: "Even Christina refrained from ecstasy over her son's having discovered the power of Christ's word, while Theobald was frightened out of his wits" (ch. 50, p. 227).

Ernest undergoes a complete turnabout after his ordination to a curacy in London. His ultra-evangelicalism vanishes as soon as he realizes "that the light of the happiness which he had known during his four years at Cambridge had been extinguished" (ch. 51, p. 229). But he attacks his unpleasant duties with redoubled zeal. The "conscious" Ernest is still dominant: "The sense of humour and tendency to think for himself, of which till a few months previously he had been showing fair promise, were nipped as though by a late frost, while his earlier habit of taking on trust everything that was told him by those in authority, and following everything out to the bitter end, no matter how preposterous, returned with redoubled strength" (ch. 51, pp. 229-230). Ernest thus falls under the spell of his fellow-curate, Pryer, who soon convinces him that "the High Church party, and even Rome itself, had more to say for themselves than he had thought" (ch. 51, p. 231).

Overton thinks Pryer "odious both in manners and appearance." But Ernest fails to see that his new mentor is quite as unnatural as Badcock. In his ignorance, he misses Pryer's veiled allusions to certain "practices" which have survived among the "most cultivated" races. On confiding to him his own sexual desires and his willingness to marry the "first woman who would listen to him," he abjectly accepts Pryer's dictum that "the priest must be absolutely sexless—if not in practice, yet at any rate in theory" (ch. 51, p. 232; ch. 52, p. 236). Ernest is particularly impressed by Pryer's scheme for a "College of Spiritual Pathology" in which priests skilled in "soul-craft" are to cure men of their spiritual ailments.[12] Imprudently, he gives Pryer all his funds

---

[12] Pryer's proposed "spiritual pathologists" reverse the principle of the Erewhonian "straighteners" who punish *physical* disease as a moral crime. The analogy remains the same, however; in each case Butler's irony revolves around the attempt to remedy "spiritual" ills by theoretical standards, removed from the ways of the flesh.

to be invested at "a place they call the Stock Exchange."

Soon, Ernest conceives a grandiose plan of his own. He will live among the poor and familiarize himself with their "habits and thoughts." But his scheme misfires. Though "good at heart," according to his seasoned landlady, Mrs. Jupp, Ernest "don't know nothing at all." He is inexperienced "in the ways of anything but those back eddies of the world, schools and universities" (ch. 57, p. 253). Ernest believes Mrs. Jupp when she tells him that all the well-dressed gentlemen calling on Miss Snow are the young lady's relatives. He fails to see that Miss Maitland, another tenant, differs from Miss Snow. His naïveté precipitates his crisis.

Ernest's moral crusade is a travesty which exposes all the deficiencies of his education at Battersby, Roughborough, and Cambridge. With the cowardice of his parents, he avoids his first prospective convert, an ill-tempered tailor who beats his wife. With an ignorance of church systems other than his own, he finds himself ridiculously embarrassed when he approaches a Wesleyan couple, the Baxters, but does "not know what he was to convert them from." With an unfamiliarity of the Gospels themselves, he is easily routed by the free-thinking tinker, Mr. Shaw, who proves to him that he does not even know his own side of the question. Ernest's final collapse comes during his visit to Miss Snow where he is found by Towneley, one of the prostitute's regular callers, just as he is about to open his spiritual attack. He slinks off, "Bible and all," with Towneley's "hearty laugh" ringing in his ears. "Then it flashed upon him that if he could not see Miss Snow he could at any rate see Miss Maitland. He knew well enough what he wanted now, and as for the Bible, he pushed it from him to the other end of his table. It fell over on to the floor, and he kicked it into a corner" (ch. 59, p.

265). But, "shielded from impurity" at Cambridge and tutored by Pryer and Badcock, Ernest still does not know the ways of the flesh. Ten minutes later he is carried off by two policemen. His past education has not taught him how to "distinguish between a respectable girl and a prostitute" (ch. 62, p. 273). Condemned to six months of imprisonment, Ernest discovers that the spiritual-minded Pryer has decamped with all of his money.

Ernest's incarceration ends the second phase of his training and marks the low point of his career. In prison an attack of brain fever forever purges away the "reasonable" religion implanted by George Pontifex two generations before. "Never in full possession of his reason" for two full months, Ernest regains consciousness by laughing at a "rallying sally" made by his nurse who promptly predicts that "he would be a man again." But Ernest must still find the way to become a free man as well. Ironically, it is in prison where, shielded from his parents and from his new allies, Overton and Towneley, Ernest can recover his freedom. For his cell provides him with the abruptly altered environment he needs in order to undo the work of parents and institutions who "hated change of all sorts" (ch. 16, p. 71): "Perhaps the shock of so great a change in his surroundings had accelerated changes in his opinions, just as the cocoons of silkworms, when sent in baskets by rail, hatch before their time through the novelty of heat and jolting" (ch. 64, p. 278).

Ernest's trust in the morality of Battersby, Roughborough, and Cambridge is gone forever. He knows that he must leave the clergy and become a layman. But Ernest does not only negate the "past selves" of George, Theobald, and Christina; his radicalism leads to a restoration of his true heredity. Realizing that he needs a faith responsive to the "dumb" voice he has failed to heed before, Ernest searches for a "criterion of truth" by which he can guide his future actions: "decision was difficult—so difficult that a man had better follow his instinct than attempt to decide them by any process of reasoning" (ch. 65, p. 282). Thus, almost coincidentally, Ernest hits upon the creed of John Pontifex: "Instinct then is the ultimate court of appeal. And what is instinct? It is a mode of faith in the evidence of things not actually seen" (ch. 65, p. 282). Ernest therefore decides to rely on the unseen "power" which he now feels "to be in him," the vital principle described in *Life and Habit* as "the desire to know, or do, or live at all." His optimism dispels all of his earlier doubts and hesitations: "He had lost his faith in Christianity, but his faith in something—he knew not what, but that there was a something as yet but darkly known, which made right right and wrong wrong—his faith in this grew stronger and stronger daily (ch. 68, p. 298). In Butler's eyes, Ernest's conversion is nothing less than a regeneration. But Ernest's passive recollection of the instinctual "grace" of his great-grandfather must, according to Butler's vitalist theories, now be translated into action. Accordingly, in the third and last stage of his evolution, Ernest enacts the precepts of his new faith.

3. The Creed of Ernest Pontifex

The third stage of Ernest Pontifex's evolution depicts the rise of his "dumb" self. To recover a "healthy ancestral memory," Ernest must, like any organism described in *Life and Habit*, induce a conscious modification which is to alter the habits of his past existence and to create a "law" for his future selves. Ernest's first instinctual act therefore is one of self-preservation; he severs himself from the "past selves" nearest to him, his parents. Although the "conscious" Ernest wavers at the thought of his weeping mother, the "dumb" Ernest has become the stronger of the two. Ernest's imprisonment has provided a "gap" which cannot be spanned by merely throwing "a plank across it." Ernest has "crossed his Rubicon," though neither so dramatically as Higgs (who must scale over a "chasm" before he can enter Erewhon) nor so undramatically as Butler (who could go overseas with his father's money in his pockets).

Prison life teaches Ernest that the crossing he must now enact cannot be effected with the help of a "plank." While in prison, Ernest learns the rudiments of tailoring and is allowed to play the chapel organ. As he returns to the outer world, he realizes that the "material bolts" of the jail have given way to "others which are none the less real—poverty and ignorance of the world" (ch. 69, p. 305). For the first time in his career, he knows that he must acquire new habits to replace those that he has unlearned. His subsequent actions show him faithful to the new "power" he feels within him. But his scheme to "sink the gentleman completely" by becoming a tailor is ridiculed by Overton, who continually reminds the reader that Ernest's new contact with poverty is as illusory as his decision to live among the poor. Overton knows that Ernest will receive a fortune of seventy-thousand pounds on his twenty-eighth birthday. Yet, as a good vitalist, he does not disturb the young man's contact with the raw facts of life. The best he can do is stimulate his sense of humor. Thus, in a highly incongruous scene, Overton counters the jobless Ernest's near despair, not by giving him a fragment of Alethea's money, but by taking him to a burlesque of *Macbeth*.

Just as Overton is about to relent by shipping Ernest "out to the colonies" with a "few thousand pounds" so that he might gain the experience demanded by Aunt Alethea's will, an unexpected development takes the young man off his hands. In his new humility, Ernest has decided to marry Ellen, the servant-girl he had defended at Battersby. Though she has become a prostitute and the mother of an illegitimate child, Ellen is, according to Overton's and Butler's vitalist standards, a fine specimen whose "good breeding" distinctly recalls that of the eugenically pure Erewhonians. Her racial origin, like that of Higgs's captors, is the product of a mythical "Ishmaelitish" crossing: "When I learned that she came from Devonshire I fancied I saw a strain of far away Egyptian blood in her, for I had heard, though I know not what foundation there was for the story, that the Egyptians made settlements on the coast of Devonshire and Cornwall long before the Romans conquered Britain" (ch. 38, p. 161). Despite these characteristics, Overton hates Ellen "instinctively," for he feels that Ernest's still undisclosed status as a gentleman is seriously threatened by his marriage. Yet he admits that Ellen's shrewd business sense should provide his godson with a much-needed schooling. He sanctions the union and demands only that Ernest not "cut himself adrift from music, letters, and polite life" (ch. 72, pp. 321-322).

True to his heredity, Ernest has emulated John Pontifex's own injudicious choice of a mate. But the renegade scholar soon learns more from selling his old textbooks than from the years of study he had spent on their content. He is happy in a life combining pleasure with utility. He has given up much. But it is his inverted renunciation, the renunciation of "unworldliness" and not the rejection of the flesh which, according to the hedonistic Overton, constitutes the true "Christ-Ideal": "What is Christ if He is not this? He who takes the highest and most self-respecting view of his own welfare which it is his power to conceive, and adheres to it in spite of conventionality, is a Christian whether he knows it and calls himself one, or whether he does not. A rose is not the less a rose because it does not know its own name" (ch. 68, p. 296).

Ernest has now rounded out his evolutionary cycle. His experience has confirmed the intuitive conversion in his cell. He knows that, unlike his great-grandfather or Towneley, he cannot be one of the "elect": "But to make Towneleys possible there must be hewers of wood and drawers of water —men in fact through whom conscious knowledge must pass before it can reach those who can apply it gracefully and instinctively as the Towneleys can. I am a hewer of wood, but if I accept the position frankly and do not set up to be a Towneley, it does not matter" (ch. 73, p. 330). Just as Dorothea Brooke cannot become another St. Theresa or Marius cannot emulate the Christian Cornelius, so Ernest is prevented from becoming a "High Ydgrunite," an "elect." But, unlike Dorothea or Marius, Ernest can rejoice in his role; he shudders to think that "if he had lived in the time of Christ he might himself have been an early Christian, or even an Apostle" (ch. 65, p. 282). For even as a hewer of wood or drawer of water, he is assured of a transcendence which, though the reverse of Daniel Deronda's, is just as much idealized. Like George Eliot's "Hebraic" hero, Butler's "Ishmael" employs his "conscious knowledge" in an act of faith.

Thus, like his creator, Ernest now bids others to worship his "dream." In the conclusion of the novel, Ernest has become an unorthodox defender of faith. He has reduced "Christianity and the denial of Christianity" into a mere "fight about names—not about things" (ch. 68, p. 299). Although he urges the Church to adopt his own version of the "Christ-Ideal," his enemies have become the scientists who deny any faith: "The spirit behind the Church is true, though her letter—true once—is now true no longer. The spirit behind the High Priests of Science is as lying as its letter" (ch. 83, p. 384). Even the literalism of Theobald's religion is regarded with a sympathy which belies the earlier treatment of the clergy: "The Theobalds who do what they do because it seems to be the correct thing, but who in their hearts neither like it nor believe in it, are in reality the least dangerous of all classes to the peace and liberties of mankind. The man to fear is he who goes at things with the cocksureness of pushing vulgarity and self-conceit. These are not vices which can be justly laid to the charge of the English clergy" (ch. 83, p. 384).

Overton describes Ernest's final creed as being "conservative, quietistic, comforting." Just as his aunt had "disliked equally those who aired either religion or irreligion" (ch. 32, p. 134), so Ernest now holds to the middle road between "iconoclasm on the one hand and credulity on the other" (ch. 85, p. 395). But if the conclusion of *The Way of All Flesh* is a defense of faith in general, it remains above all a paean to Butler's faith in "God the Known." Ellen's abrupt removal, Ernest's equally abrupt reinstatement as a gentleman, and his reconciliation with Christina and Theobald expedite the "crossing" he can now provide for his children. Having spanned the "great chasm" between his own "past and future" (ch. 64, p. 277), Ernest applies his acquired experience to ensure the preservation of the line of John Pontifex. By giving up his offspring to a healthy set of foster parents, he can convert his own modification into a law. His and Ellen's children are re-educated by "seafaring folk" well skilled in crossings. Ernest has done all he could do. He has built a bridge: "Ernest's daughter Alice married the boy who had been her playmate more than a year ago. Ernest gave them all they said they wanted and a good deal more. They have already presented him with a grand-son, and I doubt not, will do so with many more. Georgie though only twenty-one is owner of a fine steamer which his father has bought for him" (ch. 86, p. 400).

Thus, at the end, Ernest retreats. He has illustrated the workings of Butler's Evolutionary Personality, he has proved the wisdom of instinct and the unconscious, the beneficence of good breeding. Self-satisfied, Ernest retires into his second bachelorhood, stays away from society, and avoids all up-setting ties or personal claims. Ernest can now laugh freely with Overton; he can afford to be condescending to his father and to Dr. Skinner. His former pains, qualms, hesita-tions, even the "heart" which he has inherited from Chris-tina Allaby, are successfully dulled.[13] Ernest lives off his past experiences, he catalogues them and reinterprets them; he protects himself by a barrage of wit, he laughs, is amused, and waits. This final picture of Ernest Pontifex coalesces with that of its creator, aptly described by P. N. Furbank as a picture revealing "a resolute refusal of tragedy by a character naturally inclined to it."[14] But it is Overton, and not Ernest, who most resembles Samuel Butler. For Over-ton, unlike Ernest, is preaching a futile "dream": unlike Ernest, he has no descendants for whom he can provide a crossing. His wait is in vain.

Butler knew that his "dream" was a fiction. In *Erewhon* the bounds of Utopia must be crossed before Higgs can find

---

[13] On separating Ellen from her children, "Ernest's heart smote him at the notion of the shock the break-up would be to her" (chap. 77, p. 342). But, to Ernest's surprise and Overton's joy, Ellen is delighted to part with him and his children.

[14] *Samuel Butler (1835-1902)* (Cambridge, 1948), p. 113.

a new religion. In *The Way of All Flesh* the Erewhonian creed has become a timid reality. Butler returned to his "dream" with renewed passion in *Erewhon Revisited*, in a last wishful look at a binding faith of the future. But it was the fable of Ernest, bridge-builder, which culminated the efforts of those nineteenth-century writers who had tried to revitalize Victorian religion through their novels. The form of Ernest's dream was a typical Victorian compromise; the essence of his doubts, his reliance on a truth of feeling, his relativism, and his insistence on "naturalness" were Victorian as well as modern; Ernest's severance of all ties and bonds, and his ultimate repudiation of the hallowed Victorian institutions, the family, the church, and the school, were new. Samuel Butler bridged Victorian dissent and modern alienation. Unbeknown to him, his "crossing" was successful. He transported the "Nowhere" of *Erewhon* into the bounds of the modern novel.

Appendix I

THE METAMORPHOSIS of Rosamond and of Lydgate himself is presented through a kind of evolution in reverse which shows the extent of George Eliot's scientific preparation. In 1864 T. H. Huxley had proved conclusively "that many extinct reptiles had bird characteristics and many extinct birds, reptilian characteristics" and had argued that consequently both species should be classified as "sauroids" (William Irvine, *Apes, Angels, and Victorians*, London, 1955, p. 246). In *Middlemarch*, where the archaic "Dodo" Brooke triumphs over the "scientific phoenix Lydgate," a "creature who had talons, but Reason too" (ch. 58, p. 95), George Eliot turns Huxley's biological insight on Lydgate through a gradual metaphoric alteration of his wife.

Rosamond's birdlike qualities are repeatedly stressed. Her "long neck," her "warbling," and her poise, which is compared to "the movement of a graceful long-necked bird," completely captivate the young physician. He admits all too readily that "there is a bird who can teach me what she will" (ch. 27, p. 415). But Lydgate, although himself a "vigorous animal with a ready understanding," does not foresee the evolutionary lesson to be learned from his wife. Rosamond the songbird, whom he had also likened to a fanciful mermaid, suddenly assumes reptilian characteristics. Rosamond's "flute-like tones" no longer relax "his adored wisdom." Instead, Lydgate's "logic" becomes paralyzed: he begins to flinch from his wife's "torpedo contact" and feels held "as with pincers." Driven to the gambling table of the Green Dragon, he too becomes "an animal with fierce eyes and retractile claws" (ch. 66, p. 213).

Rosamond's "lash" and her "sting" also infect the behavior of another character, Will Ladislaw. Afraid of losing

Dorothea Brooke, the furious artist faces Lydgate's wife, "dangerously poised" like a serpent ready to hurl its "poisoned weapons." The snake metaphor is further extended through the Bulstrode-Raffles-Lydgate association which produces the fall of the banker and of the physician. Bulstrode sees Raffles as in a "loathsome dream" in which "a dangerous reptile had left its slimy traces" on "all the pleasant surroundings of his life" (ch. 68, p. 238). Lydgate, on the other hand, who is appalled to find Rosamond "tracing" unexpected "effects," becomes "conscious of new elements in his life as noxious to him as an inlet of mud to a creature that has been used to breathe and bathe and dart after its illuminated prey in the clearest of waters" (ch. 58, pp. 80-81).

Although detecting some of George Eliot's animalistic images in the novel, Mrs. Barbara Hardy does not dwell on their thematic significance in her "Imagery in George Eliot's Last Novels," *Modern Language Review*, L (January 1955), 6-14, reprinted as a chapter of *The Novels of George Eliot* (London, 1959).

Appendix II

GEORGE ELIOT may well have wanted *Daniel Deronda* to come under Disraeli's eyes (Arnold had likewise tried to bring *Culture and Anarchy* to the Prime Minister's attention). The erection of a Jewish state in the Middle East had a particular bearing on England's recent acquisition of Suez. Moreover, the entire question of nationality versus race, aired in the Artisan Club, was one of paramount contemporary interest. According to Professor G. M. Trevelyan: "Gladstone believed in nationality and Disraeli did not. Disraeli believed in 'race,' but he did not see why every race should demand as of right to express its genius through national freedom and self-government. His own race, of which he was so proud, throve and was famous for its own distinctive qualities, without being a nation. And so, except in the case of old established 'nations' like England and France, Disraeli preferred cosmopolitan empires of the *ancien régime*. He had supported Austrian and papal claims against Italian aspirations. On the same principle, he saw no reason why the Turk should not continue to rule over Serbs, Greeks and Bulgars" (*British History in the Nineteenth Century*, London, 1934, p. 375).

George Eliot's sentiments were largely anti-Gladstonian. Her "Address to Workingmen, by Felix Holt" was based on one of Disraeli's speeches (*GEL*, IV, 394). But she was also sympathetic to the national movements in Italy and elsewhere. Mordecai's suggestion of a Jewish state which would be "a neutral ground for the East as Belgium is for the West" (ch. 42, p. 392), no doubt seemed to her a felicitous compromise, certain to attract Disraeli. Soon after the novel's publication, John Blackwell, a staunch Tory, sadly reported that he had been unable to find out "whether Disraeli gave any utterances on the subject" (*GEL*, VI, 282).

George Eliot later hinted that "a statesman who shall be nameless" had professed to have received "a quite new understanding of the Jewish people" from her novel (*GEL*, VI, 304). The statesman could hardly have been Disraeli. Shortly after the book's publication the Prime Minister lost his office and George Eliot, the companionship of Lewes. By 1881 both were dead. But it was Balfour, then still at Cambridge, who was to take the first step toward the realization of her plea.

Index

Abelard, Peter, 168
Aesculapius, *see* Asclepius
All Souls' Day, 184
Amis, Kingsley, 229
animals, analogy to Darwinian man, 19; as basis for evolutionary ethics, 13n, 26, 34-37, 39, 55-56, 57, 251, 280-81; re-classified by Huxley, 297; as metaphors: in *Adam Bede*, 26, 34-36, 57; in *Erewhon*, 239, 273; in *Marius*, 197n-198n, 209; in *Middlemarch*, 81, 89, 297-98, *et passim*; in *The Way of All Flesh*, 280-81
Apollo, 198, 221; personified in "Apollo in Picardy," 167-68, 172; worship of, 182-83
Appleman, Philip, 151n
Apuleius, in *Marius*, 193, 198n, 200-01, 213
Aquinas, St. Thomas, 97
Aristippus, 203
Aristotle, 94, 179; quoted in *Daniel Deronda*, 121, 121n
Arnold, Matthew, 3, 5, 13, 41, 46, 51, 53, 62-71 *passim*, 130, 150n, 152, 174-76, 207, 207n, 284n, 299; compared to Butler, 227-30, 247-48, 254, 255; compared to George Eliot, 12, 16, 27, 44, 61, 62-71 *passim*, 75, 79, 102, 104, 112, 114, 127, 248, 254, 255; on George Eliot's approval of his poetry, 68; his "Hebraic" morality, 7, 65-66, 78, 83-84, 175n, 248; his religious humanism, 5, 6-7, 66, 69, 207, 207n, 247-48, *et passim*; compared to Pater,

158, 172, 174-76, 178, 180, 192-93, 207, 207n, 213n; and Mrs. Ward, 3, 4, 8n, 12, 69

works:

Culture and Anarchy, 62, 64, 64n, 299; and *Middlemarch*, 69-70
God and the Bible, 65, 69, 176
Literature and Dogma, 5, 7, 12, 63-68, 175n, 248; and *Daniel Deronda*, 64-65; and *The Fair Haven*, 230, 247; and *Marius*, 192-93; and *Middlemarch*, 65, 75, 78, 83-84, 104; and *Plato and Platonism*, 174-76, 180
The Note-books, 69n
"Resignation," 68n
St. Paul and Protestantism, 5, 7n, 64, 176
Arnold, Thomas, 229
Arnold, William Delafield, 10n, 11n, 259
Asclepius, 100, 198, 198n
Atheneum, 222n
Aurelius, Marcus, Arnold on, 207, 207n; Mill on, 207; Pater's treatment of, 159, 177, 193, 194, 206-10. *See also* Stoicism
Austen, Jane, 21, 128
autobiography, in *Marius*, 222; and the religious novel, 10-11, 11n; in *The Way of All Flesh*, 257, 258n, 259, 290, 294

Bacon, Sir Francis, 53
Baker, Joseph Ellis, 4n

INDEX